Convivialities

Also by Michael Nardone

The Ritualites
Transaction Record

As Editor

Aural Poetics
Sonic Materialities

Convivialities

Dialogues on Poetics

Michael Nardone

with Dana Michel, Gail Scott, Tanya Lukin Linklater, Shanzhai Lyric, Joshua Clover and Jasper Bernes, The Culture and Technology Discussion and Working Group, Kevin Davies, Raven Chacon, Divya Victor, Carlos Soto Román, Cecily Nicholson, Ryan C. Clarke

Talonbooks

© 2025 Michael Nardone and contributors
(see contributor copyright page for full copyright listing)

All rights reserved. No part of this book may be reproduced, stored in a retrieval system, or transmitted, in any form or by any means, including machine learning and AI systems, without the prior written consent of the publisher or a licence from Access Copyright (the Canadian Copyright Licensing Agency). For a copyright licence, visit accesscopyright.ca or call toll-free 1-800-893-5777.

Talonbooks
9259 Shaughnessy Street, Vancouver, British Columbia, Canada V6P 6R4
talonbooks.com

Talonbooks is located on xʷməθkʷəy̓əm, Sḵwx̱wú7mesh, and səlilwətaɬ Lands.

First printing: 2025

Typeset in Robert Slimbach's Arno and Nizar Kazan's Lausanne
Printed and bound in Canada on 100% post-consumer recycled paper

Cover design by Sita Singh

Talonbooks acknowledges the financial support of the Canada Council for the Arts, the Government of Canada through the Canada Book Fund, and the Province of British Columbia through the British Columbia Arts Council and the Book Publishing Tax Credit.

Canada

Canada Council for the Arts | Conseil des arts du Canada

British Columbia | British Columbia Arts Council
An agency of the Province of British Columbia

Library and Archives Canada Cataloguing in Publication

Title: Convivialities : dialogues on poetics / Michael Nardone ;
with Dana Michel, Gail Scott, Joshua Clover and Jasper Bernes, Shanzhai Lyric, Divya Victor, Carlos Soto Román, Kevin Davies, Cecily Nicholson, The Culture and Technology Discussion and Working Group, Tanya Lukin Linklater, Raven Chacon, and Ryan C. Clarke.
Names: Nardone, Michael, author, interviewer
Identifiers: Canadiana 20250114003 | ISBN 9781772016468 (softcover)
Subjects: LCSH: Poetics. | LCSH: Creation (Literary, artistic, etc.)
| LCSH: Arts and society. | LCSH: Authors—Interviews.
| LCSH: Artists—Interviews. | LCGFT: Interviews.
Classification: LCC PN1042 .N37 2025 | DDC 808.1—dc23

for Jonathan Sterne

for the spaces of listening and engagement

he created

Contents

Convivialities

> *Language is nothing but meanings, and meanings are nothing but a flow of contexts. Such contexts rarely coalesce into images, rarely come to terms. They are transitions, transmutations, the endless radiating of denotation into relation.*
>
> —Lyn Hejinian, *The Language of Inquiry*

This book begins in the uncertain space of conversation. Through a desire to enter into exchange with others – out of a sincere curiosity, in the study of poetics, to question and contemplate what we do when we write and make artistic works, to learn deeply and expansively about the details and shifting structures of this vast mesh of culture and sociality we find ourselves a part of – I began to experiment with dialogue as a form. At first I was drawn into its capaciousness: how it can hold critical inquiry beside chit-chat, how it registers moments of cacophonous thinking as well as the improvisational attunement between individuals, how it sometimes occasions utterances inexpressible when solo or incidental blurts that are surprisingly resonant. I wanted my writing to exist within such a place. I wanted it, too, to be somehow more than writing, for it to be more thoroughly conjoined with living. Through the practice of making dialogues, I began to consider how writing might thrive with *living*, how it could mark and be marked by the interplay and co-composition of numerous others, how it might even "disappear," in Fred Moten's words, "into anaxeroxic nothingness, [and] be at ease in the general and generative unease of social call, social rub, social hum, social mmmmm, social muah, social music."[1] In short, ways for writing to be *convivial*.

I first took up this word – *convivial* – to describe a condition of textuality. I was intrigued by the ways that poets, since the 1960s in particular, experimented with composing poems in an iterative way that traversed different contexts of publication and that materialized across different media. A poem, for example, might exist as a text in a mimeographed journal, as an act of speech at a site of protest, as a reel-to-reel audio recording, as a hand-scrawled text with illustration, as a score for performance by one or several performers, as a site-specific sculptural work, or as a video installation in an arts space. *Convivial*, in my mind, intoned the sociality of a poem in its traversal through various instantiations and publics. The word also spoke to a sense of interdisciplinarity at the core of making such a poetry: that the poem exists at the nexus of many cultural forms and enters into dialogue with compositional practices beyond the frame of literature, that it could be informed by and interact with these other modes of creating, organizing, articulating. I sought to cultivate this dual sense of conviviality in the works I wanted to critically engage with, in the books I aimed to edit and publish, and in the works I myself desired to make.

More recently, I've been struck by radical educator Ivan Illich's use of the term. In *Tools for Conviviality* (1973), Illich envisions it as an antidote to readymade relations. Writing against the industrial productivity and consumability of his moment, against the "technocratic disaster"[2] of the few who manage from above what is possible for the many, he warns of commodities and commodifying processes mediating every aspect of our lives. Against this destructive force (one so often opposed by poetry and art), Illich proposes *conviviality*: an "autonomous and creative intercourse among persons, and the intercourse of persons with their environment," which he considers "to be individual freedom realized in personal interdependence."[3] For him, a "convivial society" could come to be by means of "social arrangements that guarantee for each member the most ample and free access to the tools of the community" – by *tools*, importantly, Illich means not simply instruments, but also techniques, processes, social forms, and institutions – "and limit this freedom only in favour of another member's equal freedom."[4] Conviviality, in Illich's sense of the word, is thus a repertoire for attending to the commons of culture, for nurturing its robustness and capacity for difference.

Though Illich's social vision and prescription extend beyond my engagement here, there is a resonance between his thinking and the social-materialist poetics at the heart of this book. Like Illich, I swerve away from the English usage of *convivial* that situates the term merely within the setting of a feast or banquet and "seeks the company of tipsy jollyness."[5] Instead, I direct my thinking towards a discourse initiated in the word's Spanish cognate, convivir, to coexist. There is much to say about visions of coexistence in the time of ever-expanding war, climate crisis, ongoing settler-colonial dispossession, and the financialized obliteration of social life we are witnessing, in varying degrees of proximity, each day. Unlike Illich, I could never presume to propose *the* antidote to such a condition; yet, in *conviviality*, I recognize a fundamental means – a way of encountering, of listening, of reciprocity.

I connect this sense of conviviality with the Greek term ξένος (xenos) – a word Emily Wilson singles out in her translation of Homer's *Odyssey* as the crux term of the epic's narrative – which can refer to being both "stranger" and "friend." In my thinking, this dual sense in the word moves towards the being of conviviality. The "xenos figure," as Lyn Hejinian describes it, "is one of contradiction and confluence. The stranger it names is both guest and host, two English terms that are both derived from the single Greek term and are thus etymologically bound in affinity. The guest / host relationship is one of identity as much as it is of reciprocity." Hejinian continues:

> The guest / host relationship comes into existence solely in and as an occurrence, that of their meeting, their encounter. The host is no host until she has met her guest; the guest is no guest until she meets her host. Every encounter produces, even if for only the flash of an instant, a *xenia* – the occurrence of coexistence which is also an occurrence of strangeness and foreignness. It is a strange occurrence that, nonetheless, happens constantly; we have no other experience of living than through encounters. We have no other use for language than to have them. [6]

I vividly remember reading this passage over fourteen years ago – in my first months living in Montréal, upon confronting an anglophone critical culture then all too present in Canada that seemed as if it wanted to keep poetry in a locked box beneath one's bed, only to be lorded out whenever convenient to display one's mastery over the subject. Such positions and perspectives in this critical culture seemed to be yet another extension of the hegemonic forms of our era: ongoing settler-colonial appropriation, a profuse surveillance of difference and violent antagonism with it, the neglect and outright devastation of cultural and environmental commons, all set within a landscape of continuous war and perpetually manufactured crisis.

In the resonance of Hejinian's words, a different paradigm for critical practice felt palpable – one composed from the position of a "xenos figure," an interlocutor who works in relation with others to conduct inquiries into language and its encounters.

Convivialities collects moments of these ongoing inquiries in the form of a book. Each one of its twelve dialogues stages an encounter – with a writer, an artist, a researcher, sometimes even a number of people working from various backgrounds and occupations. Each dialogue focuses on questions of poetics – many concern poetry (its forms, histories, categories), yet all of them concern poiesis (making), a larger field that draws the study of poetics beyond the boundaries of the literary. Almost all of the dialogues revolve around issues of language and notation, which in their consideration extend into questions of performance, music, sound, listening, geography, politics, the transmission of cultural memory, and the overlapping crises of the present. In this undertaking, the form of the dialogue stages encounters: as face-to-face exchanges, correspondences, live forums, and all sorts of other inscriptive techniques that live between the verbal and the written. In its textures and intertextuality, my approach to the dialogues also allows for a certain critical intervention: the poet-critic as interlocutor. This is a position-taking central to critical discourse, yet it is a position-taking that welcomes – or perhaps more aptly, refuses to refuse – relation. In *Convivialities,* we are friends and strangers, guests to one another as well as hosts, visitors coming together in inquiry, in the momentary encounter of thinking and questioning and figuring together, to consider what it is we do when we compose, however it may be done.

Even if their perspectives are not unified under a single sign, the writers, artists, and researchers of these dialogues share contexts, subjects, and approaches. They are concerned with the state of the world in the twenty-first century, with the way language and art might respond to the shifting, crisis-saturated conditions of the present, at scales that extend from the planet to the neighbourhood. And they are concerned with ways we might find common ground or conviviality in these shared struggles. Throughout, they conspire to articulate tactics, poetics, contexts, and modes of relation to navigate these times and, perhaps, in the words of Ryan C. Clarke, propose a counterarchitecture. Just as each dialogue stages an individual encounter in poetics, this book stages a collective encounter between its interlocutors – their subjects, contexts, perspectives, and ways of making. It is my hope that it coheres in its refusal to be contained within a singular domain or methodology, in how it instantiates a practice of poetics that can encounter and engage with as vast an array of poiesis as possible. Such an array seems necessary to meet the needs of these present times, and to be of potential relevance to any possible future. To this extent, it is, above all, my hope that *Convivialities* be generative – towards future acts and understandings of making, towards ensuing critical dialogues, towards the conversations, encounters, and relations to come.

—MICHAEL NARDONE

ENDNOTES

1 Fred Moten, *Stolen Life* (Duke University Press, 2018), 240.

2 Ivan Illich, *Tools for Conviviality* (Harper and Row, 1973), 25.

3 Illich, 24.

4 Illich, 25.

5 Illich, 8.

6 Lyn Hejinian, *The Language of Inquiry* (University of California Press, 2000), 326.

No Fixed Positions

A Dialogue with Dana Michel

DANA MICHEL IS A LIVE ARTIST. HER WORKS INTERACT WITH the expanded fields of improvisation, choreography, sculpture, comedy, hip hop, cinematography, techno, poetry, psychology, dub, and social commentary to create a centrifuge of experience. In 2014, she was awarded the ImPulsTanz Award in recognition of outstanding artistic accomplishments and was highlighted among notable female choreographers of the year by *The New York Times*. In 2017, Michel was awarded the Silver Lion for Dance at the Venice Biennale. In 2019, she was awarded the ANTI Festival International Prize for Live Art. In 2022, the Canada Council for the Arts awarded her the Jacqueline Lemieux Prize in recognition of her contribution to dance in Canada. Based in Montréal, Michel's solo performanceworks include: *Yellow Towel*, *Mercurial George*, *Cutlass Spring*, and *MIKE*.

During the performance writing residency "So So Silky Silky Silk: Scoring *Yellow Towel*" at SBC Gallery of Contemporary Art in Montréal, with thanks to curator Pip Day, Michel and I began to work together to figure out how we might compose a score of her iterative, improvisational choreographic work *Yellow Towel*. This solo piece is exceptional for its excavation of a range of subjectivities and embodiments. As a child, Michel would drape a yellow towel on her head in an attempt to become blond and to be othered. In *Yellow Towel*, she revisits this escapist world of alter egos in a performative ritual that longs to be free of censorship. Blending austerity and absurdity, she digs into tropes of Black culture and of marginalized beings, turning them inside out to see whether or not she can relate to them. We witness her allowing a strange creature to emerge from this excavation in a slow and disconcerting metamorphosis that we follow with fascination.

Yellow Towel, in the words of James Oscar, "takes on the form of everything it sees, hears, smells – and then spits out every substance, sound, thought, every inch of mineral existence that comes its way, seeking not so much to transform it, but to explode the whole damn system."[1] Oscar emphasizes the "undeniable unspoken social urgency, charm, [and] excruciating humour" of the work, which – with the performance's experimental language and its swift movement through so many personae – drew me into its realm when I first witnessed it in 2016. I was stunned by the uncertain yet deeply felt sense of the work's form, its sense of narrative, and the open, experimental sense of its improvisational composition.

"I am always trying to run away from any pinning down of what I am trying to do or say," Michel herself states of the work. "I have made a space to kind of communicate that like a cacophony."[2] It is exactly because formulating *Yellow Towel* into the fixed state of a score seemed entirely impossible that I reached out to Michel to see if she might be interested in some kind of text-based project in relation to the performance. I became curious how the transposition of *Yellow Towel* towards the form of a score might challenge or alter our notion of the book.

In scoring *Yellow Towel,* Michel and I began with a series of questions to address the itinerant and obscure aspects of the work: What is legible in the movement of performance? What traces do its ephemeral moments leave? How to notate the duration of gesture, of utterance? To what extent, and how specifically, does the performance exceed any capacity for its documentation? While focusing specifically on *Yellow Towel,* these questions opened a number of textual and ethical issues concerning performance and inscription that are global in their concern: Who performs, for whom, to what ends? Who writes, who records? What are the techniques and technologies that mediate performance? How might a score function as a vital element of a work without fixing in place its desired fugitivity?

The following dialogue took place during the first days of our residency at SBC Gallery in September 2018 – in the midst of an array of documents, objects, and materials used in the research and performance phases of *Yellow Towel,* including Michel's personal diaries, documentary videos, and iterations of her original score – as the two of us began to imagine how they might translate the performance into the shape of a book.

MN I thought I might begin by asking some basic questions about *Yellow Towel*. I saw one performance of it here in Montréal and immediately had this sense of how exciting it could be as a textual work. Yet there is so much I don't know about the piece. When did you begin to compose it?

DM I can think of several points at once. My nephew had a big afro. My brother is, um, a Black person. (*Laughs.*) And his wife is a blond person. Their two children are fair-skinned and have various degrees of curly hair. And this nephew had an afro on top of this skin, this history. So I became curious about how he was finding his way in the world and how he identified, and I wondered, "What's it like when you don't have such clear indicators?" Obviously, we have words like *mixed race* to describe this situation, but what does it feel like? That question was one starting point. And then, somewhere around that time, I was still working at the hospital ...

MN Here in Montréal?

DM Yeah, I was at the Royal Victoria Hospital, in the maternity ward. It was my solid "I'm not letting go of this job" job, but I started thinking I needed to let go of the job. So I was wondering, "What am I going to do if I let go of this job?" My thought was, "I am going to make a kids' show." I thought I could make a good one, and one that makes money, and I like kids, so I am going to make a kids' show. My first concept for this show was that it would focus on the experience of being mixed race.

MN It's interesting because I can absolutely imagine a universe where *Yellow Towel* is a performance for children, while at the same time I know it is anything but that.

DM Yes, it is at the root of work, and I let the idea sort of spin out.

MN Can you describe your initial sense of it? Was it a character that you had in mind? What kind of performance did you imagine?

DM I wanted to make a one-hour-long, multimedia, fancy-pants but very simple, easy-to-eat kids' show kind of thingy that I would perform live. I pictured myself with a very large afro in front of a stark, black-and-white, graphic novel-like scenario coming to life in performance. So the kids' show remained an idea for a while. Then, for the Festival TransAmériques edition of *Short&Sweet* one year – have you ever been to one of those?

MN Yes! They're the short-format performances that Sasha Kleinplatz and Andrew Tay curate. I love them.

DM They are my favourite things to do. As I was preparing to do it, I was like, "Oh, I'm going to test out this idea." I got my hands on a big, reddish-brownish afro, and I wore this long colourful overcoat and had a giant umbrella I found at Village des Valeurs. The coat somehow spun me into this Jean-Michel Basquiat–train of thought – I had been watching all of these interviews with Basquiat and began to think I would do something in conversation with those.

At another point I thought I'd try out some kind of Butoh-esque white powder on my face, and I ended up getting this cheap compact from the dollar store – it was foundation or pressed powder – and it was absolutely *not* for Black people. So I was playing around with that. Around that same time, there had been a spread with Beyoncé in *Vanity Fair* or *Vogue*[3] where the stylist got criticized for doing blackface because they darkened her complexion with foundation and kinked up her hair in some of the photos. I was thinking about this, too – playing around with it inside the Basquiat interviews and the coat and the umbrella.

Anyway, I ended up doing a piece where I gyrated for three minutes, with my tits out, in my underwear, wearing a pair of creepers and the overcoat. In that instant, I was like, "This is not going to be a kids' show!"

MN This would have been when?

DM 2011. Things were really shifting in my life at that time. I left my job, and I was wandering a lot more, doing what I like to do, spending a lot of time in grocery stores and pharmacies and any store, actually, allowing myself the time to think about all of the possibilities of all the different objects and textures and colours I would see there. I had taken a huge leap, and I didn't necessarily know I was going to make a big piece. I went from this kids' show to the *Short&Sweet* piece to getting a scholarship that brought me to Vienna for five weeks.

MN I believe this was for a residency at ImPulsTanz?

DM That's right. I honestly never would have considered applying to do it, because I just didn't think I was fancy enough. A friend convinced me to do it. And I had discovered an artist who was teaching there, Ivo Dimchev, who was doing things that I hadn't realized existed in my desires to do. When I saw the works he was making, I was like, "Oh, exactly! That is exactly what I care about – what he is doing, it's possible."

MN What was it about his work that spoke to you, to the works you imagined making?

DM Oh, Ivo ... He is doing comedy and it's clearly some next-level schtick – a bit of "I'm doing whatever the fuck I want." Yet it has this incredible abstraction to it, this deep conceptualization and awareness. It's very pointed, while also being meandering, open.

MN That is something that attracted me absolutely to *Yellow Towel* when I saw it, its clarity and abstraction. The way these various, semiobscure yet exceptionally particular acts are taking place, and in their accumulation over time create this abstract ambiance that is so enthralling to be in with you.

DM With Ivo, it's super-rigorous, and it's total jackass too. It's both, and it is beautiful.

MN So you went from abandoning this kids' piece to being in residence in Vienna ...

DM And during that time, I had my brains blown. I saw fifty shows in the span of five weeks. All of this information, all of these ways of thinking. It was a big thing. It's when I officially started working on *Yellow Towel,* or perhaps I should say it's when the words *Yellow Towel* first appeared to me.

MN And did you do a performance there?

DM I did a thing, yes. I took a workshop with Ivo and he had us make solos over a week. On the first day of the workshop, Ivo had us do a writing exercise. We had to make a list of ten things we were thinking about, then narrow it down to five, then choose one from that five and write a poem about it, and this poem would be a starting point for the solo. The word that made the cut was *hair,* and I called the solo "Yellow Towel" because I would play this game when I was a kid – it seems like everything I do leads back to childhood games – I would drape a towel on my head and pretend like I had flowy, bouncy hair à la 1980s Head & Shoulders commercials. This was the first official nugget of *Yellow Towel.* It had morphed from the kids' show idea to a performance about my hair.

MN How did the piece evolve from that point?

DM When I left Vienna, Ivo said, "You should keep working on this. It's great what you are doing. You should keep going." At that point, I think I applied for a grant to work on it some more. Now, I realize I'm saying a lot of things at once, but they are all tied together. What I was trying to say earlier was that this was really the first time I was wandering about without a specific direction in mind. In fact, what I did know is what I *didn't* want to do: I didn't want to tour, I didn't want to court producers, I didn't want to have to sell a thing. Honestly, I just wanted to fuck around and work on this thing.

MN It's interesting to hear you cite wandering through grocery stores and pharmacies and engaging with the things in these kinds of places as you were starting to compose the work. Yesterday I realized – as I watched you organize all the performance materials – that just about everything you use is a banal object from such quotidian commercial spaces – a roll of paper towels, a container of cream cheese, vacuum cleaner attachments, hair-care products ... It struck me because in *Yellow Towel* all of these things are charged with a wild oddness, with a kind of supernatural power. I also noticed that maybe you were a bit shy or hesitant about bringing them out of their suitcases –

DM For sure.

MN Why was that?

DM Well, I've spent five years being so particular about how these things are seen. I've been keeping the secret of these things. Like this, for instance! (*Picks up a felt hat that has the face of a frog.*) I have this frog in my pocket, holding all of the rubber bands, throughout the show. And nobody knows! (*Laughs.*) Does everyone get this kind of pleasure? I know it's always been there for me for as long as I've been alive. When I was a kid, I would hide two of my McDonald's fries under a napkin and, when everyone thought I was done, I'd be like, "Nope!" And I'd sneak those two little fries back out. (*Laughs.*) I can't believe how satisfying that was. I don't know why. Perhaps it gives you something extra to bend around in the tedium of living? Anyway, I take so much pleasure in objects, in organizing them and thinking about them and dealing with them. Especially this set of objects. I've been allowed to fully express my desire to hide them and care for them over these years.

MN This hiding you speak of relates to the choreography of *Yellow Towel* in an interesting way. There's this thing where you hide your own virtuosity in the piece. Or, to put it in perhaps a better way: you hide your capability to do stunning and incredible bodily movements throughout the work. And then, in the moment it explodes out into the piece, you often cover it again, hide it.

DM I am often faced with this question from other people: Is it dance or is it not dance? Or: Is she an amazing performer or is she crazy? While I am hiding this and hiding that, I can't say the same for my person. I perform well under pressure, and my intuition is sharp – I know that much. I know I can react well to a thing. And I know that I like jokes. It's embarrassing to say it, but listen, I like to be funny. I like it a lot. It's very important to me.

MN I mean, *Yellow Towel* is absolutely hilarious at moments!

DM I know those things are there for me, and that I can rely on them. What happens with my body comes as a shock to me, too.

MN How do you mean?

DM I think of it through the frame of raves and Caribana. They are places where my body moves and does things, and I don't know how it does them. I realize, "Cool, so I have some kind of natural-ability thing happening," but it's not to a point where I'm like, "Oh, I am an amazing dancer." In performance, I don't often know what my body is doing. When I look at documentation after a show, I may realize that a certain turn, for instance, makes a good photo but – and I'm not talking about this ego-wise, I'm talking about my choreographic analysis of what my body is doing in the work – it's not a situation where I'm doing all these moves and I've written them for my skill to appear at specific moments, no.

People can talk about it from the outside however they want to talk about it. All I can say from the inside is that I am working in a joke space and in a what's-happening-with-my-body space. If something hurts, for instance, that's going to affect the way I am going to do it. I don't shut that down. I let that talk to the work. I let all of the things talk to the work, and it produces something. People seem to express to me that it works. More importantly, though, I register from the inside that something intuitively makes sense about this manner of writing movement.

MN What struck me so deeply in seeing your work is the fact that it's as if every movement and every utterance are constructed from layers and layers of history, histories. They are always partially obscured or in the process of becoming legible, and they are charged with new valences of meaning as you embody and intone them. How do you do that?

DM For me, it's a matter of putting the body in at the very last second. When I was preparing the work, I was giving it lots of time, doing all kinds of thinking, and, as I said, spending a lot of time wandering. And when I'm doing research, I'm cloaked in an invisible Velcro suit. Or a magnet suit. I'm in constant osmosis mode.

MN Osmosis and Velcro!

DM You see where I'm going. I'm soaking everything up like a goddamn Christmas fruitcake. Soaking it all up. I'm touching materials, talking, thinking, getting super-swollen with all the information. Then the emergency of the performance wrings out from me what is necessary. I set up very specific tasks for myself, paths, timings based on music. I know I work well under pressure – it's when I have the most clarity.

What came out of *Yellow Towel,* out of my body, was exciting to discover, because I knew I was increasingly interested in what came out of improvisation. But *improvisation* is still not good enough a word. I knew I was most interested in how a body reacted in the time of performance after having worn this soaked-fruitcake suit.

MN How does this differ from the way you thought about composing choreography prior to *Yellow Towel*?

DM The way I was working before – I would go into the studio and I would improvise, and then I would watch videos of it. I would find interesting things, but, overall, it was boring. It's now embarrassing to me, this conception of dance where I work my moves and find cooler ways of doing them. It has nothing to do with anything I care about anymore. I don't mind seeing certain people do it, but there was definitely a moment when I recognized it didn't fit with what I wanted to do.

MN There is a productive problem here that's interesting to think about as we begin to arrange the score for the work. On one hand, you're saying that the way that you like to work is by absorbing things – absorbing and having lots of information enter you, pass through you – and then using this to respond in some kind of way in performance. On the other hand, at some point you have to organize the information and all that you've absorbed and some aspect of your response to it. How does structuring come into play? I'm curious if there has been a shift in how you think of the way *Yellow Towel* is organized and the way that you have composed your solo works after it?

DM I feel like I found a kind of organizing principle with *Yellow Towel,* and I'm feeling it. It's still there in [my more recent solo performance] *Mercurial George,* but what has shifted is time. I've become more reckless. The soaking period is the same, but that moment when I initiate running the mop through the squeezer is happening later and later. That's what I've noticed. I'm constantly upping the ante. And then sometimes I find out, wow, okay, yep, the ante was too high! That was way too close!

MN Does that shut you down, or does that intrigue you?

DM It never shuts me down. I'll keep taking the joke further and further. What I've found out is that I have a great time in this space, but in terms of a research practice, I realize I could be a little less ridiculous. I could be a little more productive if I was a little less ridiculous.

MN I imagine that you have to push through some far-flung boundaries in performance to realize perhaps you need to take it back a step or two.

DM Exactly! As you're talking about choreography, I'm picturing now a pinball machine. Maybe my work is a pinball machine. (And maybe a pinball machine is not like this at all. I am often confounded by contraptions.) The machine is the text-score, the objects, the music choices, the light, and I'm the ball. But my ball is a thick sponge ball sloshing through the system. Whereas for most choreographers I talk to, the choreography applies only to the sponge passing through the pinball machine, for me, the whole pinball machine is choreography, and the machine is for me more important than the sponge, or it's where I spend the most time.

MN In the work, there is an array of embodiments and accents that come through you. I'm curious if, in developing the work, did you see these various embodiments as characters?

DM I don't think of them as characters. I think about it as me reacting to different circumstances. In the most basic way, that is what's happening. It really is me reacting to different circumstances. What's happening is that I'm embodying a mental state that is mine. I'm letting it communicate with the rest of me. I am physicalizing what is actually fucking happening, and normally we need to contain these things. I've allowed performance to be a place where I don't have to contain these things. I think the reason why it looks real is because it *is* real. It's not mimicry. It's been difficult. I've had some hard questions come up when I've performed it.

(*While talking, they drift over to a screen playing various performances of* Yellow Towel.)

As time went on, I realized I had to be more careful about the language I used around the work. The kind of casual way that I could talk about what I was doing to myself or to people who know me was and could and did get used as weaponry in the mouths of other people when they deployed the language. It shaped the work in a way that I didn't anticipate, and once those words were out there, it was immediately too late. I still don't know how to handle what I triggered and where to place it, because I also find it all very fascinating. In a way, I'm content with the language that was used, because it ricocheted the work exactly where I was trying to get away from, and that was interesting to watch happen.

MN Can you give an example?

DM For instance, my big thing was, "This is my 'Black piece.'" This is very true for me, but when I say it, I know exactly what I mean.

MN And that's a huge space for other people to infer into –

DM And that's exactly what happened. In a way, it's good that I left it that way. I opened the door, and it was wide open for exactly the opposite of what I meant … For instance, this situation right here. (*Refers to a video of a* Yellow Towel *performance that is playing on a screen in the gallery.*) I can tell you exactly what's happening from the inside, where the clothing came from, what I'm doing. But this person, this shape, this character thing, when people talk about it, it's a crack addict. It's an unhoused person on crack. I opened the door for that by calling it my "Black piece," apparently.

MN I'm curious, though, as to whether you mean for that to be one of the valences – or do you not have that in mind at all? And by *valence* here, I mean the different resonations that echo out of the work, as in this being one of the embodiments that is intoned, but just one of them.

DM Well, yes, that's why I still have a confusing time with all of this – because of what we discussed earlier regarding the sponge suit. I can't deny any of these things.

MN So is the problem, then, the fixing of the embodiment of it being your "Black piece" only to that one interpretation of it?

DM Yeah, and the sadness I have around that is I was never trying to *prove a point*, but it proved all kinds of points front and centre, up, down, and around. Just the fact that the word *Black* was used and I do some of the things I do in the work ... Had I not said anything about *Yellow Towel* being a "Black piece," I wonder how it would have been read. It's not that I wasn't being careful, I was being generous. Also naive.

(*They begin watching the initial moments of a* Yellow Towel *performance.*)

MN If you were to describe this section of the work and this embodiment, what are the ways you would think about it?

DM Well, I'll begin with the jogging suit ... Wait, to go back to what we were just talking about, I want to say I also think it's important that what is happening here telescopes, that people bring in information to me based on what they are seeing. That is super important.

MN It is, in a way, that next level of steeping that you talked about earlier, which you get to play with and within.

DM Yes, it's really important. I don't want to turn that off. But the jogging suit: I bought it many years ago for a different project. It was for a musician to wear so they could disappear, but I never ended up using it for that after all. Then, a couple of years later, I was doing a work-in-progress thingy and was three months pregnant. I was still a high-risk pregnancy, so I think I wasn't ready to share the information yet with people. So I was digging through my stuff, and I was like, "I need the biggest clothes I own." I felt like I needed to hide, so I busted this jogging suit out.

MN It's totally a disappearing suit.

DM Okay, there is stuff that happens on the inside of the clothes, but I won't talk about that. But on the outside of the clothes, in this particular section, I wrote a short score. There is a path, a diagonal, and at the far end of the diagonal there is an inflatable toilet. I have this text about house music – which pulls up all kinds of memories, as I have a deep history with this song, Chuck Roberts's "My House," from my rave days – and the point is to get from one corner to the toilet while saying the text. Except I haven't memorized the text, so part of it is about seeing how I remember the text while doing the diagonal. So: I gotta say the text; I gotta make it to the toilet; I'm doing it with this kind of accent or affected way of speaking; that's it. The body that comes out of it is a body that is dealing with serious memory challenges and dealing with having people watch those memory challenges. That's kind of a skeleton of what's happening there. This is all very far away from a person who has no home and who is on crack.

MN For someone to see that into what you are doing is to see only one of the vectors that intersects with that diagonal.

DM Exactly. I see what the intersection is, but that intersection is not made up in my mind for the same reasons it's made up in other people's minds.

MN It's an important aspect of the composition, its aboutness. What this section is about is someone walking from offstage, across the stage, to a toilet –

DM While trying to remember something, with a bunch of strangers watching.

MN In that sense, it's exceptionally literal. However, in that movement, there are all of the valences, all of the things that you have soaked into this procession, into this diagonal, and they of course resonate, but they are a tangent outward from the score of the crossing and the remembering.

DM And also, the way I work is – was it with you that I was talking about memory holes this morning?

MN I don't remember! (*Laughs.*) But what about memory holes?

DM It's about the way that information serves me or comes to me, the tie-dye effect of it all. The timing is not linear. The first thing that someone wrote about this work when it was still in progress was that it's about Trayvon Martin. His shooting had just happened. I didn't know about it yet, but then I looked into it and obviously followed the story. But I don't know; I can't discount butterfly effects.

MN It is a resonation because you create a space where such things can be read and interpreted into the work in so many ways.

DM But with the memory hole, sometimes I'm soaking information in, and I don't know exactly when it comes out. So I feel I'm not 100 percent in control of my output.

MN It relates to this work in that, along with all of the embodiments, movements, and gestures – and how one might project onto them all different forms of age and abilities, from childlike to elderly – there is also this protean thing that happens –

DM *Protean*, what is this word?

MN The word has many associations or connotations, but, in this sense, I mean it specifically with regard to Proteus, who was a shape-shifter. I mean it in regard to all of the different transforming bodily instantiations that are brought together through *Yellow Towel*. I think of the protean in *Yellow Towel* on several levels – race, age, ability, as I mention – and also with regard to gender performance and representations of sexuality across a wide spectrum. Throughout the work, you do these things that are explicit in a certain way, and yet you somehow extract the sexuality out of them in a certain way. It's both overt and also diminishing at the same time, if that makes sense. Is that something that you think about in terms of the performance?

DM Yes, of course. This is something people have asked me about and that people have written about the work. Sometimes they discuss "androgyny," and some people have described my "lack of fear to be ugly." But that's not how I conceive of it. I'm definitely not aiming for any kind of anything. Definitely not androgyny. I'm attempting to hold all of the things that are in here and let them exist. People have asked me, "How can you allow yourself to be seen in such an ugly way? As a Black woman, especially, it's so brave that you ..."

MN That language feels quite off, no?

DM "Ugly," yes. "Not sexy," yes. Whatever. I'm not shocked. From the inside, in terms of how it feels, I can say I felt powerful and exploded in those moments they are citing. I felt fucking gorgeous. I felt extremely sexy. I was all the things, all the moods. I'm not trying to seduce anyone, so that means I can exist in a way that is attractive to me.

MN I'm curious how that bleeds into life outside of the performance?

DM As in, why can't that sensibility exist for me all of the time?

MN Yes, that's it.

DM I've watched myself have the courage to morph into someone that feels closer to what's happening in here. (*Places hand across chest.*) And I don't know how this person inscribes itself in the world. It's not so neat.

MN What's it like for you to continue to perform a piece like this? I imagine it being complex, because on one hand repeating the work seems to go against all of the exploration that you have written into its score, but on the other hand, you have composed a choreography that is a structure you get to play within and, perhaps, explore the (possibly minute) differences you come up against from iteration to iteration.

DM That's it. When I premiered the piece at the Festival TransAmériques, I thought of it as a one-shot deal. I like to work in this way, and formats like *Short&Sweet* are perfect for me, because that's how they work – you try something out and then move on to something else. This is something I admire about the visual art performance world: there's a thing, it happens, and then that's it. At the same time, maybe this doesn't make total sense for me, because I do love repetition, and I like things to live for a long time.

When I started to be invited to tour *Yellow Towel*, I thought, "This does not make sense at all." The whole question was, "How can I react to something I've already reacted to?" I wondered if all the subsequent moments then would be fake, wouldn't feel right. I thought, "I don't get why, but I guess I'm going to do this thing." There were seven months between the premiere and the next run, and before that second run, I did a one-week residency with Peter James and did a showing of the work, and I was like, "Oh, nope, it's new again, I'm definitely experiencing this thing again for the first time." My experience of the work went in and out of that feeling. Especially if there were several months between performances, it came in and out of making sense. In fact, last year I really got into a place of feeling and thought, "Oh, this is a whole new situation. I'm probably going to stop touring *Yellow Towel* now," but it's like brand fucking new again.

MN What was it that made it feel that way? Was it a personal thing?

DM Yeah, I'm a different person. Things have really shifted in my mind, and I've made all kinds of new learnings. That's one thing. And on a smaller scale, I'm so sensitive. Every floor in every theatre is different. There's different dust. The light. Everything is different. The energy in the room is different. The country I'm in, what languages they understand. Everything is different all the time. Because I'm a person who is so sensitive, I can be affected by such small things.

MN Are there specific shifts or moments that stick out for you in the strings of performances of the work? For example, "In this one particular performance, I got this one segment right," or "What happened in this other performance was really unexpected and it really worked." Or is it that such analysis doesn't register, because you're so in the thing that the comparisons from one iteration or context to the next don't really map against one another?

DM It's both. This is what I love about getting to do this stuff. It's so living. There are so many negotiations. Sometimes I'll think it feels really good to say this in one particular way, and then I do that same thing another time, and I am hit by the fact that I am breaking cardinal rule number one, which is "NO FIXED POSITIONS." Don't hold on to anything. I stole that from Bruce Lee, I believe, and I've adopted it hard-core.

(*They begin to watch the beginning moments of two different performances to compare them: the first from the US premiere at American Realness in January 2014, the second from the performance at the Venice Biennale in June 2017.*)

MN Do I remember correctly that you told me the show begins offstage?

DM Yes.

MN How deep or far back does it go?

DM Generally, I am in the changing room, and the stage manager says, "They are ready for you"– that's when it starts.

MN Can you describe where that is in relation to the stage?

DM It depends. In the performance we're watching, it's just at the back of the stage and a little bit off to the side. At other times, I have to come down some stairs. When there's a ways to go and I've started the show offstage, sometimes the stage manager isn't quite sure how to deal with me, because I don't say to anyone that I'm starting. In starting, it means I stop being polite, basically. By that I mean I'm not going to say all of the things you need me to say so you feel like you're okay, you know what I mean?

MN Is there a way you like to allow yourself to become visible to the audience?

DM Hmmmm.

MN Because in the two videos I watched yesterday, you definitely lurk a little offstage for a bit.

DM You can see me lurking?

MN Yes!

DM Dammit!

MN But I'm looking for it; I'm watching exactly for those details. I don't recall seeing or recognizing that when I saw it in person. But I do remember thinking, "Is this starting? Has this started? Does this performer know where they are? Do they know the performance has started?" (*Laughs.*)

DM Are you asking me those questions now? (*Laughs.*)

MN No! But I am curious about how you choreograph the start.

DM Well, they say, "Are you ready?" and I follow them, and I take my time to make it around to the stage. I take my time to hug that corner, basically. It depends on how I'm feeling that day. Sometimes I can just walk around that corner onto the stage, and other times I'm like, "Oh, wait." There are all kinds of systems. It depends! It depends on how noisy the public is. I generally like to come on while everyone is still talking, and I can kind of slip in. So I'm listening for the right moment, when I feel like maybe no one is looking or I can slip in among the chatter. Sometimes it's dead silent in there because they are very polite or because the usher has made some kind of gesture that tells people the show is starting. In that case, it will take me longer, because I have to find a way to make myself feel like I am slipping in unnoticed. I guess I'm always trying to slip in naturally, casually.

MN I've now watched four recordings of *Yellow Towel,* and the length of time from you slipping in and being visible to the audience until the time you make a first utterance – it varies greatly. I'm curious if there is something scorable there?

DM There definitely is. When I come around the corner, I know that the curtain tends to be very soothing. So I allow myself to be soothed by the curtain. Generally, I'm negotiating my proximity to the curtain and, depending on where people are sitting, I'm negotiating that sensation – trying to gauge what's happening in this space while being comforted by the curtain. Also, I'm negotiating my feet – but, wait, this maybe sounds …

MN Please go on! This is the choreography.

DM Okay, so I'm negotiating the curtain. I'm finding a way to make it from behind the curtain to inside of the curtain, and I'm trying to do all of this without anyone noticing. Except the whole room is looking at me! That's a big-ass negotiation, right? And I'm thinking, "How do I feel about all of this? How close is this person? Is it a smooth curtain?" Sometimes the curtain texture can make me feel comfortable, or not at all. And then there are all the other things I'm factoring in: Am I hungry? Am I tired? All of this affects how long it takes me. Sometimes my foot might get caught. Sometimes there is another curtain that I am trying to close behind me so no one sees backstage. I'm negotiating the aesthetic space.

MN That's it; you're engaging the material aesthetic space, right down to its most quotidian elements.

DM Exactly. And also, there's a writing in how I am trying to deal with my feet and my knees, in the bending and opening of the legs and knees, how I'm trying to blur it so it's not too sharp. I've spent a lot of time at the curtain, and sometimes when I'm there, I can see my shadow, and I spend some time looking at my shadow. It depends on how tight my hood is tied. Also, the number of nails I've glued on will affect the pacing, as I allow myself to be soothed by the sounds of the nails on the curtain's fabric. So I go from hugging the curtain to working from the curtain down to myself. Then I try again to make it away from the curtain without anyone noticing that I am moving my feet.

MN The term you are using – *negotiation* – seems key for your sense of choreography. If the main plotline of these initial moments in *Yellow Towel* is to enter and move diagonally across the stage from curtain to toilet, then, in this instance, the negotiations are each obstacle and information point you confront along that line.

DM It bounces between "the choreographic" and what I need to do this job I'm trying to do.

MN And here, at the start of *Yellow Towel,* what I sense you're performing or relaying is something cosmogenic. You seem to be initiating an entire universe of movement and sound.

DM When I'm in and away from the curtain, I am working myself up to a place where I can feel like I can make a sound. I'm saying, "Ummmmm, uhhhhhh." I'm thinking, and I'm playing. Then it's choreographic. I'm writing. I've been warming up a little – "So, ummmm, so" – I'm working my way up to saying, "Hello."

ENDNOTES

1 "Yellow Towel," *Neon Lobster* (website), neonlobster.org/dana-michel.

2 "Yellow Towel."

3 Editor's note: It was *L'Officiel Paris*.

Can Struggle Be Shared?

A Dialogue with Joshua Clover and Jasper Bernes

FOR OVER SIX MONTHS IN 2012, TENS OF THOUSANDS OF students across Québec went on strike to protest the government's plan to increase university and college tuition fees by 75 percent. During these months, the strike was supported by a number of protest actions, including mass demonstrations that shut down Montréal's downtown, bridge blockades, and "casserole protests" that brought entire neighbourhoods out on the streets to bang pots and pans in defiance of the government's emergency measures to quell the student uprising and limit protestors' rights to assemble. It was a militant moment. The protests and related actions quickly surged beyond the right to education to focus on issues such as police violence and impunity in Montréal to the industrial exploitation of the environment and the current economic order that is based on this devastation.

The following is an excerpted transcript of an open dialogue during an event entitled "Can Struggle Be Shared?" that took place at the Sense Lab in Montréal on June 24, 2012. The gathering brought a number of Montréal students and activists together with Bay Area poets and antagonists Jasper Bernes and Joshua Clover to discuss student and social movements in Québec and California.

Joshua Clover is the author of seven books, including *Roadrunner*, as well as *Riot. Strike. Riot: The New Era of Uprisings*, a political economy of social movements, with recent editions in Spanish, Italian, French, German, and Swedish. A former journalist with *The Village Voice*, *The Nation*, and others, he is currently professor of English and comparative literature at University of California, Davis, as well as affiliated professor of literature and modern culture at the University of Copenhagen. Jasper Bernes is the author of *The Future of Revolution: Communist Prospects from the Paris Commune to the George Floyd Uprising* and *The Work of Art in the Age of Deindustrialization* as well as two books of poetry. He teaches for the English department at the University of California, Berkeley, and lives in Oakland.

For years, I have admired the poetry and critical writings of Clover and Bernes. Their involvement within various anticapitalist, antiracist actions in the Bay Area as well as student struggles more broadly in California, and their overall theorizing of the relationship between poetic practice and political organization to confront the overlapping crises of our times feels crucial to understanding the social dynamics of these last decades. Upon hearing the two would be in Montréal to witness the unfolding of le Printemps érable / the Maple Spring, I organized a space for the two to enter into conversation with folks involved on the ground with the protests here.

To initiate a dialogue, I asked Joshua and Jasper the following questions:

> Recognizing a common ground against the restructuring of educational institutions according to the imperatives of the financial industry and the militarization of the university campus as a means to enforce these imperatives, what are ways to unite and fight these mutual struggles in California and Québec? What tactics might be enacted to further develop networks of dissent?

I have edited this excerpt of the exchange to focus on the Québec and California student movements, their relationships to the Occupy movement, and, finally, the larger economic crisis in which they occur. Due to the policing of activists during the student strike, dialogue participants chose not to identify themselves by name in this published dialogue. To offer some framing, though, I will note here that "LL" is a philosophy graduate student, "SL" is a Montréal activist and organizer, and "CL" is a Montréal-based musician and activist.

JC These movements and struggles tend to move in waves and rise and fall somewhat unevenly. It's a bit of a moment, I think, of decomposition in the Bay Area after the high drama birthed on the campuses where Jasper and I have both recently found ourselves, but also at Occupy Oakland, which we were briefly proud to call the Oakland Commune. The fall, especially September and October, were times of great struggle and drama and seeming import there. And now it's a little bit more of a decomposed moment. So we were incredibly excited to go someplace where it was more composed and to get a sense of what's going on here, which frankly strikes me, I think strikes all of us, as self-evidently, fantastically important, but also something that's not being covered particularly carefully in the US press, if covered at all.

So we figured the way to know about it was to come here, which was a little hard to schedule, but we managed to pull it off, and people here were very supportive and encouraging. Michael set up this event, and we didn't really know what it would be, and we still don't really, but I can tell you a bit about it. I came up with the title, and I sent it to Jasper to see if it was okay with him, and Jasper said, "It's a pretty good title, but why is there a question mark? Of course struggle can be shared."

We talked about this and I basically agree, but I didn't want to have that be a closed question, because I think for me really fundamental issues continue to present themselves in ways that show struggle can and can't be shared, both across space and different places – Oakland and Montréal to name just two – but also across various kinds of social boundaries, whether they be class structures, whether they be from inside the university to outside the university, to the space of work, to the space of nonwork of the unemployed – and particularly the things that present themselves as possible places of unity, but also limits to unification, obviously things like demands. If you have a university-specific demand, say, does that open to other struggles, or does that cordon you off from other struggles? These are issues that have been very aggressively debated or aggressively ignored in various spaces in which I found myself organizing for the last three years, and the optimistic answer is always: well, yes, of course struggle can be shared, and for two obvious reasons. People want it to be shared. Nobody wants to struggle alone. And then the fact that people in quite different places or communities are subject to shared forces, most obviously a catastrophic global economic crisis and the ways it presents itself, albeit differentially, in various places.

So that's more or less sort of the framework or the set of puzzles that we see going forward: on the one hand saying, "Well, the movement in Québec has already grown extraordinarily larger than the movement in California has been in this recent passage," and yet the questions remain of what are its limits, and how do people here conceive of moving beyond them or how do people conceive of those limits, and how do people think of those questions here? I think there are specific flashpoints around these questions. I think the question of demands and how they work and what people's relation is to them is important. I think the question of people's relationship to the state and to police repression, and how people articulate their relationship to them, is a fundamental flashpoint. I think the relationship to labour, the relationship to organized unions – be they student unions or labour unions or so on – become fundamental areas of debate, and so I want to offer these more as questions or as places of discussion and contention that have arisen.

JB One of the things that's interesting to me is that the struggle here in Québec, from what I can tell, abbreviates a transformation that happened in California. If you look at something like Occupy Oakland or the Oakland Commune, there are a couple of different streams that flow into it. One is a student movement that we had in 2009–2010, and the other is the antipolice movement that basically emerged around the murder of Oscar Grant by Bay Area transit police. When the student movement was happening in 2009–2010 – and it wasn't particularly large, but it was pretty intense – there were a lot of things happening that were interesting, at least from the perspective of the United States. There was a much greater degree of ferocity, and new tactics and new ideas got put on the table.

One thing we talked a lot about during the student movement was how we wanted to link up that struggle with struggles in other places and sectors and to thereby escape the university. We realized that inasmuch as we remained confined to the university, things would die there. And that's probably because none of us – at least the people who I was consorting with – really wanted to preserve the university as such. We had a pretty negative view of what the university does, its function in a capitalist society. We didn't think of it as an engine of liberation. In fact we saw it as this thing that reproduces class society. So it really wasn't as if we wanted to struggle to preserve the university. No, we wanted to generalize antagonisms towards society as it is currently constructed, and the university was the place where we could do that. Nonetheless, though we often talked about how we had to link up with struggles in other spheres, beyond the university, that never really happened, and we were not successful at getting off campus, as it were.

But what did happen was that, eventually, a year and a half or two years later, after the student movement had largely come and gone, Occupy Oakland emerged, and that strategy of occupation which we had pursued during the university protests found a much larger arena. Many of the same people who were involved in the first round of things at the university were also involved in Occupy Oakland, and a lot of the ideas that were put forward in the context of the student movement re-emerged in the context of Occupy Oakland. That's only one of the streams that went into it, of course. Occupy Oakland had a very different class composition and social composition, which makes it more interesting in many ways than what happened in the universities. In any case, Occupy Oakland was, in many ways, the realization of a certain desire for generalization which we had during the student movement. I think we were happy about that. But here in Québec it seems that what has happened is that there's a student movement and then partly through the passage of the special law, there's this moment of generalization in which it becomes a larger social uprising, one that's no longer confined to students or student issues.

LL The first thing that strikes me is that there's a continuity between Occupy and the student movement that's taken for granted, and, with that, the theme of debt between the two. I want to ask this question to everyone, what they think about that connection, because I was part of the Occupy camp in Montréal, and that was, for me, very obviously mobilizing and radicalizing. Then when the student movement started to really snowball around the end of March, I saw a lot of my friends from Occupy not participating, because it wasn't their thing. They had some other struggle.

So along the theme of "Can Struggle be Shared?," does anyone see connection between the Occupy camps in the States and up here? Do we have maybe a separation between the two?

SL I think the effect of Occupy Montréal was negative on the student movement. In comparison to places in the States, with certain strategic tendencies and ideological dogmas – pacifism being a particular one – in Montréal, these tendencies and ideologies have been, at least historically, less prominent in terms of radical scenes. Certainly, within the anarchist milieu in Montréal, the question of pacifism has largely been resolved, at least in terms of people who have been engaged continually for several years.

Basically, what Occupy Montréal did to a certain degree was give pacifism a renewed life. I think it's interesting that Montréal – a place that has a militant tradition of its own, Québec in general having a very militant tradition – imported this pacifist model from the United States, which in a lot of ways, I think, did not make sense in the context here.

JC One of the things that's really striking with what's happened in the Bay Area – and Jasper started to get at this – was, in fact, the order was reversed: it was not that there was this Occupy thing that broke out and then there was a student movement. There was this largely student or university movement in 2009 – and then there's the antipolice movement as well around the murder of Oscar Grant – which formulated, among other things, or didn't formulate but chose occupation as a tactic.

But because there was a student movement before Occupy that did influence Occupy and really fed into it around particular axes, it did, indeed, change the tenor of Occupy Oakland, as far as I know, compared to all the other Occupies. Occupy Oakland was both a fairly militant movement and also a pointedly antipolice movement because of the murder of Oscar Grant. That really shaped Occupy Oakland and its initial principles: that there would be no politicians allowed there as politicians, and there were no police allowed, and there would be no negotiating. We actually never violated those principles, and that set up quite a different dynamic.

There was a different relationship to pacifism or to the police exactly because there had been these two movements, including a student movement that fed into Occupy. Now, that said, things reversed. There was Occupy and there was sort of a revivification of these student movements or campus movements, and then it very much did go exactly as S said: there were the local Occupy movements, let's say Occupy Davis, which is the town where I work, and then Occupy UC Davis, which is the university where I work in that town. These two Occupies had largely different politics and struggled around different specific concerns, and I wouldn't say they supported each other so much as set up a complicated dynamic that led to disintegration fairly swiftly. It would have disintegrated entirely if people didn't get pepper-sprayed on global television, which managed to hold the movement together for a couple of months in shared misery, fame, and lawsuits.

JB Observing all of these movements over the last year, I think one thing you can say is that self-organization on its own is not enough. In Egypt, you see people self-organizing in order to protect businesses. You see neighbourhood assemblies that are self-organizing for the purpose of explicitly reactionary forms of politics. Similarly, the Occupy encampments had very different characteristics in different places. Some of them were actually quite sympathetic to a kind of libertarian, quasi-racist element, and some of them were completely antithetical to that. I think that's probably what we're going to have: these forms – like protest camps – which spread and are then filled with political content. Some of that content is not going to be good or pretty. You can't just separate out the question of the content. The forms or tactics may be spreading, people may be occupying squares or they may be doing casseroles or whatever, but fascists can have casseroles. Fascists can occupy buildings. Fascists can have a Black bloc. These things on their own are just a shell.

When I talk to people in Egypt and in Greece and Spain, in all places where there are neighbourhood assemblies – and I think this is actually a really powerful thing, I'm totally supportive of the neighbourhood assembly as a way to empower movements to take next steps – but they complain that some of these assemblies are liberal, some are kind of chauvinist, some are not doing anything, some are really conservative, some are procapitalist. And that's what you're going to get, these forms of ambiguity. Self-organization on its own isn't necessarily going simply to produce emancipatory potentials.

I think Oakland was really interesting, because there was a very explicitly anticapitalist and antipolice and antistatist content there. I think a lot of people wanted Oakland to be an intervention into the whole Occupy movement, which had these politics that were either ambiguous or, in some cases, unambiguously problematic. And you can see, looking back, that those principles central to Occupy Oakland ended up changing the character of the movement overall.

CL I think it's really a stretch to draw a connection between the student strike and Occupy here in Montréal. Of course people here are taking inspiration from what they saw in Oakland and in New York City in terms of the direct actions that took place, but the historical conditions in Québec are very different than in the States and even than in the rest of Canada in terms of having a very rooted and long-term struggle for free university education.

The student strike that happened in 1978 revolved around that demand. In 2007, there was a huge effort to make a strike also, and at that time it didn't take root. In the fall of 2007, there were significant demonstrations that students were trying to build around. At that time the government of Québec was increasing the cost of tuition for students. There was a huge effort then, and it didn't work in terms of achieving significant popular support and organization.

There are a million ideas on why it has worked this time, but I think, to be honest, one of them is pretty straight-up: persistence. There has been massive popular organizing on campuses and in communities for many years that went into this. And, of course, it speaks to one of the unanswered dreams of a very specific period in Québec: the demand for free education, which dates back more than a generation, and that's something that a lot of people believe in quite deeply. So it seems like Québec society collectively didn't successfully address, or that victory didn't happen around, the "The Quiet Revolution," which I think is not an accurate term. It was a very loud period. At that time one of the demands was for free university education.

Every place has its own history, and I think Québec's history very much informs what's going on. But, of course, in the global era, in the global moment, people are watching what happened in Egypt and watching what happened in New York City. I think we also can't underestimate the fact that there's long-term nuts-and-bolts organizing, and tons of underattended meetings, cold days flyering, and demonstrations that were very small a few years back that went into building this. That's the case anywhere of trying to build a movement. I think it's important to not overromanticize what's happening in Québec, but more to just understand that it's tied to very particular history and experience that speak to political struggles in Québec that go back generations.

JC There have been some really interesting, eloquent accounts about the vertical, by which I mean the long history of Québec, both before this moment and the long organizing that has gone into this moment, but there's also this horizontal line, e.g., global economic crisis. I want to think about this situation, what it allows and what it necessitates. Capitalism produces two things in this crisis: one, it produces debt, which is why debt is an important thing to organize around, but if you just organize around debt, you get a debt jubilee so you can start from zero and start generating your debt again. The other thing capitalism produces in a crisis is unemployment.

I think a fundamental question for me is how student struggles meet in a mode of political engagement with a surplus population, with those who are not employed, with those who are excluded from the job market. I'm not saying that's the only political front in any regard; I'm saying that the question of unemployment and the unemployed as political agents should present itself to us very strongly as we think about the horizon of the next five or ten or fifteen or twenty years. For me that's a vital question as we think about what can happen there.

JB Even if the students manage to fight off this fee increase, what's going to happen five years from now? We can see that there's this process of austerity grinding away across the entire world, and one victory here or there isn't going to alter that. We're in a situation where society as it's constructed is radically incapable of meeting people's needs. Which means that, rather than simply fighting back against austerity measures, one thing we can do is learn to provide for each other. This is something we need to do, especially in the university, where even if you manage to get a degree, there are no jobs at the other end. So what if, instead of only trying to preserve access to the university, we tried to take over the university and use it for other purposes, for the purpose of meeting these immense forms of social need?

I think that this was what the Occupy movement was about, at its best. What's striking about Occupy is that, contrary to the desires of a lot of organizers who were in it from the very beginning, it articulated no real demands. People wanted it to eventually. That was the vision which the organizers had for it: people would get together, they would have a general assembly, and they would figure out what their demands were. But that didn't really come about. Instead, Occupy became about directly meeting people's needs. It became about mutual aid. It became about unhoused people feeding each other and figuring out how to survive. It became about figuring out how to take care of each other in a situation of social breakdown.

A Collectively Authored, Ever-Unfinished Landscape

A Dialogue with Shanzhai Lyric

SHANZHAI LYRIC IS A POETIC RESEARCH AND ARCHIVAL unit focusing on radical logistics and linguistics through the prism of technological aberration and unofficial cultures. The project takes inspiration from the experimental Englishes of shanzhai T-shirts made in China and proliferating across the globe, to examine how the language of counterfeit uses mimicry, hybridity, and permutation to both revel in and reveal the artifice of global hierarchies. Through an ever-growing archive of poetry-garments, Shanzhai Lyric explores the potential of mistranslation and nonsense as utopian world-making (breaking). Their work takes the form of poetry-lecture, essay, and installation. In 2020, they founded the fictional office entity Canal Street Research Association in an empty storefront on NYC's counterfeit epicentre Canal Street, a site whose complex interplay of hustles probes the limits of authorship and ownership.

I first encountered Shanzhai Lyric's work through a performance-lecture they gave as part of the *Loosely Assembled* exhibition curated by Danielle St-Amour at Montréal's SBC Gallery in 2019. As the duo (Ming Lin and Alex Tatarsky) read a collage of particular garments and passages of theoretical writings from photocopied book pages, audience members were welcomed on the runway – one of their ongoing series of reading apparatuses designed in collaboration with the NYC- and Brussels-based architectural collective common room – created down the centre of the gallery to select, try on, and read from the archival T-shirts. The ensuing demichaos was exhilarating. In it, one could sense a number of things: the all-pervasive tongue of capitalist jargon rubbing against a breaking point in the system, the interpersonal joy in the affect of this rupture, the facade of individual authenticity fading into a foreground of collective mimicry, a momentary soft architecture of reformulated relation that was revelatory.

Since this collective reading, I've been following with wonder their work from installation to installation, performance to archive. There are several elements of the overall project that continue to draw me in: its social and ethnographic dimensions; the way it knits together in a complicated texture various art historical genealogies with poetic practice; its succinct and wild materialist poetics; the way it explores a kind of linguistic realism that is resonant with histories of found poetry; and its emphasis on the circulation of language, with and amid so many other commodities, and the array of meanings that are made through the process of that circulation.

The following dialogue – focusing on the contexts of the Shanzhai Lyric project, their recent explorations through the Canal Street Research Association, and the cultural-linguistic scraps they weave into a living garment – took place in the autumn of 2021 between New York City and Montréal.

MN What initially drew you towards these shanzhai garments and their language? How did that evolve into the initial stages of the Shanzhai Lyric project?

SL Ming was living in Hong Kong, documenting errant architectures. Hong Kong, being at the base of China, receives the bulk of mass-produced Chinese goods that filter through it before being distributed all over the world. As a result, there are lots of informal markets pawning off of its excesses, and shanzhai shirts are one of the things that you frequently see. There are whole street markets dedicated to secondary or tertiary markets of those shirts.

Simultaneously, Alex had been thinking about spambot poetry and about multilingual translation and the translation of apparent nonsense, specifically in the Soviet-Jewish context of diasporic peoples who may not have access to an "original" tongue or mother tongue, so instead they write in an imagined or invented mother tongue. How do you translate a language that is made up and that is collaged of references or desires or intense longings to communicate? The things we both had been thinking about came together in this exciting way through the apparently nonsensical meaning-making structures of shanzhai writing. We were like, we could think about this forever – everything is in it: questions of property and ownership, access and values, language and hybridity and global cultural exchange and hierarchies, and the myths around consumption. So we've been thinking about it ever since.

Anyway, we were offered an opportunity to go to Beijing, and that's where the project started. Knowing we were about to enter the firewall, we downloaded five books to bring with us. *Shanzhai: Deconstruction in Chinese* by the German philosopher Byung-Chul Han was one of them. It became really instrumental to our thinking.

We had of course been familiar with the idea of Chinglish for a long time, but it didn't sit entirely well with us. The word *Chinglish* has a derogatory implication, and fails to encapsulate what are often very beautiful and hilarious, ecstatic phrases. We wanted to think more about why the language of shanzhai garments was so enchanting.

MN This makes me think of Fan Wu's statement about shanzhai language as being something one looks at, laughs at, and moves on from, that it is ubiquitous and rather easy to not even acknowledge beyond a passing glimpse, yet, when you actually look at it and begin to think about it, you begin to see all of these elements you mention.

This leads me to my next question: Who, generally speaking, composes the language on these garments? And how are they composed?

SL Actually, it's still an ongoing inquiry of ours and there isn't one answer. One of the many things that was cancelled in 2020 was this larger research program we had designed where we would spend a bunch of time in South China trying to gain access to these various cottage industries where a lot of these shirts are produced, and then make our way from there to the Museum of the Counterfeit in Paris, which has been a long-term dream of ours.

MN Museum of the Counterfeit?

SL It's this fascinating and quite antiquated museum that was founded in 1922 by the Union of Manufacturers, an organization started in 1872 to combat an influx of fake goods – mostly pharmaceuticals – that were flowing into France from Prussia. They wanted to show examples of "real" versus "fake" items to warn the French public of these dangerous foreign items. At some point, the museum board was taken over by a consortium of luxury brands. The museum's collection is largely comprised of goods confiscated at the border and is used today to train border guards to identify counterfeits. We're very interested in how this demonstrates the direct role definitions of authentic and copy play in global nation-building apparatuses.

We have our theories about where this language comes from, and there's evidence in the language of many different processes going on – for instance, text and imagery directly lifted from a luxury brand's design with alterations that appear to result from the use of certain software or be personally edited in to avoid copyright infringement or to comment or innovate on the design. We've had many conversations with people involved in the design worlds in Hong Kong and China, but we have not had a chance to visit a factory. So there's this degree to which it remains mysterious to us what the physical infrastructural conditions are. Of course, the conditions are different from garment to garment. But the methodologies that we've talked to people about sound like a kind of chance poetry, a human-machine collaboration that leaves a lot of room for creativity: the translation techniques being used, the various procedures of retyping, this one approach described to us of searching on the internet for a particular word and then collaging together the text and imagery that come up. So let's say a designer searches for a word – *freedom* was the example given to us – they see what text the internet pulls up, and then think visually in relation to the text to make a composition on the garment. So there is this blurring of the line between poet and designer, akin to concrete poetry that treats the text as pattern.

It's interesting to us that this question of authorship is so central to people. It's usually the first thing we are asked. We have ideas of how the text is made – and you could probably come up with similar ideas – but this question of "Who are these people?" is really a question about intentionality. And what's underneath the question a lot of the time is, "But these are really just mistakes, right?" You're over-ascribing intention.

To us, it doesn't feel that way. We're not claiming to know what anyone involved in the process was thinking or intending to communicate. We're trying to describe a phenomenon that the circumstances of global production have made possible and to read within all of these dynamics the different insights that arise in response to a contemporary experience. So the question of intention, or the fact that there is so often a question around authorship, is in and of itself really intriguing to us. If there is any kind of talkback with an audience, the first questions are always: "Who did these? How do you know that's what they were thinking? Aren't they just errors?" We're interested in the assumptions behind those questions.

MN For me, I was simply interested in imagining the space in which there exists a kind of board room next to the production room where people are making these shirts, and inside the board room of this "cottage industry," as you say, there are these investors who look at a T-shirt and read "AIL PALACES ARETEMPORARY HALACES" and they all nod their heads and say, "Yes, yes, this one is good, let's make three thousand of these." At some point, some individual or group of individuals is making those decisions, and I find that particular point in the production to be fascinating.

But I love your point about authorship and the poet-designer. Here, I am thinking about the search engines involved in the process, and then also the nation-state's own particular regulation of those search engines, how they are involved in the writing as well. It's really a vast apparatus of inscription we're talking about here.

SL That's what the glitches reveal, right? It's a diffuse and distributed chain of command that is not so much hierarchical as it is horizontal.

MN It's the "meshwork of glitch," to quote Fan Wu again, involved in this chain of command.

I want to ask a question about the English on these garments. I sometimes think that it's as if global capital itself is speaking upon or through these garments and that the "English" syntax and spelling we encounter is its particular accent. Based on your interests in the various aspects of multilingual translation and creation of new or nonlanguages, I wonder how the engagement with the textuality of these garments has impacted your relationship with English.

SL It's not only English, it's also French, Italian, Spanish, and transliterations from Cyrillic. There's a lot of Pinyin – Romanized Chinese words – as well as lorem ipsum or nonsense filler text reminiscent of Latin.

What's coming to mind in thinking about the appeal of garments that say, for instance, "SAMPLE TEXT," is that a hollowing out of English is also a demonstration of English as the global language of selling stuff. And that the text itself doesn't matter as much as the demonstration of imperial tongue, of a tongue that signifies power, access, the possibility of luxury, the possibility of riches. "SAMPLE TEXT," is a canonical example of that. It is delightful to see a shirt that so nakedly displays this function.

It's like a deferral of desire, because a garment can state all these aspirational things, "PARIS!" or whatever. But then you get the garment, and you're disappointed. It's like the potential is never realized. But "SAMPLE TEXT" leaves that open. Insert your desire here. Imagine whatever you want into the form of this, these letters. It's great.

MN This meaning-making in the hollowing out of traditional linguistic norms makes me think of Dohra Ahmad's anthology *Rotten English,* which speaks to vernacular modes of trying to undo imperial sense or imperial meaning-making at a syntactical level.

SL That's the main thing that we've experienced in talking to people who make or distribute these garments, an irreverence and casual rejection of caring about English as a meaning-making language. The attitude is pretty much like, I don't care. I don't care what it says, and I don't care that it's wrong. The shirt looks cool, and I like the appearance. So the English is reduced, reduced or elevated, in some way transmuted into image, which is really curious and delightful.

The other day we were talking to some folks who are all doing different kinds of research on shanzhai, and Zairong Xiang offered that he would describe this attitude towards English as one of "radical indifference," which is great. Radical indifference as an everyday strategy of resistance. To demonstrate radical indifference towards the correct form of an imperial tongue means that you're not even giving any energy towards rejecting it; you're just like, I don't care. I can't be bothered.

MN I love the framing of Shanzhai Lyric as exploring the interwoven state of linguistics and logistics. This, I think, is a vital way of considering language that I would like to see more of on different historical and geographical scales. It's a concern that appears in some critical writings, but I think in this creative work you're exploring the subject critically with an important depth that is not often materialized in other modes of critical discourse. So I simply wanted to ask what drew you towards thinking about logistics and linguistics together?

SL When we were first in residence in Beijing, where the project was really born, we were also involved in various distribution practices as art practices. While distributing coffee through Kate

Rich's Feral Trade network, we were thinking about how objects move around the world and how to situate art practice within this flow of goods. So the relationship with logistics was there from the beginning. When we began developing an exhibition framework for looking at and reflecting on and celebrating these garments, it was implicit that the inquiry would extend into how they were being circulated.

Also, we're excited about the flattening out of category. We don't fully identify as artists, and it's curious to us that the work continually finds a home within arts contexts. We tend to think of ourselves more as paralogisticians, because what we're doing is moving things around – and out of necessity! We now have four hundred poetry-garments in the archive, and part of the practice is perpetually finding new homes for them, because we don't have a warehouse.

And the Feral Trade project is also a critique of the art world. Coffee and other provisions travel on what the artist Kate Rich calls the "hot air" of the art world, the excess baggage of the global circuit of curators and artists travelling to and fro who have surplus space in their suitcase. By tracing the dispatch routes, Feral Trade ends up becoming a portrait of the excesses of the art world. Similarly, poetry-garments in transit become a tracing or portrait of a certain moment. So logistics enters into the project on multiple levels. On our website the metadata is part of the story of these shirts. How they circulate is as important as what they say or what they don't say.

A lot of the research of the past year has been observing global trade flows as they manifest in the space of a single block, Canal Street. Pre-pandemic, we had wanted to follow a single item around the world, but given the circumstances, we couldn't. When we started occupying a storefront on Canal Street, we realized that we didn't need to travel because those movements could be studied right outside of our door. Canal Street is a cacophony of languages and cultures where vendors predominantly from East Asia and West Africa peddle bootleg luxury goods to tourists from all over the world. It is a main artery of New York City, has served as a landing pad for immigrant communities for centuries, and is the site of what is considered the first free African American community in North America.[1] Canal Street was built atop a creek channelled to flow from Collect Pond – once the largest freshwater reservoir for the Lenape peoples and, later, the Dutch and English colonizers. The original Canal Street industry was oysters and the policing of street vending that began with the harassment of the oyster carts has carried down into the discriminatory policies towards African American and immigrant street vendors that continue today.

The myth of the authentic, the question of real and fake, when you think about it, starts to seem like it's at the heart of everything that governs our lives. Who determines what's real and what's fake? And who are these definitions used to criminalize? The criminalization of the "fake" happens at the level of a bootleg bag and also happens in the militarized maintenance of borders. This is very much on our minds, because borders are the ultimate fake thing – arbitrary lines invented to criminalize and contain certain people for the benefit of others. And so the movement of counterfeits across borders is where you can really see the fakeness of the nation in action, and how dedicated the nation is to presenting itself as real through various violent activities.

In more recent times, authenticity also plays a role in the neoliberalization of the city. Canal Street has this lore around it as one of the last holdouts of authentic New York grit. But what makes it authentic, which is something that landlords and the government don't seem to appreciate, is the informal economy of fake goods. It's the thing they're constantly trying to eradicate or sterilize, not appreciating that it's what gives the neighbourhood its desirable "authentic" character. In relation to the street markets, it becomes very visible how the police exist solely to protect landowner property. During the pandemic, when the stores here were boarded up, there were no more police, because the police had no businesses to protect. And so the street markets really came to life. And as soon as businesses began reopening, the police returned and were stationed on the block 24/7, because they had people – not even people to protect – because they had people's *property* to protect.

Street vendors represent the genuine possibility of upward mobility. If the "American Dream" is a thing that could possibly exist, it exists in the informal economy, because you come to this country and you do not own property and you do not have the means to own property, and so you sell things out of your coat or from a rug on the ground or from a small cart and that's the way to accumulate capital and to maybe one day own property that you will then pass on to your children. That's the heart of the myth.

MN This makes me think of Moscot Glasses, which is not too far away from you there, and the whole mythos of somebody's great-great-grandfather, a newly landed immigrant, pushing his cart of eyeglasses around the Lower East Side and today, look at this giant store with his appearance across it on Delancey Street.

SL We're making our way in that direction with the Canal Street Research Association project. Heading west to east, we hope to conclude at Essex Market, which is where Mayor La Guardia basically pushed all of the street vendors to, as a way to regulate the informal economy of the streets and make it less visible. The original Essex Market had no windows, because they wanted to conceal immigrant vendors who were considered a blight on the city.

MN I'm often astounded by the municipal political discourse of invoking and celebrating diverse forms of urban life while at the same time always trying to sanitize and regulate and police to the maximum that which is supposedly central to the composition of this living. It obviously exists beyond the municipal level and functions at the level of the nation-state and the union of nation-states. Yet the urban municipal level is one of the clearest frames for seeing such a process.

I want to attempt to draw two questions together that arise from your last statements. There is a sentence from Caroline Busta that you quote in your essay in *The New Inquiry* about "metabolizing the surplus of one's environment," how fashion metabolizes the surplus of one's environment. It makes me think of how you are enacting a kind of countermetabolism in the Shanzhai Lyric project. The thought that rose up with that first one while you were speaking was about the life of Canal Street during this brief interregnum of the streets in the midst of the pandemic and after the George Floyd protests. I'm not sure how exactly these two points connect, but I thought I might offer them up as a kind of partially connected question-thought.

SL The way that you phrase this question or offering, connecting that quote "metabolizing the surplus of one's environment" to acts of theft as rebellion, really prefigures the situation in which we had access to an empty storefront for free. Salient images in the media of the uprisings, like police cars being set on fire, and the so-called looting of luxury goods from luxury stores right here in SoHo, are in some sense what "tore apart the nation" and showed where the divisions in terms of values and perception of reality lie. Because to us that was an ecstatic moment to be stealing these extremely valuable and yet utterly worthless items – to be metabolizing the surplus of one's environment by redistributing the goods.

This is precisely what shanzhai philosophy is. Etymologically, the roots "shan" and "zhai" translate to "mountain" "hamlet," a place on the edge of town where bandits can take the goods from the centre of empire and redistribute them on the margins.

MN One thing I wanted to ask you about is something that emerged from seeing Alex's performance at The Kitchen a few days ago, and it concerns the poetics of the scrap. I realize Alex's intoning of this phrase is speaking to the specificity of the work they're doing as a solo artist outside of the Shanzhai Lyric project, but it was something informed by this collaborative project that runs concurrently to it in an important way. There is a rich historical discourse on the fragment. I never realized this until I started to think about the scrap and how it applies to the Shanzhai Lyric project, but it struck me how the fragment has this masculinist aura to it – as in "I broke off this piece of my grand oeuvre," that this remaining piece of a glorious past totality is something to be lamented. In my mind, the scrap laughs in the face of that. I wanted to ask you if the scrap is something that you've been thinking about in terms of this work, because it obviously relates to garments as much as it does the linguistic issues that are present throughout the work.

SL Yes! Everything is chewing on the same questions, but taking different forms. Alex was teaching a class on the poetics and politics of rot last year and talking a lot about scraps. The students were developing different practices of saving scraps and finding tenderness for the scrap. This one really wonderful student in the class said, "I just don't feel right calling them scraps. I think we should call them scrawps. We should have an 'aw' for them inside the word. When we say 'scrap,' it sounds too much like crap; it sounds too dismissive. I think we should start calling them scrawps." So we started calling them scrawps.

The scrawp has a tenderness that the fragment can elicit as well, but you're right, a scrap is scrappy, right? There's a different ethos in it. Scrappiness. Often you need to be scrappy when you don't have the same access to resources. And then the other thing in relation to the garment is, well, the commedia dell'arte figure of Harlequin. He dons such a beautiful garment composed of colourful scraps collected from friends, because he can't afford fancy clothes of his own. It involves noticing and loving scraps enough to save them over time and to figure out what the composition of scraps into a whole wants to be. Scraps form a whole where the seams are still visible.

This is something we've been thinking about for a long time: how shanzhai garments make visible the seam, the seams of production, as well as the places where the seams unravel. This metaphor inspires us as a way to approach structures that seem impenetrable, that seem unbreakable. Usually there's a way that you can find where the seam was constructed. Then, perhaps, you can also find or notice where the seam is unravelling. Then, maybe, you can even figure out where you could tug on the thread and help accelerate the unravelling so that a different kind of composition might become possible. So that's exciting to us in terms of thinking politically about how structures come to be, and how they might be undone. At the level of language, the unravelling of tongues makes possible a different way of describing and therefore experiencing and therefore imagining.

We've been working with the architectural collective common room to develop these different reading apparatus for each iteration of the project. These reading apparatus are often drawing from tropes where we witness text and textile in action. So for instance, we've built structures based on a runway, a clothing line, a newspaper stand, a billboard, a wall. But another trope we've picked up on is the trope of the heap, as something which is ubiquitous in informal markets – the heaped-up goods. We've found that the heap is often the most exciting structure for people to pick through. It's perhaps the most inviting; it's what people are most drawn to it and willing to engage with. It's also very nostalgic for a lot of people in the sense that for some, it's like going through Grandma's closet. It's this informality that makes people want to engage. The heap is the best reading apparatus in terms of being the most functional, because people know how to read it. While it seems counter to legibility, it turns out to be the most legible way for people to connect with the garments and their language. It invites you to be active in making legible in a way that you choose.

This somehow relates to – and this is very little-known – the fact that the name of the Shanzhai Lyric project was inspired in part by Lisa Robertson's "The Value Village Lyric," which also speaks about this kind of flattening of the codes of luxury and a space that calls on consumers to engage in a new way with garments and to find their own mode of making legible, emancipated from the norms of branding, on the clothing racks.

MN I adore Lisa Robertson's writings on fashion – both the variously scattered pieces she writes from time to time and the excerpts of *The Baudelaire Fractal* that focus on thinking with some particular garment.

The thing about the heap, too, in hearing you speak about it, is that it intones this whole tradition of minimalist sculpture and participatory works, also. For instance, Robert Smithson comes to mind (*A heap of Language,* 1966) thinking about the heap, but so does Félix González-Torres (*Untitled [Portrait of Ross in L.A.],* 1991).

SL We've been thinking about Félix González-Torres a lot. Part of our practice is restaging or producing bootleg versions of various ephemeral art pieces. Literally the whole New York art world from the turn of the century on has deep connections to Canal Street. You hear these stories about so-and-so finding this piece of metal at a junk shop on Canal Street. Like Richard Serra found his first piece of iron on Canal Street, David Hammons bought the plastic moulds to make the snowballs for his *Bliz-aard Ball Sale,* Louise Bourgeois bought latex at Canal Rubber, Jack Smith salvaged his trash sets from the street, Nam Jun Paik and Laurie Anderson repurposed Canal Street electronics for sound pieces, Dan Flavin got his neon here ... and Duchamp found his urinal here. Or rather, Elsa Baroness von Freytag-Loringhoven did. The list truly goes on and on.

MN I love this quote where you write about how the shanzhai mode of production could be considered to operate in the tradition of Chinese landscape painting and calligraphy. It's an incredibly bold assertion, and absolutely fitting once the dynamics of production and authorship in these practices are brought together in conversation. So I simply wanted to think about various textual, poetics, and imagistic traditions that you feel like you're in conversation with – where do you see affinity, where do you see conversation with specific aesthetic movements or tendencies, or even particular artists? With affinity, there's always a speaking back to, or critique of, I think, that's important to acknowledge, so affinity does not need to mean clear correspondence or admiration.

SL The thing that comes most immediately to mind is the very recent history of Canal Street where, during a summer of pandemic and uprising, storefronts were boarded up by landlords seeking to protect their property. On the one hand, this perpetuated the hoarding of space, but on the other, what was apparent to us was the way it turned the city into a massive scroll. As soon as the plywood boards went up, various signatures, tags, posters, and all kinds of commentary were thrown up onto them. Like an ancient landscape painting on a scroll, which, as Byung-Chul Han describes, invites collective inscription from subsequent owner-authors, the plywood pieces become loci of collective inscription, challenging the notion of private property and the attendant idea of a single owner-author.

It also feels similar to modes of discourse on the internet. For instance, with memes and comment boards, the original is lost and the work is ever-changing, ever-accumulating as alterations become forms of commentary, resulting in this collectively authored, ever-unfinished landscape. That also feels really in line with what Byung-Chul Han traces as a shanzhai lineage from a landscape painting tradition that proposes a different relationship to authorship and originality. The communication modes of the internet are actually returning to this mode of collectively authored and commented-upon work.

In terms of other traditions, we often think of Zaum writing in the poetry of the Russian Futurists. *Zaum* can be translated as "beyond sense"– not nonsense but beyonsense. There's something being communicated: that language, as we might think we know it, is insufficient to communicate. You have to go beyond sense. You have to break the word, or recombine the word, or be residing in an imagistic or sonic landscape, in order to communicate more fully a certain experience.

And also, there is Dada, and thinking about both Eastern and Western forms of Dada, or thinking of Dada as not solely a European male tradition but as a way of relating to text as image. We have right now these large neons that we found on Canal Street and one of them says "DA." We think it's from a company called VEDA but we arranged it to say "DAVE." Then we felt like that made our space seem too much like a start-up. So we layered them up on top of one another so that it just reads "DA," which feels better on many levels, *da* meaning an emphatic, ecstatic "yes" in Russian. But also meaning nothing: da da da da da da.

MN It also has a series of meanings through the Sanskrit – "to give," "to sound," and also, as symbol in the Puranic tradition, "a ruin" – all of which are significant in T.S. Eliot's "The Waste Land," as "DA" is what the thunder says throughout the poem's final movement.

SL See, associative methodologies always work!

We also look to artists who employ strategies like bootlegging and mimicry as a way of reclaiming. There is no definitive history of Canal Street, largely because of the illicit nature of the activities that have transpired here or the unofficial status of many people who work here. Therefore artworks become the street's main archive. Restaging or bootlegging is a means of telling lesser-known, unofficial, and unsanctioned histories. We think of artists like Elaine Sturtevante, who bootlegs iconic male artists' work, such as Oldenburg's *The Store*, to reclaim the narrative.

We also think of different modes of discourse where the commentary is the work. For instance, a Talmudic relationship to text bears some similarity to the relationship that Byung-Chul Han draws to Chinese landscape painting, where a central image becomes increasingly surrounded by comments over time. The commentary becomes the work. That feels really resonant with the shanzhai garments, where an image is often surrounded by accumulating text and commentary, and that commentary is the work. Then anyone engaging with it can inscribe themselves into it with additional commentary on the commentary.

MN This is how I was approaching your work or making sense of it when I first encountered it in Montréal. At the time, I was working on an essay about the circulation of various drafts of Aristotle's *Poetics* in the Mediterranean during the Middle Ages, and I was fascinated by this text – one that was dictated and assembled from a kind of lecture or live event of teaching (an acroamatic work) that then gets translated into Syriac and then Arabic, and with these translations, all of these commentaries are added into the text itself and into its marginalia, and, very similarly to Talmudic texts, you have a main text (one often altered in its copying) and then generations upon generations of commentaries upon it that bear the history of its use and reflection and circulation over time.

SL The marginalia, exactly, which bears the architectural, geographic resonance of the margins. On the page and in a city, and in a country and in the world, what is the marginalia?

ENDNOTE

1 David Berman, "North America's First Free Black Settlement in Our Neighbourhoods," *Village Preservation Blog* (website), May 25, 2022.

We Need to Ground It in the Real

A Dialogue with Cecily Nicholson

"THROUGH FACT WITH TEXTURE, ATMOSPHERE, AND affect," Cecily Nicholson's poems compose the possible syntaxes and slogans of collective resistance. Her first two books, *Triage* and *From the Poplars,* are palimpsestual and polyvocalic studies of imperial violence's perpetual encroachment on lands and lives. They articulate how solidarity might be materialized in language and in action against such forces. Nicholson's following book, *Wayside Sang,* thinks with the fugitive movements and networks of Black diaspora and Indigenous displacement to establish a ground for convergence, for communion, for chorus. Set mainly in the rural, Nicholson's fourth book, *HARROWINGS,* connects with Black intellectual and art history in relation to agriculture. Considering movements organizing for food security, set within a local agricultural enterprise led by people who were formerly incarcerated, the book also contends with "the farm" as a tract of colonial advance. Nicholson's new book, *Crowd Source,* was published in the spring of 2025. She is the 2024/2025 Holloway Lecturer in Poetry and Poetics at the University of California, Berkeley, and the author of four books including *From the Poplars,* recipient of the Dorothy Livesay Poetry Prize, and *Wayside Sang,* winner of the Governor General's Literary Award for Poetry.

I first met Nicholson in the summer of 2013 when we were invited by Juliana Spahr and David Buuck to take part in the Beyond Oakland program along with poets Anne Boyer and Marie Buck. Two things struck me right away: first, the particular mixture of sensitivity and conviction of her perspective on the overlapping terrain of the social and political from her grounded experience of working in one of the most complex communities in North America ravaged by settler colonialism and global capitalist accumulation, Vancouver's downtown eastside; second, her capacity to transmute that engagement into a lyric practice that is at once jarring and fractured, yet also always somehow mellifluous, replete with breath and togetherness.

Readers of and listeners to her poetry are drawn in to want to travel with Nicholson, however terse the terrain, for the spaces she opens through her work.

The following dialogue dates back to a live exchange Nicholson and I recorded during 2017, a few months before *Wayside Sang* appeared in print. Originally, we had intended to prepare this dialogue for a scholarly volume emerging out of a conference on Vancouver poetry, but we then decided to direct this exchange towards Buuck's *Tripwire: a journal of poetics*. Our exchange arose because I felt that her shattered, graceful, rough-hewn yet graceful lyric-documentary works did not yet have the readership they deserved. That situation has since changed, yet the conversation offers a striking view into how, with whom, and for whom Nicholson has been able to compose her polyvocal, palimpsestic works. Her development of a poetics of relation, of community-based practices that are anchored to the page yet rove beyond it, are central to this book's overall undertaking.

MN I wonder if we might begin by discussing Vancouver poetics, or what it means to compose works on the unceded xʷməθkʷəy̓əm, Sḵwx̱wú7mesh, and səlilwətaɬ Territories known as Vancouver. When we originally talked about doing this dialogue, its destination was for a publication emerging out of an academic conference on contemporary aesthetic communities in Vancouver. I think both of us felt some hesitation to contribute to that forum, though.

CN The one piece of feedback that struck me was – and it's a typical thing that happens in academic contexts – about the way the conversation was framed, that the conversation itself fed into academia. It doesn't matter; you can't have grassroots dialogue in spaces that are not accessible to community to get there. Unless you're moving through academic channels, or if you were invited and had somebody paying you to go, it wasn't possible for people to be there and represent. So I was aware of that, too, that perpetual divide in terms of who gets to represent any place away from it. Certainly, with Vancouver this plays out.

MN The form of the event immediately forecloses any possibility of the kind of grassroots dialogue of which you speak.

CN I think so. I think it's that notion of – how do I say it? – it's that those people who are really entrenched in the local, the people who are the most Vancouver, are the ones who are the most immobile (and who are, at the same time, often the most subject to displacement, institutionalization, forced migrations). I mean, with love, I am interested when people are trying, but I do think – and I realize I'm generalizing – that academia often fails when it tries to connect to and enact non-academic community. They are coming from too remote a place socially to grasp what's practically needed. It also has to do with the communication, with the methods of gathering and how we come together. The material barriers are a perpetual problem for all that we imagine ourselves doing.

MN Yes, and mobility arises in terms of the circulation of works, as well. The phrase that you used earlier about "the most Vancouver" of the Vancouver poets – I feel like one has to do a lot of work in relation to other readers, other poets, in order to get to that milieu. There are people I look to in Vancouver, and who are always reading the work of Vancouver poets, and so I know to look out for the work of Annharte and Mercedes Eng, and to track down what was published in those old Tsunami Editions, and to read Dorothy Trujillo Lusk.

CN Good examples. And Maxine Gadd, similarly. They are prominent in certain ways because writers lift up their work and remind us. Otherwise, their works don't circulate in the same way. There are historical divides that are gendered, racialized, and certainly classed. One of the lovely things about the Kootenay School legacy is that the school has always been concerned with class. I mean, it's failed in some other considerations, but its consideration of class is an important legacy in Vancouver poetics. I feel like that doesn't function in the active way that it needs to these days, across experience, as we are even more defined in this city by the stratification between rich and poor, and, overwhelmingly, as so many art and literary representatives come from the academy, through the academy. You don't often hear from writers of my generation or younger who aren't somehow connected to universities. That's an incredible limitation when we think about who accesses, and succeeds at, this kind of education. I wonder about it. In Canada, I'm barely published outside of Vancouver. I want to think for a minute, because perhaps I'm missing something, but I'm pretty sure you'd be hard-pressed to find my work anywhere east of Calgary.

MN I think it's an issue in Canada where poets who are committed to exploring diasporic and internationalist affinities and commitments in terms of poetics and politics simply don't have a place in the cultural apparatus here, which is vehemently nation-centred. They may have their singular site, their city, but if they want to be read outside of it, there has to be some kind of network forged outside of Canada.

CN Yes, and things are shifting right now for me in that way. I am spending more time south of the border and embracing my own personal history in terms of ancestry and forced migration and displacement and feeling some deep affinity with works in the

US. I recall you introducing me to Fred Moten's work years back, and as Mercedes Eng and I head to New York in the spring to visit him and community there, I think on new friendships. I think of friendships in Detroit. And in the Bay Area, Tongo Eisen-Martin, such a lightning bolt. Meeting him felt like meeting new family. I think of Aja Monet and Jasmine Gibson. I appreciate Juliana Spahr and David Buuck, who have made space for me and my work. It's an odd shift, as my work these days finds more resonance perhaps in those directions as opposed to central Canada, even though I grew up in rural Ontario. Then again, the conversations continue. Christina Sharpe and Dionne Brand were in town from Toronto recently and, somehow, I ended up at the same table for a moment or so. I mean, I've been reading Dionne Brand since I was a kid, terrified, coming to Toronto in my teens, sitting with her poetry on the Greyhound bus to the city, it was critical for me. And all the brilliant work, Katherine McKittrick, Robyn Maynard, I mean the kind of practices that Black women intellectuals are doing right now and that we're able to access in this moment, is moving. That shift isn't just a mainstream push or pull around literature. It's a resonance from multiple communities foregrounding experiences of Blackness, embodied – we're using different language, we've multiple locations, influences, and affinities, we are global in our relations, and I also belong to this.

MN I'd love to hear what you've been up to in Detroit and Windsor while you've been writing *Wayside Sang*.

CN The book runs through Windsor to Detroit. The cities are twinned in a way, but it's always been about Detroit for me. I've been going there for decades now. When I was young, I went just a couple of times, but later, kept getting called to visit. Part of that evolves out of limited narrative I have around my birth father's movement. He was a travelling musician, among other kinds of work, and he was often crossing that border, at that place, although I didn't know that until later in my life. I've needed to think about and spend more time in that space to gain a better sense of it, and of myself there.

In Vancouver, we certainly have a lot to face in terms of the cost of living and the idea of affordability, but we sure have resources when it comes to art production. There's so much infrastructure that's threaded through by the province, by the state, and by the municipality, and that is actively a part of how art work and art world conversations occur in this locale. It's not to say that Detroit doesn't have government funding influences – the private foundation model does seem to be much more prevalent – however, there is this real dearth of infrastructural support, right through to a lack of good public transit. What I've witnessed over the years has included some really humble and humbling practices, examples of community, incredible collaboration, and use of materials, the rise of lost and derelict and things broken, refashioned, with social and non-capitalist purpose. And being in a majority-Black city, it means that almost everywhere you look, there are people that can see me. I'm a mixed, light-skinned Black Canadian citizen, I think through my mobility and privileges – including the history of my education and diction – yet I feel freer there than in Vancouver. It's confusing. I feel a debt to the city. It seemed necessary to finish this recent book there, to let a neighbourhood suffuse the last bit of process as I wrote by an open window during one long summer month, resting, where Detroit meets Hamtramck.

MN *From the Poplars* reads, for me, as a site-specific work in that it is focused on Poplar Island, a small island near the delta of the Fraser River, close to Vancouver. Is *Wayside Sang* similarly site-centred as a work?

CN I struggle because I'm compelled to do that, but I couldn't quite do that with this narrative. It's a narrative that travels roadways, crosses borders and land. There are some site-specific efforts concerning the areas and road travel that I'm undertaking in these multiple narratives, not just my own narratives. The writing does work through some of the place names, thinking through territories, through migratory routes and waterways, things we can think of comprising the ecology of a place. It is a ways away from the West Coast. If anything, there's some interplay of the prairies, because I was also thinking through my relations to fathers and brothers, somehow come through there. My only Black brother lives on the prairies. Also, a musician, he's in this book somehow. Although it does deal with specific locales at moments, *Wayside*

Sang is definitely not the specific study that *From the Poplars* is. I needed the narrative to not be fixed this time around.

MN Yes, the reason I ask is because I think of that site study as a central part of your poetics – the exploration of space's composition, its strata of history and rhetoric and contestations. I read *Triage* as a book specifically about the downtown eastside, about the various spheres of power and resistance that intersect there, but perhaps that's an impression I put onto the text knowing you and your efforts parallel to writing.

CN No, you're not the only one. I didn't make that overt when I wrote *Triage*. It's more in retrospect that I realize, of course, that's so much of what it's about. I mean, certainly there are more obvious narratives that are working through being present in a neighbourhood – those are entirely about, in, and of the downtown eastside. Now that book means a lot to me, actually. I suppose all our first books will mean a lot to ourselves in the long run, right? It really was an achievement post-traumas. I look back on it and feel really, not proud, well, maybe it is pride, I don't know. Something. A sense of survival and thriving beyond. But it is situated, for sure.

With *Triage*, I don't know what got into me, but at that point I was just starting to enter into art gallery spaces, and realized that I'd missed a great deal in terms of the relevance of visual culture. I was thinking a lot about that while I was writing the book. I picked up a camera for the first time and began to see protest as an aesthetic, or to see the aesthetics of protest. And I began realizing that, again, I'm so naive – there are whole threads of history I've missed. I realized I was completely hindered by politics, by the idea of politics. I did not realize that questions about "politics" have also been a way of marginalizing aspects of art history. I was trying to figure out some things about art and the art world, and as I worked on that process with poetry, I realized that poetry, somehow artificially, in a really disturbing way, gets separated out from these spheres – again, related to issues of class, and the notion that access diminishes quality. So with *Triage*, while it's working through and is of the downtown eastside, and of trauma, it is also trying to figure out entry points to a world of art. The more experimental parts of it – not really in terms of form, but in terms of language in that book – have a lot to do with that.

MN When were you writing *Triage*?

CN It was published in 2011, but the work for that book got underway in the early aughts. I started working in the downtown eastside in 2000, and I was writing poetry out of necessity pretty much right away. The book was a long time coming. Work seems to come together for me a lot faster now, in terms of the writing, what I do with it and where it goes. Part of it, maybe, is confidence. Part of it is that time presses harder and harder. I think I'm also less caught up with the need to pore over things. I realize that sometimes people are interested in what you're saying off the cuff, you know. I'm trying to find balance and to practise.

MN I remember when we first met how impressed I was in hearing you speak. I admire so much your capability of talking about the context where you've been engaged and the people you've been working with over the last decades. Your groundedness there permeates your language about it. Can you say more about that? It's something I struggle with, but it's also something I'm perpetually intrigued by – who speaks? what are the practices of listening involved in this kind of collective work? what are the modes of engaging with others, on behalf of or in connection to a place, in relation to other sites and activities?

CN If we're of a community, we know who of a community can speak back and be supported in doing so. We know that. The thing about the downtown eastside at this point, for me, is that it's been almost eighteen years that I've been working on that ground, within networks that connect there. That's not to say that my legitimacy in terms of representation has grown just because of time, but my relations and my security in knowing that I am also of that community has. I have process for reporting back and process for reporting out. When I am mobile, when I'm being invited to represent things – commonly from a quote-unquote minority position – too often we're called upon to represent widely.

I've been working in the federal prison system for several years now, but the people I'm working with have been at it for over thirty years. Every time I'm invited to talk through related issues – concerning Blackness, concerning disability, trauma, and mental health – you feel an urgency. You don't want to not speak. If you're present, you don't want to not take that space if you're the only one there who will honour your communities. You always have to have a sense of who you're indebted to, who else could be there alongside you, should be there instead of you and doing a better job. You need to figure out what you can do to support that work and make those connections.

MN You said earlier that you started working in the downtown eastside upon moving to Vancouver in 2000. What brought you there in the first place?

CN I guess I had an uncritical vision of being an activist at the time. I'd been aware and learning more about violence, particularly for racialized and Indigenous women in the sex trade. I wanted to do a PhD at the time, so that was in the back of my mind. I was moving with my partner, now my husband, and both of us had some visions about cities that we loved. One of the first decisions we made was not to stay in the States. I had a job in Indiana at that time. We had just fallen in love. You know that moment. I knew I couldn't go back to Ontario. We had two cities in mind – Montréal and Vancouver. At the time I had French in some small ways, but not professionally, and I was really worried about what that would mean. I'd never been to Vancouver, but I thought: ocean, mountains, why not? I should go at least once. I found a job at the Women's Centre within months. And that was it. I still work across the street from there. For seventeen-plus years, I have spent the greatest percentage of my time literally on that corner.

MN What's the corner?

CN Columbia and Cordova – it's been my vantage of Vancouver. Now I don't live in the city anymore. I've been evicted twice, and not for anything we've done wrong; it's the nature of the city. I won't move back to Vancouver. I feel it's unlikely. I feel very angry and haven't recovered from the Olympics. There are uncomfortable places in Vancouver for me at this point.

MN Did you know much about the writing community when you moved there?

CN No, I didn't. I had heard of Fred Wah and I think I'd heard of Wayde Compton. There was very little else I can think of that I would have known. But I also wasn't really a writer then. I was one of those people who had always written, but I kept it to myself. So I didn't arrive thinking, "I'm gonna be a writer." That wasn't even a priority. But what happened was that I got here, and within a couple of years I was involved in the university system. I met people, and began to pay attention to poetry publicly, and started coming out to events. I didn't find communities of colour therein, couldn't find Black poets or audience at the time. I did connect to the Kootenay School poets and their poetry, although I was never a part of their collective. I was interested in and engaged by the people there. A favourite person from day one was Jeff Derksen, a really critical figure to me. Of course, many others! What drew me in most was a desire to be part of these conversations.

MN So Derksen was someone you began reading and exchanging work with – who else?

CN Early on, Wayde Compton, Rita Wong, too, amazing people I was fortunate to encounter. Also, Larissa Lai and later Steve Collis.

MN This would have been the earlyish or mid-2000s?

CN Yes, around 2004 to 2007. My first public reading was, I believe, 2008.

MN I love your "The Quality of Light" essay you wrote for Stephanie Young's series on poetry and money, where you detail your personal history of writing and reading poetry through the conditions of labour and work and service.

CN Well, that was a funny thing to come at, to think through with that lens. It was helpful, actually. I learned about myself. It could have been longer, but then I was like, "Oh, this is just getting embarrassing." To reveal like that, I mean, I don't typically talk about myself in writing – that's the first time I've ever done that.

MN What I like so much about it is how clearly you think through the material conditions of writing, of the means and for whom one writes. On that note, can you describe the work you do with Gallery Gachet? I know you're involved in so many formations and networks of organizing, and to single it down to the work in that one location is an insufficient way to come at all the work you do. But visiting you at Gachet and walking around the neighbourhood with you, I feel I gained this deeper understanding of the language of your poems, their material context.

CN Gachet is my paid work. So the ways in which that dominates our lives do matter, but fortunately my heart has been committed for six years to the work I'm doing there. I'm an administrator – I think it's quite boring at the end of the day, but I have learned that administration and how you construct a program or programs is not by any stretch a neutral way of managing or being behind the scenes. Gallery Gachet straddles social and arts practices. We're a mental-health resource, but we're also a gallery and an artist-run centre. We run a public-access gallery where we host five to seven exhibitions each year. Three or four of those will be juried, and work with artists that we put in dialogue with our communities. Then two or three of the exhibitions are always based in community and partnerships longstanding. The work is predominately visual art. We do performance a lot in the space and, not surprisingly, a lot of social-practice stuff happens. And we do a lot of stuff scattered across sites, so we are increasingly not working just in the gallery – everything from parades to workshops to pop-up exhibitions and performance work in public spaces. We're trying to gain a better understanding of public art, and trying to break down what makes certain art public art.

MN Yes, and experimenting with a public art that doesn't uphold the formations of the social as they already are. This is something I've been thinking about often, how so many social-practice-based works mostly reinforce the already-existing parameters of art and aesthetic cultures.

CN That's right, and because of that we're very careful about who we work with and bring into the gallery. One of our ongoing partners has been the artist-curator Carmen Papalia, a real leader in terms of trying to think through ideas of access. He's a non-visual learner, self-described, who makes use of amazing interpretations of a disabling world. He was actually the first person to publish me. Many years ago, he ran a journal called *Memewar* with a group that worked out of Simon Fraser. Anyway, he's one example of some of the wonderful people who are able to do work in and of our community as they get to know a plurality of who that community is, and somehow help interface in broader art-world conversations and problems.

MN And you've also been inviting writers into the space, I believe?

CN Yes, I've been able to do literary programming in the space as well. We've hosted Jasmine Gibson, Tongo Eisen-Martin, Juliana Spahr and David Buuck, Marie Annharte, Mercedes Eng, Otoniya J. Okot-Bitek, Jordan Scott, and others locally. One of the more influential series in recent memory, in my mind, in this city, was REVERB: a Queer Reading Series. They just disbanded after four and a half years, but that was a crew of people led by the writers Leah Horlick and Estlin McPhee. They curated queer writers and did so in ways that engaged questions about access for audiences and readers, and what it meant to situate themselves at Gallery Gachet in the downtown eastside, considering who attends and how. They did amazing work, and they were just building and building – physical access, environment, figuring out good childcare, figuring out ASL, figuring out queer ASL ... and withstanding necessary critique along the way. There are all kinds of moments around Gachet, centred in it, that have been just amazing. And then we're a resource, also, for the social movements of the neighbourhood. So when there's a paint-in or when there's banner making, when there's a need for a parade, a report to be designed, or support for communications, people know they can call on us. It's been important to have some of that work in the space. That is part of my work. I suppose I could talk about my volunteer time or the other things that I do – filtered through what that community deals with. A lot of residents and former residents experience policing, surveillance, carceral logics and systems, formerly or family-wise, or are at-risk of, and so I've been concerned and involved with work and organizing within prisons and without, extending notions of community to understand what's separated out, to resist what these systems try to do. An example of that is with the Memorial March Committee.

MN The Memorial March, is it for Missing and Murdered Indigenous Women?

CN It's for Missing and Murdered Women and two-spirit + and is led by Indigenous matriarchs and organizers. I'm quiet in that circle, but I am a helper through the years. Sometimes the work is not about organizing, it's about being organized, allowing yourself to be a part of being organized. At this point, I help coordinate the guardians for the march; the guardians are what one might call marshals in another setting. We have guardians, all connecting through the downtown eastside community, and many are living in the neighbourhood. I think that march is one of the most stunning aesthetic examples of Vancouver – a presence and commitment through the years – in terms of the sound, songs, the Women's Warrior Song, and the drum, the uniformity of messages, the many works that flow through this moment, the complexity of regalia, the leadership of matriarchs, and the movement in the streets, orchestrated and organic. There are so many ways to consider it. I'm also involved with a group called Joint Effort – we try to find ways to connect with incarcerated women and to connect them with their communities outside of prison. For the march each year, Joint Effort goes in to the prisons bringing materials for quilting. We bring out finished smaller pieces that get sewn together in a banner, and every year that banner is part of the march. We photograph each piece, as well as the banner, as well as the banner in the march and the people who march with it, and we take that documentation back to the prison to remind the women of their connection. These are small textile works and they're very humble, but they connect us somehow in these moments. The march will never call itself a protest. It does interrupt the major flows of capital and all the things that a good protest can do, while memorializing. I cannot write much about this. There will be shades, there will be corners that get occupied by what's relevant to my everyday, but I really can't write about a lot about this work. It goes back to those questions, which are ethical ones, about representation and being grounded, of being of communities and speaking to that. I will listen and lift. I can work through practices and methodology, I will collaborate.

MN It's interesting when one's own engagement allows them to realize the responsibility of not speaking, of not representing. I want to say, though, I'm amazed in the midst of all these efforts how quickly you've moved from first reading to first book to the two books you've written since!

CN It's funny, because it's not like I have more time to write. It seems I make decisions and they're supposed to set up that possibility of having more time to write. For instance, like taking on the Writer-in-Residence position or getting support from an arts council, which have been new experiences for me of late. They're wonderful, and this is not a complaint, but it's confusing, because it doesn't seem to work like that. It's not like there's more time.

MN I imagine that the work you do with Gachet never stops, because the community is constantly going and that never stops.

CN That's true, that's true. And everybody's got my cellphone number. But definitely there's a lot of respect for my time – I get calls when I need to get calls. Someday I look forward to being a volunteer in the community, to just being a volunteer. I look forward to someday not representing an organization that has relationships with governmental bodies, such that myself as an individual can't not represent some things publicly. I look forward to that, because I think what's happening as I age and tire a little bit in that weary sense is that I don't think my activism is as sharp. Sometimes I'm not able to answer these calls. And they're not just coming from downtown, of course. And I just can't jump to it in the ways that I used to. Part of it is that I'm accountable to a home network, as well, one that keeps me healthy. Part of it is that I am engaged in wage labour, particularly. But I think it's heralding maybe a different time for me coming in the next decade, and I think that will be about writing and about creative and collaborative organizing work. It's always going to be necessary to be in the street, or to support people in our streets, to be a live part of movement. Can't skip that step – our relationship to frontlines and land defence, that's always going to be there. Being a witness has other responsibilities to it. Collective, creative work can have powerful, relevant outcomes. I think about that these days as an uninvited guest on these Territories. I don't just want to thank people. I don't just want to name who I am and what I think I'm up to. I want to think through what is relevant to the Tsleil-Waututh, what is relevant to the Musqueam, to the Squamish. I feel that way foremost embodying Black and femme experience, realizing violences of state and borders, I want to be relevant.

MN Will you discuss the relation between your engagement with these with regard to the syntax of your work? I ask because I am interested in how your work combines a mix of syntactically dense and technical language – which might signal to readers a kind of impersonal affect or distancing effect – while at the same time it inhabits this grounded, self-present mode of direct speech, which I read as emergent from the forms of address that I imagine are central to the work you do as an organizer and activist.

CN That's interesting to hear, because this is the kind of analysis I cannot do. I'm not so deliberate in terms of strategy. I'm just trying to do what's necessary, and that's going to keep changing. I don't think it's something that I can map out.

MN Anytime something arises as being necessary, there's always a site, always a situation, and always others involved to respond to and with.

CN Exactly. It's one of the early lessons I learned from Derksen. I remember him reading a very early collection of poems for *Triage*, and he asked me to consider several things. One was that I had a ton of quotation marks. When I did a reading once, my first reading, actually, at the Railway Club for the Short Line Series (also organized, at the time, by Carmen Papalia), every other line I was like, "Quote, duh duh, duh, duh," and I did that for the whole reading. He said, "Maybe just let it go, let the quotes go." But that led us to talking in particular about the idea of texture, how our affective language and psyche and concerns and personal observations, how all that sprawling stuff is situated.

What it was, in part, was a materialist argument for poetry, that we need to ground it in the real. He didn't use that language, but I love this idea of texture. I feel like texture happens as an interplay. It cannot be so interested in the self; the I is not that interesting for me, unless it is part of broader networks, media, and relations. Anyway, my heart is trying to do with language what feels necessary. I'm never going to be accountable if I write a book that's so cerebral, and so entrenched in isolated material, in terms of the words on the page itself. It's not enough for the work to only succeed there. I am grateful for the kinds of conversations that are possible, for the kind of people who study and are actively concerned with poetics. Yet I am ultimately concerned with movement, and I'm looking to people – to kinds of land and community-based, relational practices that are of the page, even if anchored to a page.

Contrary Motions

A Dialogue with Raven Chacon

RAVEN CHACON IS A COMPOSER, PERFORMER, AND installation artist from Fort Defiance, Navajo Nation. As a solo artist, Chacon has exhibited, performed, or had works performed at Los Angeles County Museum of Art (LACMA), The Renaissance Society, San Francisco Electronic Music Festival, REDCAT, the Vancouver Art Gallery, Haus der Kulturen der Welt, Borealis Festival, SITE Santa Fe, Chaco Canyon, Ende Tymes Festival of Noise and Sonic Liberation, and The Kennedy Center. As a member of Postcommodity from 2009 to 2018, he co-created artworks presented at the Whitney Biennial, documenta 14, and Carnegie International 57, as well as the two-mile-long land-art installation *Repellent Fence*.

A recording artist for more than twenty-two years, Chacon has appeared on more than eighty releases on various national and international labels. In 2022, he was awarded the Pulitzer Prize for Music for his composition *Voiceless Mass*. His 2020 Manifest Destiny opera *Sweet Land*, co-composed with Du Yun, received critical acclaim from *The LA Times*, *The New York Times*, and *The New Yorker*, and was named 2021 Best New Opera by the Music Critics Association of North America.

Since 2004, he has mentored over three hundred high school Native composers in the writing of new string quartets for the Native American Composers Apprenticeship Project (NACAP). Chacon is the recipient of the United States Artists Fellowship in Music, the Creative Capital Award in Visual Arts, the Native Arts and Cultures Foundation Artist Fellowship, the American Academy's Berlin Prize for Music Composition, the Bemis Center for Contemporary Arts' Ree Kaneko Award, the Pew Fellow-in-Residence, and is a 2023 MacArthur Fellow. His solo artworks are in the collections of the Whitney Museum of American Art, the Smithsonian's American Art Museum and National Museum of the American Indian, LACMA, the Getty

Research Institute, the University of New Mexico Art Museum, and various private collections.

In this book's dialogues, I have put an emphasis on artists and writers working multi-modally across aesthetic disciplines, and Chacon stands as a paramount exemplar. His work is informed by many genres of making – from free jazz to metal, sculpture, and social practice, historical narration to activist intervention. I wanted to enter into conversation with Chacon to consider in particular his score-based works and the various listening practices those works articulate. Within this terrain, I was particularly interested in thinking through the ways in which Chacon negotiated more traditional musicological themes such as counterpoint and notation, all the while extending these themes into historical, cultural, and performative contexts often marginalized within musicology. To this extent, his decades-long engagement with land, territory, and resonance is exemplary of an overall critical listening practice that I'd like to think of as being central to this book.

During the summer of 2022, Chacon and I met for a series of discussions regarding the trajectory of his compositional practice and the various listening practices involved in the composition of his scores for performance. The following exchange, edited and abridged, accompanies the folio of Chacon's scores in *OEI #98-99: Aural Poetics*, which I edited and published in Stockholm in 2023. All of the score compositions that we discuss are included in that volume, and are additionally accessible via Chacon's website, spiderwebsinthesky.com.

MN I'm curious if we might begin this exchange by thinking about context and the ways in which your scores make contexts resonate. It's an element I find particularly fascinating in your work: how your compositions tend to draw attention to musical and extra-musical histories, site-specific issues, as well as epistemologies of sound, listening, and performance. Is this something you think about within the frame of context? Or is there a different way of conceiving this facet of your work?

RC Perhaps the best way to describe it is through the idea of counterpoint, which is a method for composing; I'm not sure when it started, perhaps as early as the 1500s. But then you had Baroque composers, Bach especially, who would work with two lines, with some kind of polyphony: one line going up and the other one going down, sometimes they are moving in parallel motions and other times in contrary motions. The interactions between these two melodies influenced the rest of the piece, especially the harmony. Composers from this period were developing rules about how counterpoint could work, rules regarding how one shouldn't go in parallel motion at a certain interval, or how one should move between contrary and parallel motions, or how chords evolved out of two melodies working with and against each other.

I've been thinking about this idea of counterpoint extending to other parameters of making music. For instance, a group of musicians who have never been in a concert hall before – that would be a contrary motion. Bringing in a group of people who never imagined themselves playing music on such a stage, what does that do? Or, another example, putting musicians in a neighbourhood that is their neighbourhood but separating them so that they have to play at great distances from one another – that is some kind of counterpoint.

I haven't developed my own set of rules for this yet. I think of many of my compositions as a long-time study of – well, I don't want to call it "social counterpoint," but what I am fundamentally interested in are the dynamics of the musicians in a context: who they are, where they are geographically, the specific site in which they are performing, and the history of that site and its surrounding geography.

MN Contrary motions – I love this phrasing. It speaks to the sounds themselves, while at the same time intoning the historical, geographical, and discursive elements of the compositions.

RC An interesting aspect of Baroque studies in counterpoint is resolution. Composers experimented with progression towards a resolution. It's why you have these cadences that move through episodes of dissonance and consonance; the contrary motion has to resolve itself by coming back to some kind of parallel motion, ultimately arriving at a resolution that culminates the phrase and the composition. There is some hope in that complexity. I'm not saying it's trying to wrap everything up in a nice bow. The resolution could, in fact, be continued conflict, or the recognition of conflict. Nonetheless, it's arriving at some kind of point of – I am trying to think of a better word than resolution, something more provisional. Maybe it's position. The work arrives at a position, or a position comes into focus where the players are, where the audience is, and where anybody else involved in that musical situation is as well.

MN The shift from resolution to position feels important. There is a sense of recognition in it, a sense of recognizing different perspectives overlapping in the space in which one is making music and all of the various social trajectories that compose that space.

RC Exactly. *Drum Grid* (2010) might be one of the best examples to describe how that happens. In that piece, there are musicians (who might not identify as musicians) and they are distributed across an entire neighbourhood, with each person standing at a different intersection. They are not playing anything complicated, at least not initially. They simply play single hits, each striking their individual drum only once, but still they are collaborating, making sounds together. How that sound is interpreted – as music, as protest – is where the audience becomes involved.

MN *Drum Grid* brings to mind another term that, like context and counterpoint, I see as fundamental to many of your scores: relay. This sense of relay is related to context, because the sounds and the actions to perform them are interpersonal, they are travelling through the musicians. There are often acts of reception taking place from musician to musician – reception, interpretation, and then a retransmitting out into the world to produce some kind of music-making. Another aspect of relay involves different kinds of spatial listening: tuning to a site, an environment, a context of musicking, and sensing out how to interpret the dynamics of that space in a sonic performance. That, too, is a relay. *Mirror Quintet* (2003) does this kind of relay, and so does *Echo Contest* (2005). And there's *Music for Voice* (2003), which has such an intriguing sense of relay in it. There's the percussive sounding, coming from the movement of the four performers each rubbing a ball across the surface of the drum in different patterns, and then that sound is relayed through the musician interpreting it by mouthing what they hear. Is that mouthing an actual vocalization or a bodily-facial gesture they perform as if the percussive sound being made on the drum is, in fact, emanating from their mouths?

RC It's not to be uttered, but something always emerges. The players always have this urge to let some sound escape when they are mouthing it. It's bound to happen. There's a feedback loop with this idea of relay which happens in some of these pieces. I'm thinking of another piece, for amplified piano, *Nilchi' Shada'ji Nalaghali* (2008). Initially, the piano player is holding down indicated keys to initiate a drone. They're not making sound with the keys, but they're opening up the hammers so the drone changes. But once the drone starts going and there is feedback, then the pianist, in order to keep it from getting out of control, has to find new positions, new "chords." A pianist who was playing this piece told me that there is a noticeable shift where the drone begins to play the pianist.

Music for Voice works in a similar way. Once you start vocalizing, it becomes something that perhaps you can't stop. Or it starts becoming its own secondary music, and then the rubbing on the drum has to respond to it. Even though there is a gesture that indicates how the players are supposed to rub the drums, it only refers to motion and not to time or pace or speed, all of which might influence how one performs the mouthing. It's a physiological feedback loop with the instrument.

MN This brings up another aspect of many of your scores: the way they create environments or conditions for their players to – well,

I'm not sure of a better way to put it – to figure it out. From your scores, the performers receive precise directions that are often wonderfully open to so many degrees of interpretation; the structure affords them a great degree of autonomy in figuring out a singular instantiation or experience by means of the score. How they choose to relate to the score and to one another and to the site and to the extended sphere of those listening is all open to the navigation of that singular encounter. *Music for Voice* is a wonderful example of this.

In this regard, I think of an early piece of yours, *Duet* (2000). In one of our first discussions about your work, you said something about how the rests in that piece are not meant to be considered as silences, or that they're not exactly "rests." Can you elaborate on what you meant there?

RC I believe I said that *Duet* is not about hearing silence, in the way of John Cage's *4′ 33″*. Or, perhaps I should say, the idea is not to hear the ambient sounds that compose a supposed silence, which has been the interpretation of Cage's piece. *Duet* is interested in exploring the interactions that are possible between two people. The score is the organizer of a kind of telegraphing. Normally in a duet, the two musicians would interact completely by listening, but this composition requests nonaction. What this piece seeks is to have other senses be involved in that listening, while respecting the rest events within a shared pace. For each of the performers, there becomes an acknowledgment of their partner's presence, of every nuance of their nonaction.

MN Listening becomes more expansive. It moves beyond the ears.

RC Yes. Even though *Duet* was one of the earliest pieces I wrote, it has a theme that has continued with me all the way to today – the idea of aligning, of something aligning with something else. A more recent piece, *Compass* (2021), also explores this idea of reading the pulses and paces of the world around us. There are things happening in nature, and then there is music. And somehow we can read these things, we can be a part of them and then respond, and the aligning of the musician with the rest of the world is what creates the music.

MN *Duet,* as I think about it, also has a complex sense of counterpoint embedded in it.

RC Yes, there is a counterpoint in *Duet,* the counterpoint of dynamic. Even though there are no notes being played, there is still an indication of "volume." There are rests that are *forte.* There are rests that are quiet. There are crescendos and decrescendos, as if the rests are becoming louder and softer, more and less intense, meaning the performer could intensify or calm whatever it is they are contributing to this shared musical relationship, allowing another inaudible interplay to be read or felt. But there are no actual instructions for *Duet,* its subtitle *"for two musicians"* nods to the language of the convention of standard notation; all of the information is there, but it requests an awkward silence if one sees it only as a contradiction of musical symbols.

This kind of exploration of dynamics and alignment appears in other works, too. For example, my piece for the Kronos Quartet, *Journey of the Horizontal People* (2016), has accented rests in the beginning so that everybody can align before they begin. This idea of amplified silences has been important to me. It's in an early work and installation, *Field Recordings* (1999), where I would find quiet places and make a recording and then turn those recordings up to their maximum volume. It's also in a recent work I showed in the 2022 Whitney Biennial, *Silent Choir (Standing Rock)* (2017–2022), in which I recorded a silent protest that happened at Standing Rock. It's the sound of six hundred people on a cold day, quiet and still, staring at the police. You can hear the presence of all of those people as a confrontation. You can hear the weight of them being silent. This is what *Duet* is also about, about organizing those moments of presence and exploring the intensities, or degrees, of how that presence is to be felt more than heard.

MN I have a question for you concerning overlapping communities and the possible tensions you've experienced through being in dialogue with, but also being claimed by, different communities. I'm thinking of your training, immersion, and response to various strands of twentieth-century new music, and how that connection comes into balance or conflict with the Indigenous contexts you're immersed in – ones that new music often gestures towards, or even extracts from, without much critical reflection on such engagements. And when I say "Indigenous contexts," I mean Navajo communities, of course, but also pan-Indigenous communities, too, that you've come into relation with through collaborations and other efforts.

RC The Navajo part of me, if we are talking about musical influences, my entry into that is through my grandfather, who is a singer of Navajo music. The majority of my knowledge of how Navajo music functions is through him. When I think of things like pitch, for example, or scales, these are things I don't prioritize at all, at least not in my chamber music. Having a sole singer, like my grandfather, singing either a song that is very old – who knows how old, hundreds of years maybe – or one that he came up with on the spot, I don't see a difference there. It's malleable or fluid. If he sings the same song twice, it's going to be different each time. But it's still the same song. There's nothing fixed about any of that music for me; I think that, in itself, has become an influence.

As far as my training in music, there were many separate trajectories that I didn't know could ever overlap. There is one trajectory that's simply about playing music and wanting to play in a metal band as a teenager. There's another one that focused on making experiments, and that goes back to being a young person in my bedroom playing around with cassette tapes, trying to build guitars and drums, things like that. And then there's a third that was prompted by the piano lessons I took as a kid, which developed into this naive or misguided idea that in order to be a professional musician, you had to study music – as in, study notes, study the Western canon, and go into a music program. That's what I did, because it's what I thought you had to do.

I had no idea that these trajectories could overlap until I went to a place like CalArts for grad school and found out about sound art installation and, yes, a lot of the experimentation of the twentieth century. There were a few composers who allowed me to see that there could be overlap, like James Tenney, Alvin Lucier. What I learned there was that compositions were experiments, processes, ones dealing with some other kind of phenomenon. Maybe they are more about sound and timbre than musical form. Maybe they are even more conceptual. Maybe they are dealing with something that is extramusical, such as history or even some kind of spirituality. All of this was incredibly intriguing for me and helped me to understand what kind of works I could make.

MN Studying your works over these last weeks, I realize that they are constantly founded in a sense of listening. Of course composers are listening, musicians are listening. Yet I think of a body of work that explores the ranges of and possibilities for listening as vast as yours, and I'm curious how that begins to develop as a field of exploration in your compositions.

RC That's a really good question. I guess I have a certain skepticism about listening. Perhaps it comes from this discourse that emphasizes the listener from the point of view of the audience and focuses on listening for sound, meaning to listen only for the timbre of the composition. Although I am interested in both of these elements, I'm more interested in the interactions between all of the people involved in the site specificity of the performance.

Once I started learning about other composers' ideas about listening, I became even more skeptical. For example, someone like Pauline Oliveros. I have faith that her intentions for deep listening were aligned with what I think I am trying to work towards. However, there are those who, I think, have perhaps misread her works and have begun to think of deep listening as an opportunity to go somewhere and simply capture the environment. I'm thinking of people who are, like, "let's go to the desert and do mushrooms and, you know, do a ceremony with a shaman in New Mexico." My homelands are ground zero for that type of shit, but this kind of mentality is apparent in many other less explicit ways. So I'm skeptical when I hear someone say, "Oh, I'm deep listening (trademark) certified, I went to a workshop!" I want to ask, "What are we listening for?" It's something I am still thinking through.

MN Deep listening is, fundamentally, extractive. It seems to hinge on the concept of a privileged outsider who can show up and guide by means of a well-esteemed methodology, all of which strikes me as being closely related to a colonial epistemology.

RC *Field Recordings* addresses this. The work magnifies and amplifies the land, which could mean, by extension, magnifying and amplifying the people who have stewarded those lands. It could then also mean that these places are dealing with encroachment or violence, or that violence has happened in these places. The sonic result of oversimplification could remind the listener of violence. There's a question concerning fidelity in the work, too, as it's not really a field recording. A field recording is supposed to contain information, it's supposed to document. What *Field Recording* does is completely blow out this aspect. There's a respect for low fidelity in my work. Or maybe I should say that the concept does not need fidelity. In fact, low fidelity can be a vehicle for the concept.

MN I'm interested in the way you model modes of listening in your scores and performances. You are modelling modes of interaction and sensing between one another, and that implies a need for the performers to figure out a situation together. In this frame, audience listening becomes not a listening for content only, but a listening to understand how the performers themselves are listening, and how they are figuring out the moment's interactions, creating alignments and counterpoint in the space with one another. This is a kind of contextual listening, a formal listening that situates the contents of a work within a larger terrain of the composition. When an audience member seeks to understand the interactions between the players through this contextual listening, that is when they become a part of the work's modelling.

RC For me it's often a question of time, of timekeeping. How does one's perception of time come into alignment with others, whether it's an audience of two hundred or it's four people playing together, all of whom have vastly different tempi. It's always interesting for me to talk to people who conduct or direct my works. I love hearing how they attempt to use the score to mediate all of the people involved.

MN This makes me think of a comment you made about the score being its own conceptual vehicle that works in relation to the performance and the recording. Can you discuss the relationship between score, performance, and recording and how the score exists in the constellation of these things?

RC In more conservative music schools, the score is taught as the way that music has to be organized. The so-called Western Tradition – Mozart, Beethoven, Bach, etc. – put music into a score so that the music was fixed. Everything was a score, or the score was *the* document. There's not a lot of room for interpretation in that. On the other side, there's the idea of transcription. I sometimes come from a skeptical and cynical place regarding transcription, because ethnomusicology often tries to put so-called world music, or all of the other musics that exist in the world, into that rigid system of Western notation.

The place I like to be is in the middle of that feedback loop, thinking about how a score might be both a transcription and a composition (or a prescription). For example, the piece *Ella Llora* (2002), where I transcribe the recording of a person crying, and then it ends up being given back to a singer to perform – this dynamic ends up in a lot of my other pieces too, but maybe not through as literal a process as that one.

MN I'm thinking about these comments in relation to what you said about your grandfather earlier, about him singing and you, as the listener, not knowing if the music is one hundred years old or if he was making it up just then, but also not caring about this difference and being present to the music. That's interesting to think about with regard to this transcription/score dichotomy and being present to the current resonance. Perhaps your composition *... lahgo adil'i dine doo yeehosinilgii yidaaghi* (2004) is playing at this interstice between transcription and score as well?

RC It is. We should talk about that piece, as it might bring together a lot of these ideas. It too has its own kind of cynical reasoning for existing. It was inspired by Cornelius Cardew's *Treatise* (1963–1967), a composition that is famous for not having instructions, for being a score that is open to interpretation. Musicians are allowed to play it however they deem they should. They may come up with a logic regarding how it should be realized; that's one approach. I know of others who just show up, see it for a first time, and immediately begin to play through it.

While *Treatise* is a masterwork, and I of course appreciate it, it made me realize that I don't like graphic scores that are open, like, for example, a squiggle or a circle or an inkblot on a page, and someone says, "Play this." If that is a way to make music, then what are people's assumptions about what those symbols mean? Are people assigning logic to notations that have no logic or that had a logic that has been lost?

Around the same time I was thinking about this kind of composition, I was going to a site on the west side of Albuquerque that is a petroglyph park. On that side of the city, there's a whole row of inactive volcanoes, and 1,000 or 1,500 years ago, Ancestors made drawings into the volcanic rock. The city built a freeway through part of this area twenty-five years ago, and then people began taking the petroglyphs home and putting them in their yards. Finally they made the area a protected site. I used to go there a lot. I spent the night out there quite a few times, and I would sketch the petroglyphs. These drawings served as the inspiration for the *... lahgo ...* score. None of the drawings I made were directly placed into the score. I made alterations. But I wanted to see what would happen if somebody applied the *Treatise* process and said, "Just play it," this kind of thing I'm very much against. I was interested in seeing what kinds of preconceptions the score might produce, because they are so clearly North American Indigenous symbols.

Somebody once asked me a question about whether or not they should be hearing Navajo music inside my music. This pissed me off at first. It was a good question, though. It got me thinking: Is it possible for any ensemble to show up and start making music that is inspired by Indigenous sound or melodies? That's what *... lahgo ...* does or can do – be a prompt to make those sounds, to organize them as music, but a score that takes the burden off of me to give specific instruction.

MN There's a lot of presumption that will go into negotiating the symbols and their sounding out in the space of playing. It must be fascinating to see what happens when people confront that presumption in their own sound-making, in their fellow players' sound-making, or as an audience member.

RC I strongly believe there has to be a good reason to use graphic notation, meaning that it should relay or solve a musical idea that Western standard classical notation can't. I am a believer in the five-line staff, even though it's a Western tradition and it's something that most of the world doesn't follow or need for their music to exist. I do think it's still one of the best ways to relay to a musician what to play, as a visual marker for pitch and time. On the other end of that, there are a lot of things that standard notation can't do, and that's why one uses graphic notation or text. Or maybe you simply have to record a demo and give that to another musician, and they learn it, that's just as good. And then there's improvisation – you show up and play together, and it doesn't have to be notated or fixed.

MN It's interesting to think of *Whisper Trio* (2008) in relation to *... lahgo ...* because of the intentionality in that piece for someone who is a non-Indigenous person, or really, I guess, a non-Navajo (Diné) speaker to co-confront the language in that score and give voice to those words. An intriguing element in *Whisper Trio* is that one hears oneself speak a language and make sounds that are deemed, for various reasons, in danger of extinction. That is a provocation towards an interesting experience of self-listening.

RC *Whisper Trio* is one of my favourite pieces. It hadn't been performed for a long time until quite recently, but lately there have been a number of performances. The singers often write to me, and they say, "How do you pronounce this word?" and "How does this one sound?" or "Am I doing this right?" Every time I have to tell them that it's not about getting it right, it's about trying. And the fact that they are whispering, that they don't have to enunciate out loud, that's going to be a safety net for the singers. Often the singer's confidence with the words will determine the loudness of the piece. So there will be peaks of loud and quiet whispering that didn't have to be notated into the score. That's the variable part of it.

Have you ever heard Alvin Lucier's story of how he came to make *I am sitting in a room* (1969)? It's an inspiration behind *Whisper Trio*. He made his piece because he stutters, and the way he sought to smooth out his voice and get it to equalize itself was through the piece's repeating, echoing structure. I was thinking about this with both *... lahgo ...* and *Whisper Trio*. What these two pieces exploit is the knowledge that it's likely not going to be a Navajo person performing it, not a person of that culture or community. And because of that, I'm interested in the variations, in the things that put the performer in a position to make sounds that they wouldn't ordinarily make.

One last thing I'll say about *Whisper Trio* is that listening is absolutely crucial, because the performers all have to end together. So not only do they have to be listening to their own voice attempting the words, they are also listening to the attempts of their two collaborators to try to understand where they are in the score. Each performer has to do a solo and should provide the space for the other two to do a solo. These solos, then, displace the other two performers in time. They must listen to understand where the others are in the piece to time it so they can end together.

MN I wonder if we might discuss a work of yours that, I think, plays with the notion of the solo set against a group sound, *American Ledger no. 2* (2019). It's a fascinating composition.

RC It is the most complicated piece I think I've ever written.

MN The instructions are complex!

RC It takes quite a bit of organizing. The series was intended to be very narrative, exploring how a score in the form of a flag might tell the story of the land that the flag has come to represent. So for the United States, it would look like the US flag and it would tell the story of the United States, or the land where the United States is. *American Ledger no. 2* went a bit beyond that. Not only does it tell the story of Oklahoma, of Tulsa in particular and the story of the Black Wall Street massacre, but also of the movement of tribes into Oklahoma, ones displaced from other parts of the country who, in turn, displaced the tribes that were indigenous to Oklahoma. Basically, the score narrates cycles of in-and-out movement specific to that place, that region, and they are enacted as the motions of the performance.

There are people walking around in a circle, and they are making sounds. The instruments that they use are limited; there are only so many materials or instruments available to make the sounds of the work, and yet everybody is required to make these sounds. This means that the performers have to share the instruments but also, eventually, take the resources for making sound away from each other. The only way to end the game – although I try not to call it a game, but it ends up having a kind of game dynamic – or the only way to exit the piece is to accomplish the making of all the sounds outlined in the score. Otherwise a performer can end up stuck within the piece and being a remaining participant. And there's a burden if you end up in the piece for too long, because if that happens, you have to perform an accumulation of sound events. There are huge inequities of duties if you end up being a remaining participant. Each performer has the materials to relieve themself of responsibilities, but at the same time, you're placing that burden onto somebody else. Usually when you're making music together, everybody is working towards the same goal, but in this piece, it becomes very individualistic inside of the group sound. The group sound is there, but it's as if there were twenty-four solos composing it.

MN How fitting a formulation for the United States and its fantasy of individualism. One has to select which violence they are going to enact within the space – I mean, it's not a literal violence on a larger socio-political level, but it's mimicking such dynamics in the space of a music performance. This is also a very American dynamic.

RC Yes, exactly.

MN These dynamics fascinate me. Whereas other works might model a mode of relation that, in the disaster of imperialist capitalism, in the extractive nature of it, could perhaps provide an antithesis to it. Or an opening against it. This composition, *American Ledger no. 2*, is attempting to model the mode of relations that imperialist capitalism forces upon us.

RC That's exactly it. And there are other sonic elements to it that I'm remembering now. All of the performers have a whistle, either a police whistle or a train whistle. Then, to define the boundaries of the performance space, there's a bugle player on one end and a person with a megaphone in the opposite corner. They are, in a way, policing the boundaries of the performance. It's a very complicated piece. It's different than anything I've ever made before.

MN There's something very compelling about the process: in working with site and its resonance, in composing sounds that one doesn't necessarily like, sounds that are antagonistic, and relaying those or altering them in some significant way in their relay. That, too, creates contrary motions. How did site and place come to be a core component in your works? Is resonance a term that is significant to you in thinking about site and place?

RC History is definitely a motivator. When I was part of the collective Postcommodity, every time we did a piece, the process would be similar. We would get an invitation to do a project, and we felt it was our responsibility to research as much as we could about that place, starting with who the Native peoples are or were in those places, what other colonial history happened there, if there was slavery there, if there were other kinds of displacements, if there were incidents of building or destruction based around capital and the marketplace, and thinking about economic influences present in that area. It was always a site-specific response. Very few of those Postcommodity pieces ended up getting made a second time.

For me, this site specificity got me thinking about another musical term: transposition. If you take a scenario, a composition formulated as a response to a specific space, for example, the city of Pittsburgh, and then attempt to transpose it to, say, New Orleans, for me that becomes an interesting dynamic; ultimately, the medium I'm working with is going to be the collaboration with other musicians. It's going to be me who is transposing myself into these other places where musicians and musical practices already exist. There is a lot to think through here in terms of the dynamics that is going to be complicated and provocative.

MN I'd like to conclude by discussing *Dispatch* (2020), because it feels like an alignment of many practices and trajectories in your work. It's a collaborative work, composed with Candice Hopkins, that is meant to instigate and resonate through further collaborations and responses. Standing Rock is the immediate context to which the work responds, and in this focusing it opens onto larger concerns of US imperialism and white supremacy.

RC *Dispatch* tries to learn about listening, about what sort of practical information and survival information is inside of listening. Going back to the issue of deep listening we discussed earlier: listening is not simply an action to calm us or allow us to meditate, it's an actual survival sense that we have. How does that inherent sense fit into the feedback loop of music-making? How much of it is an improvisation? *Dispatch* thinks very literally about improvisation, about what real-world applications practising improvisation tactics and responses might have. It considers what role listening plays in someone deciding to take action.

Dispatch is also a culmination of thinking about counterpoint and these interactions between performers and testing out ways to compose those interactions, document them, transcribe them, and then represcribe them through the score. The relaying and the filtering that are central to *Drum Grid* and *Mirror Quintet* are also in *Dispatch*. You have a call to action that is going out to specific people or the general public, one that says, "Come to this place, we need help over here," and people come, or they serve as another relay for that call to action. And in this call, there might be noise, or misinformation, or some negative outcomes. That's what happened at Standing Rock, you had people say, "Come to Standing Rock, shit is going down." And then other people are saying, "They are shooting at us." Sooner or later, one isn't sure what is really happening. So *Dispatch* is a self-examination that speaks to the importance of sound as messaging, how important it is to have some accuracy, some legibility. And of course, in *Dispatch*, there are opportunities for counteractions, counter-surveillance, and for making noise as a tactic of distraction. All of these elements come into consideration when accounting for the dynamics of organizing, whether it's activism or some other kind of gathering.

One thing that Candice and I always talk about in this work is that we want to make clear it's not a guidebook for organizing or activism. It's more of a work that tries to understand the dynamics of who is involved, who is leading, what happens when groups gather. Then, as a work of music, it focuses on what happens when this becomes a sonic or a theatrical prompt.

MN To this extent, I think of it as a work in close affinity with Ultra-red's *Ten Preliminary Theses on Militant Sound Investigation*

(2008), though *Dispatch* is more clearly situated, at least initially, in an aesthetic context. Both are interested in, as you phrased it, "real-world applications of listening," and I want to think more about that.

In *Dispatch*, there is the real-world application in that it invites one to consider how they are tuned to a social formation. It brings to my mind the moment of insurgence that happened here in Québec in 2012 during the student uprising, and how all the various banalities of everyday life – who gets to speak, who gets to control the social modes of informational relay, who gets to inhabit the city and its streets, squares, and neighbourhoods, and how – were suspended and brought into question during an extended and energized moment of several months. This kind of rebellion alters the sphere of the senses. I recall experiencing this in numerous ways, but most thoroughly through the sense of hearing. On the streets, the moments of alignment, as you call them, were audible. And with them, there were all of these moments of aligned difference; different perspectives were being voiced against one another while also standing together in order to perpetuate the rebellion. Within alignment there were all kinds of contestations and difference, too. A gathering could be convivial and celebratory at one moment, and in the very next be challenging and destructive because of the fractures between people who were supposedly aligned. There were all kinds of false reports perpetuated by the government and the media in order to contest, or cancel out, or create further division so as to push forward their own agendas. I describe these dynamics because *Dispatch* listens to the way in which the relay of this convergence happens in real time.

RC I've never thought about it in this way before but, moving from our conversation about counterpoint, the goal of counterpoint, traditionally speaking and in some of my works, is resolution. Whether that is an actual resolved solution or not, it is at least an ending of the piece. *Dispatch* offers this process in reverse, where the resolution is that everybody first gathers and then branches out into several alignments, misalignments, or in aligned difference, as you put it. *Dispatch* is interested in counterpoint, but its intention is to create discussion, new branches of possibility, and to see what the artifacts of that branching might be in terms of music or theatre. Perhaps another way to look at *Dispatch* is that it's trying to find a way for the audience to be part of this shared experience. It's not that the audience is there to listen to the musicians who are engaged in a different kind of listening or planned interaction, it's that everybody should be involved in the same alignment of what's happening. Thinking about the critique of deep listening, of its privilege, of envisioning a very serene location in which to do it – this is one of the reasons why we made *Dispatch*. What happens to deep listening when you're at Standing Rock and they have sirens going all night and the water hoses on you?

Dispatch emerged out of these types of questions, but listening has been important in a lot of my work – in *Whisper Trio, Whistle Quartet, Mirror Quintet, Drum Grid, Echo Contest,* and so on. Listening is the area of shared experience that a composition tries to mediate. I have written these compositions primarily as an experience for the people who are performing them. They are all about creating relationships between the musicians. The audience is sometimes understood as secondary in this process: what they hear is whatever it is that comes out of the shared experience of the performers.

Tracking the Traffic of Glyphs Across Oceans

A Dialogue with Divya Victor

DIVYA VICTOR IS A TAMIL AMERICAN POET, ESSAYIST, AND educator. Her writing, editing, and research focus on twentieth and twenty-first century poetry and poetics, with an emphasis on innovative and experimental forms and poets who undertake representations of trauma, both systemic and intersubjective. She is the author of *CURB*, which won the 2022 PEN America Open Book Award and the 2022 Kingsley Tufts Poetry Award. It was also a finalist for the 2022 CLMP Firecracker Award (Poetry). Divya is also the author of *Kith, Scheingleichheit: Drei Essays, Natural Subjects, UNSUB*, and *Things to Do with Your Mouth*. Her work has been collected in numerous venues, including *BOMB*, the New Museum's *The Animated Reader, Crux Desperationis: International Journal of Conceptual Writing, The Best American Experimental Writing, Poetry, The Yale Review, American Poetry Review, The Atlantic, The New York Times Magazine, The Seagull Reader*, and *boundary2*. She is currently an associate professor of English and writing at Michigan State University, where she is the director of the creative writing program.

The following discussion concerning Victor's book *Curb* took place between East Lansing, Michigan, and Montréal in early autumn 2021, a few months following its publication. Because we initially considered circulating the video recording of our live conversation, the exchange begins with my extended introduction to Victor's work, focusing specifically on *Curb*; I have included some of that here before transitioning into our dialogue.

I first encountered Divya Victor's work just over a decade ago through the Troll Thread publishing collective, of which she was then a co-editor. I remember feeling thrilled by her work and wondering: who is this writer? I was interested in the conceptual rigour of Victor's poetics, which worked outside the main lines of that era's discourse of conceptual writing. I was interested to see work that made use of some of the dynamics present in that discourse towards interrogating cultural practices and processes, especially documents. Her work engaged information genres in which language is deployed to regulate and police and surveil and commit violence against bodies. I loved that Divya's work was taking this on, engaging it from a periphery, from what was then a margin. I saw in Divya's work a writer working from within the US empire on discourse centred in the US, but using her work to counter it and its rhetoric, while looking to establish dialogues with writers across several hemispheres.

To offer a brief introduction to my own reading of *Curb*, I remember confronting the title and being surprised by it, its referencing such an unpoetic and banal object. Then, in reading the work, I was struck by how Divya's fiercely internationalist perspective put under scrutiny such a thing as a curb, how she observes and thinks with the quotidian edges of everyday living: lawns, sidewalks, front doors, sites where familiar interiors meet social exteriors. Here, Victor shifts our attention to dividing lines – between neighbours, between intimacies, between exposures, between languages, between world views – to consider how where we are separated is also where we enter into relation. *Curb* is both lyric and documentary. It's multilingual, and multilingual within English, while also bringing into its textuality other languages such as Tamil, Hindi, Urdu, Sanskrit, and Latin. It is grammatical poetry. Yet it is one that situates its grammar of ongoing imperialisms and the everyday violences against those surveilled as "other" in the post-9/11 United States.

I believe Divya has written an incredible and necessary book to be reading right now, and I also believe that it is one that clearly articulates a model for poetry, for poetic practice that she has been developing over the last decade – in terms of its lyric work, its research, the documentary poetics, the personal engagement of the work, combined with grammatical and linguistic exploration. I believe it is a model that will resonate far and wide in the time ahead.

MN Thank you, Divya, for the gift of this book, and thank you so much for joining me today.

DV That was a disarming introduction. You did warn me, but I was not prepared. As a poet writing from the periphery, as you said, Michael, it has been a life-giving experience to have you keep me company in the periphery for a surprisingly long time. Kithship in and because of poetry.

We could wade into our discussion with *Curb* by highlighting what you observed in your introduction – writing from and within the periphery. The inscriptive practices emerging from globalization draw connections to the medieval, to the scribes responding to the texts that they are merely copying. Writing in the margins has been a way of resisting or responding to the dominant narrative. Writing on the edge is where inversion happens. That is important for *Curb*, which is a book that examines the edges of domestic and public spaces as battlefields. The edge, however clear-cut and sharp, is the most ambiguous space: on the body, at an ecological zone, in built environments.

In terms of urban planning, the street's curb forms the margin, drawing a dividing line between the private and the public. The question of why you are moving on the sidewalk, and the question of who you are when you are in public during that act of movement, are central to *Curb*.

There is a line from *Curb* that could be a working title for this dialogue: "tracking the traffic of glyphs across oceans." This is a line from the poem called "Pavement," in which I am reckoning with the death of Divyendu Sinha. The poem is written, in part, as a response to eight minutes of footage of Sinha's wife, Alka Sinha, who is in a courtroom in New Jersey during the sentencing hearing for the assailants whose assault caused the death of her husband. She is moving her hands delicately across the line of her script. How important it is to her that she doesn't miss a word. How wondrous it is that she is maintaining this bodily practice that we sometimes retain from childhood when we are trying to learn a new language. It was important to me that we pay attention to this image of a woman reading in a juridical context. The preciousness of every single word in Alka's testimony – I wanted that as my charge when I wrote *Curb*. So I am, in fact, "tracking the traffic of glyphs across oceans" as a poet belonging to English in some ways, but in my trafficking, I am then also betraying so many other languages. As a poet, I am ferrying language across the oceans. So both of these things: both the periphery (the margin, the edge) and the labour of trafficking in glyphs are important ways for me to think about *Curb*.

MN I remember coming across a question you wrote in a text related to *Curb*: "How can poetry be a space in which my family survives?" There is an arc in your poetry of the last decade in which you interrogate documents and the histories instantiated in them in order to locate kith across time and geographies.

Curb takes up the incredible work of addressing specific generations of kith – of wanting to enact them in and through poetry, protect them, allow them to be convivial in the face of depredation, and support their vital exchange for generations to come. I'm wondering if you might discuss the generations that are involved in this book and maybe describe, if you're willing, your own experience of your family's movements that are documented in this book.

DV Two political touchstones come to mind that could help us think about kithship, the importance of multigenerational or transgenerational documentation, and poetry as a kind of survival. The first: in 2021, we have a generation of people in their twenties who have been shaped entirely by post-9/11 events and policies. That is a whole generation of immigrants, Arabs, Middle Eastern folks, South Asian folks, children of immigrants who are defined by the acute suspicion that results from the exercise of post-9/11 freedoms for Christians and whites in the USA. The second: the conspiracy theory of "white replacement," which is this idea that inclusive citizenship acts, immigration policies, foreign policy, voting reforms, and all of the work around empowering and enfranchising voters is related to the replacement of whites in this country. So both of those are important conceptual anchors for me when I think about what a generation means and why a poem can be a kind of space where one can write for the protection and the survival of one's kith.

I began to do the work "of" *Curb* in 2001 when I migrated to the US as an eighteen-year-old. I landed in the United States in April of 2001, and the World Trade Center attacks happened when I was barely gaining my footing in the country. I suddenly found myself sobered in my view of the American dream. I felt rejected from participation. As a writer, I see myself among those in that post-Patriot Act generation. That moment sets up a new frame for how we relate to documents, how we relate to information and data, and how we relate to becoming information and data for the sake of the (supposed) security of others.

As a poet, the question I have is, "If my family and I have become information and data for the protection of those who have a dominant position in the United States, then how can my work offer a counterpoint to the use of bodies as data and information?" That helps me think about my relation to the documentary. The lyric offers a necessary dimension to understanding the document's place in time just as a shadow applies to the body, just as a shadow allows the body to know where it is in relation to the sky and the earth. I think of the lyric as the shadow of the document. This is where the document exists in space and time. The lyric shows you the shadow that is being created by that location.

MN The post-Patriot Act generation of writers you're describing, this is something I've been attempting to articulate and describe over this last decade. This new relationship to documents, the new relationship of bodies to information and data, and the spectre of security that you're describing – this is what initially drew me towards the discourse of conceptual writing in its moment, in the hopes of taking some of the tactics for composition discussed there towards a space of engaging such issues.

First, I know there has been an extensive history of white self-deputization in the United States since its initial colonial settling. I think, though, white self-deputization takes on new forms after 9/11 – in terms of the extent to which individuals permit themselves to regulate others' lives according to white supremacist beliefs, and also on a structural level in terms of group organization, media support, and the mainstreaming of white supremacy within US party politics. This is a terrible and necessary terrain in which to explore language and its relation to bodies – one that I see as being a central consideration in *Curb*.

And second, I know this too has a much longer history, but for me and my coming into awareness as both a politicized being and a person engaged with literature, the post-9/11 landscape illustrated the impact of language on bodies to a monstrous degree. Here I think to Iraq and the "weapons of mass destruction" – the way a ruling class with their array of journalists ready to partake in and give the greatest of amplitudes to their fabrications, the way in which corporations were lined up and ready to profit to a maximum on these fabrications, and how together this assemblage of individuals and entities deployed a succinct language to push through a narrative that was absolutely fictitious. I think every day of Donald Rumsfeld, the formidably monstrous rhetorician who looms at the threshold of the post-Patriot Act generation you describe.

DV Rumsfeld radically opened up the range of interpretation to which a human can be subjected as an object of information extraction. This, of course, is the foundation of the rationale for torture. His statement, "There are known knowns ... there are known unknowns" – that is an interpretive range. Any person can become a known known or a known unknown. He's talking about the imagined "weapons of mass destruction." In the wake of 9/11, the brown, Arab, Sikh, Muslim other became deputized, rhetorically, as weapons of mass destruction in their singular human form, either as a known known or known unknown. Deputize: as in, ask someone to be responsible for someone else; to act in another's stead; to become an embodied cipher.

South Asians and Middle Eastern folks became embodiments of this awful Rumsfeldian interpretive range: on one hand, the model minority, the known knowns; on the other hand, the known unknowns, the monstrous other, the terrorist, or the various slurs that are used to identify us. The equivalence drawn between the bodies of my kith and the speculative void of the weapon of mass destruction was key in defining that generation's self-knowing.

As a poet, Michael, I don't want to perform as a "known known" – writing poems with all of the exotic tropes, writing to assuage American guilt or ignorance. You know this. It's a horrific obligation. I'm refusing that. In *Kith*, I wrote about my refusal to italicize myself and what I know. So I refuse this performance of being a "known known" – this kind of safe entity that can be brought into literary festivals to present an experience of

South Asian identity. But I also want to be able to refuse being a "known unknown": this kind of nebulous darkening at the horizon, this horde, an undefinable mass, this "dusky peril" swarming in. I think *Curb* is trying to refuse both of these formulations for our weaponized condition as brown immigrants.

MN Alongside of known knowns and known unknowns, there's another important quality that plays as central to the white supremacist violence you discuss and document in *Curb*, which is *misrecognition*.

DV Misrecognition is central to this book, and to living right now. I am frustrated by everyday practices of misrecognition and the crude attempts to recognize the other in the terms of the self. You can be at a bar, and someone will say, "Where are you from?" And it can ruin your fucking night. It can really ruin it. Can I actually read you something short from an essay I've recently published at *The Yale Review* that summarizes some of what I'm trying to get at with this problem of misrecognition?

> Crimes of violent misrecognition are routinely perpetrated against South Asian Americans. In 2001, Balbir Singh Sodhi was shot outside his own gas station in Mesa, Arizona, by a violent racist who mistook him for a terrorist. In 2012, Sunando Sen was pushed under an oncoming subway train during his daily commute in Queens, New York, by a woman who made no distinction between Hindus and Muslims, and blamed both for the September 11, 2001, attacks. In 2017, Srinivas Kuchibhotla was shot at his favourite after-work bar in Olathe, Kansas, by an anti-immigrant nationalist who thought he was an undocumented Iranian. In 2021, five members of the Muslim Afzaal family were mown down by an Islamophobic man in a pickup truck in London, [Ontario,] leaving only the family's nine-year-old son alive. Balbir *ji*, Sunando *da*, Srinivas *gaaru*, and the Afzaal family were strangers in the neighbourhoods where they lived, worked, and owned businesses. They were seen and then *unseen*. First they were "recognized as not belonging, as being out of place," as [Sara] Ahmed writes, and then they were misrecognized as strangers (a terrorist, "Muslim," "illegal") in a way that led directly to their deaths.

There is overwhelming evidence for what Ahmed writes in the kind of work that the stranger does in building the nation. So much of the maintenance of the sovereignty of the nation-state depends on acts of misrecognition – that is overwhelming to me. This takes me back to my earliest memory of understanding how a body politic is composed: in 1998, Rishi Maharaj, who is the son of Trinidadian immigrants, was assaulted and very badly injured by a group of people in Queens. When he was being beaten, one of the assailants said to him; "This will never be a neighbourhood until you leave."" In the police report, they mention that he apologized until he lost consciousness. So much is staked on that misrecognized body. Misrecognition has fatal consequences. And it became unbearable to me. It became unbearable that we were not talking about it here. So *Curb* comes out of that difficulty bearing something like this.

MN Here I think of Sureshbhai Patel, an Indian man who was visiting his son in Alabama, who for no other reason than being in public was assaulted and partially paralyzed by three police officers, only one of whom was charged. I think of his words – "No English, Indian Walking" – which you devote a single page to, these words in a large font upon it. What his words and what you're describing above attest to is something you describe in *Curb* as "the fear of walking as a stranger in your own neighbourhood." The next thing I want to ask you about stems from your ability to balance and put into conversation these specific instances of quotidian life and violence in tandem with the larger structural frames to evaluate and engage and form resistance against such violations. You give form and give language to the possibility of thinking within these two frames at once, and it's incredible work.

I know there are generations and lineages and trajectories of documentary poetics that explore such a terrain and framing, so I am wondering if you might discuss who is a model for you in terms of making a work like *Curb*? Muriel Rukeyser comes to mind when I think of your work in terms of the way in which you give voice, give breath, give life to lives lost. You give a name to these figures against their being lost in time. I don't know if she is particularly someone you are interested in, but I'd love to hear you discuss some examples and models of this terrain you are exploring in poetry.

DV Rukeyser is certainly a starting point in the documentary genealogy. But I came to her later and her approach is more investigative than mine is, and more prone to needing the investigative agent on site in a way that's quite distinct from someone like Reznikoff, who refused a physical relationship to the site. His understanding of spatial connection was intuitively diasporic. *Holocaust*, for example, comes out in 1975. The Eichmann trial transcripts came out in the early 1960s. So there is a belatedness to his response to the catastrophe, and there is, of course, documentary distance and mediation. Famously, of course, he refused to return to Israel with Marie Syrkin, his wife, who was at that time writing for the *Jewish Frontier*. Syrkin encouraged Reznikoff to begin the *Holocaust* project, "while he was still obdurately producing more *Testimony*." She hoped for "lyrical threnody." That is not what his *Holocaust* becomes.

I think I am much more moved by – and Todd Carmody's work shows this – Reznikoff's implicit siding with Arendt's argument against sentimental Zionism as a formative feeling behind diaspora. I admire that a lot in Reznikoff's work.

For me, as an Indian woman writing in the context of both US and Indian empires, writing in allyship to Kashmiri freedom and Palestine, I have to hold my contradictions together as a witness, as Reznikoff had to hold them, I think. I'm not suggesting an equivalence, but I am saying that I think of him as much more of an elder to me than Rukeyser, in terms of the various contradictions he had to manage.

MN That's right. Reznikoff is someone who has been present for you for a long time.

DV Yes, for a long time. I study him as a mimic, as a scribe, just being a kind of stupefied copier of his work. Like in *Hellocasts* and in *Partial Directory of the Unnameable*, I learned a lot from his understanding of how poetry and evidence function as distinct but similar discourses that build a lived identity. I think he is the chap who is helping me think through what Wendy Brown calls "wounded attachments" and also Brown's warning against having psychic injury be the driving force behind what makes us sovereign. I'm interested in that. I have a deep respect for Reznikoff's approach and for his particular flavour of objectivism. And also his love for what he calls "the daylight meaning of words," which refuses the mandate of "literariness" – which I read as a disinterest in assimilating into the mode of the WASPy lyric and dominant ideas of verbal beauty.

I also love his commitment to the common table, to the idea that the poet speaks at the common table, and not upon the dais, not upon the stage, not upon the pedestal. That is an important part of documentary writing as I see it – that it has to stay with the chorus, that it has to stay with what remains common, rather than what becomes proclamatory. That's also why Reznikoff is so important to me.

MN This being a poet of the common table, of the chorus – it works against the projectivist model of declaration, of the world funnelled through the singular body and declaimed upon all. Instead, we have the poet who exists in deep relation and whose voice is a point in constellation with other voices, and who always situates that relation, that context, that constellation of other voices.

DV Yes. Refusing Olson's singular "ear" or the fetish of breathing – how to fetishize breath when writing about the dead?

MN In *The Language of Inquiry*, Lyn Hejinian writes about a model of transitive poetics that I always understood as being counter-projectivist, anti-Olsonesque. As opposed to being declamatory, it's convivial – a mode of composition based on active listening and exchange, of improvisational thinking together through all the moments of harmony and dissonance. Being a poet "of the common table" articulates this in such a clear way.

One of the questions I want to discuss with you concerns not specifically the multilinguality of the book, which I want to get to, but also the variations of English, of Englishes that are present in the book. It's something I sense as emerging out of your living amid a variety of Englishes.

DV Let's talk about Englishes. Biographically, I am constantly losing and reacquiring Englishes. I had to lose Indian English when I migrated as an eleven-year-old; then I took up Singlish when I lived in Singapore on and off. I also code-switch into Tamil Indian English, which is different from what we think of as a dominant strain of globalized Indian English. I then gave up predominantly living in Singlish, attempted American English and kept code-switching between US English, Singlish, Tamil Indian English, and a more generalized British postcolonial formation. And everything – lexicons, dictions, accents, intonations, pacings – all of these things are constantly being impacted in that kind of tender, sometimes bloody, place where my location and my articulation meet.

Curb and *Kith* are invested in refusing the idea of language as private property and refusing the idea of linguistic identity as something that can be owned by a nation or state. I want to go beyond what Kamau Brathwaite has helpfully theorized as nation language. Folks like me, who were learning from Caribbean and Black poets, needed that – what Brathwaite identified as an English that is like a "howl, or a shout, or a machine-gun, or the wind, or a wave."[1] But, in a moment where globalization is, of course, killing us, we need to go beyond it. We need the language of the howl to also embody the silences, the various Englishes, the pit of silenced or erased voices of documents. I've appreciated Dohra Ahmad's term "rotten English." It is such a useful umbrella term for global Englishes. I especially enjoy the way it refers to ripeness gone over. It is language beyond its utility for profit. What do we do with rotten fruit? What do we do with the rottenness that is English, with something gone over, beyond ripeness? You don't even need to pluck it. It's fallen. Not even the animals will touch it.

MN I want to say how amazed I was by your incorporation of Hindi in "Estates: Last Offices Concerning the Curbs of the Body" in *Curb*. There's the first poem in the sequence where you connect the "him" with the "hum" – in Hindi, "we," the plural collective pronoun. Then you connect "beyond the sea" to "videshi" (foreign or foreigner) – forming two words tied together, in meaning and in sound. You feel this connection deeply in your juxtaposition of them. And then the "sanse" (breath) with "sense," one following the other. So in "Locution / Location," a prior poem in the book, we have this incredible lyric working and unworking, this movement through these various Englishes. Then, following this, in "Estates," the reader encounters a lyric work that ties together different languages, different grammars, different scripts, even.

DV I'm so glad we're talking about "Estates." To state the biographical fact: growing up in India, my supposed mother tongue, which is Tamil, was ousted or usurped by English, which was the medium of instruction for the school I went to. But then I had to reckon with the secondary problem of Hindi nationalism, which then tried to usurp Tamil from me and my family. As a result, I identify as an illiterate Tamil. It's a horribly problematic position that I am trying to reclaim, because as I've said elsewhere, how can I be so articulate in the language of the colonizer? Which is also my language, and the gift I gave to the colonizer. But how could I be so ill-equipped in the language of my most immediate kin? Hindi becomes this bridge language for me to assimilate into my South Asianness more broadly because of all of its connections to Urdu and Hindustani and Farsi, right?

I think the comfort with a plurilingual environment, to use Caroline Bergvall's term, is in one's ability to switch as frequently as possible without being punished.

MN Then, in an earlier poem in *Curb*, "Pavement," you perform an exceptional tying together of the poet and the subject of the poem through the conjunct letters – the *vh* and *yh* that are written in Devanagari. Here is an exceptional example of what I was alluding to earlier as the grammatical work that's taking place in your poetry.

You're mapping your negotiation with this language and incorporating that into the poetic work. You're bringing the reader with you into that negotiation of the other language. That's an incredible moment, because when I see the *vh* and *yh* sounds explored in this figure you are detailing of the poem, I realize: that is the sound of your name. *Di–vh–yh*.

And that is where a connection is being formed between the man whose death you're witnessing and yourself. It is a hinge into relation. Here, there is a phonemic relation that serves as a starting point for making kith that's documented there.

DV Thank you so much for recognizing that moment. I've been waiting so long to talk about this piece. It is a grammatically unique moment, which has a certain theorization of kithship, as you say, Michael, through the pure phonemic coincidence of our names. Divyendu and Divya. *Vh* and *yh* together. The unique Hindi aadhe akshar vaale shabd (conjoined consonant or vowel units), the idea that you can halve a consonant as a way of connecting it to another – it's so gorgeous. The idea of connection that is merely phonemic – it's both so beautiful and, importantly, so limited. When I was researching Divyendu Sinha's death as the result of an assault in New Jersey, I kept wrestling with the fact that there were no conclusive definitions for this assault. It was not labelled a hate crime. The assailants were minors and were clearly in a difficult place themselves. "Pavement" was the poem in which I had to wrestle with the horrific truth that no matter how much I theorized imagined community within my work, I would ultimately remain a stranger to those whose lives become evidence for that theorization. Sometimes, all you have is the flimsiest filament-thin connection of two consonants linking up at a point where they are halved. Sometimes, all we have is a glyph connecting us. The *vh* and the *yh* – *vyha*, that's it, that's what Mr. Sinha and I have in common. And yet, I can bear something like witness in particular to the reportage around his death. And that is enough of a connection. The thinnest of bridges, right? I always think of that ligament between the *vh* and the *yh* – the thinnest of ligaments. I think as a minoritized writer writing from two empires – both the Indian and the US empires – I needed to know that that was enough.

MN I'm curious as to how this might relate to the ghostly "the" that exists in relation to variations of the third person singular pronoun ("he" and "his") that also exists in this poem "Pavement"?

DV The "the" is a drum in the poem. It is a drum followed by a kind of longer sibilance: the "his," the extended *S* sound and the extended vowel sound of "my" throughout the poem. It was a procedural tool. I was struggling with whether I would like to maintain the personal pronoun or an impersonal pronoun; that is, a choice which has an ethical valence or charge to it. So if you read (an earlier draft of) this line, "I forget his name walking up the stairs" – who is "he" to me? There is already a problem for witnessing, which demands a definition of that witness-object relationship. "I forget the name walking up the stairs" – so he's not mine, I could never claim a relation to him. But "I forget the his name walking up the stairs" there is this trip, a stumble, a stumbling on the choice between the article and the pronoun.

Can there be a stumbling witness? How do I, first, refuse to self-deputize as a person living between two empires or within two empires? How do I, at the same time, know that writing itself is a problem for witnessing?

MN It's incredible that you are able to present that stumbling in such a precise way.

I wonder if we can conclude this dialogue thinking about the continuities and ruptures in your work over this last decade or so. I'm curious what are the continuities that you see yourself focusing on, what are new things that are coming up in your work?

DV Troll Thread was definitive for me in my twenties. It was a testing space – something between a Petri dish and a forge. The pace of Troll Thread's publishing model was important, because it heightened the import and the stakes of the work. What that early contact offered me was this idea that one is "always making books." This became central to my practice at that time.

How can I summarize the arc? It's a decolonial arc, really. It's an arc that begins with a severe devotion to the field. In *Things to Do with Your Mouth*, I am reckoning with the Western canon as it has defined me along various axial points in my identity. I was disappointed in the way the arguments around conceptualism played out, its neglects, its binaries, its various absolutisms, the declarations of the post-ness of it. I thought it was embarrassing, intellectually. I think I'm more comfortable now not writing against something, not writing into a field, but really writing and devising terms that I want to pass on to folks I think who are possibly like me, who don't feel seen in institutions, or recognized within literary communities.

Curb is written for those who started reading me when I wrote *Kith*. That was it. *Curb* was written for like twenty people, and my family was among them. My grandmother and my father read *Kith*, and they said, "This is probably beautiful. I love the fact that you wrote this. I don't understand a lot of it." I asked them what were the parts that they understood, and my grandmother said, "I understood the parts where I cried." I recognized then that I needed to take both affect and sentiment extremely seriously, because they have epistemological functions for the self-realization of those in the diaspora. Affect and sentiment are not relegated to the rubbish heap as I have been taught. These are articulate formations – they show us what has been taken from us; they are eloquent manifests and registers of postcolonial grief.

I wrote *Curb* with urgency, because I felt that I was living in an emergency in a dangerous, amnesiac United States. And because my grandmother – whom "Locution / Location" is about – is getting old. I wanted to write a book she could understand and love before she dies. Ultimately, my work is shaped by strategies and values of what bell hooks calls "keeping close to home," and in trying to understand what that could mean for people who are not from the United States, what that could mean for people who have no home. How do we keep close to it?

ENDNOTE

1 Kamau Brathwaite, *History of the Voice: The Development of Nation Language in Anglophone Caribbean Poetry* (New Beacon Books, 1984), 13.

An Alternative Set of Procedures

A Dialogue with Carlos Soto Román

CARLOS SOTO ROMÁN IS A POET, TRANSLATOR, AND PHARmacist based in Santiago, Chile. He holds a masters in bioethics from the University of Pennsylvania and studied at the Jack Kerouac School of Disembodied Poetics at Naropa University. While living in the United States, he was a member of the New Philadelphia Poets Collective and a MacDowell Colony fellow and curated the anthology of US poetry *Elective Affinities*. In the United States, he has published *Philadelphia's Notebooks, Chile Project: [Re-Classified], Alternative Set of Procedures, Bluff,* and *Common Sense*. In the UK, he has published *Nature of Objects*, and in Chile, he has published *La Marcha de los Quiltros, Haikú Minero, Cambio y Fuera, 11, Densidad (d=m/V),* and *Antuco*, the latter in collaboration with Carlos Cardani Parra. He is the translator of the first Spanish-language version of Charles Reznikoff's *Holocaust*. His book *11* was awarded the 2018 Santiago Municipal Literature Award.

I first came upon Soto Román's work when Gauss PDF published *Chile Project: [Re-Classified]* on September 11, 2013, the fortieth anniversary of the US-supported coup d'état which overthrew Salvador Allende's government and led to the installation of Augusto Pinochet's military dictatorship. Soto Román's book forensically depicts and remanipulates the language that permitted, justified, and stood as a document of the political terrorism, disappearances, executions, and interrogations of the era and calls on readers to reckon with this history. In my mind, it exemplifies an important tendency of poets working against the grain of conceptual writing in order to make legible and scrutinize the rhetorical practices of US imperialism and its ongoing catastrophes.

To this extent, I wanted to invite Soto Román to reflect on the wider terrain of Chilean poets making works in the era of the dictatorship, a time when literary production was routinely censored and it became dangerous to articulate certain views in any kind of public way. Poets had to innovate formally in order to avoid censorship, and the contours and specificities of this tradition are a significant and vital contribution to poetics globally. In drawing together the arc of his own work within the context of this poetic tradition in Chile, I was particularly curious to hear Soto Román reflect on the fact and facticity in poetry at a time of increased misinformation campaigns and the political production of alternative realities.

The following dialogue took place over a series of live conversations and written exchanges between Santiago and Montréal in the autumn of 2021 and spring of 2024.

MN Perhaps we can begin by focusing on *Chile Project [Re-Classified]*, as it was through this work that I first learned about your poetry. There are numerous facets I'd like to address: how it blends a number of genres such as documentary poetics, found text, erasure, and artist's books; the various voices and hands articulated in the work, and your relation to them in the construction of the book; and a more general question about composing from the position of the perpetrator, which in this instance is the various individuals involved in the US government's campaign to implement and support a right-wing dictatorship, political oppression, and state terror in Chile. I wonder, though, first, if you might introduce *Chile Project [Re-Classified]*, discuss its composition, and explain what it means to "[re-classify]" – quoted, importantly, in square brackets in this work?

CSR *Chile Project [Re-Classified]* is part of a trilogy composed of *11*, *Chile Project*, and *Tercera Estrofa* (*Third Stanza*), the last of which hasn't yet been published. When I first began working on *11*, I reviewed multiple sources and materials related to the coup in Chile (the "11" of the title refers to the date of the coup, September 11, 1973) and materials related to the US government's involvement. That's how I came across the Chile Documentation Project in the US National Security Archive, which is a repository of declassified secret documents and one of the leading nongovernmental repositories of national security documentation obtained under the Freedom of Information Act (FOIA). The documents I found immediately had an impact on me – the way they were severely altered, modified, intervened, censored, redacted. It was a very dramatic and graphic representation of the events those documents were telling about, or maybe it would be more appropriate to say "hinting about," since the information was so obscured. Two things happened: first, it was impossible to make sense of the words because of the severe redaction, and second, the parts that were not that censored turned out to be well-known information or, in many cases, irrelevant. The irony and the uselessness of this declassification were evident. This compelled me to respond in a certain way to the kind of "violence" the documents were exhibiting, so I spent a long time thinking about how to adequately reply to them. I realized the only proper way to do it was by replicating the same tactics, the same procedures, but trying to subvert them. That meant responding to the perpetrators and to the violence of the documents with their own language, so I decided to erase, to white out everything that hadn't been redacted by the many hands that touched those documents, emphasizing the horror contained in those pages. That is, I left visible only the traces of their redactions. So the "re-classification" is more like a turn, or should I say *détournement*, where the same gesture is used to express the opposite.

MN I tend to think of *Chile Project* as a field of documentary poetry, but I'm not sure if that is the framework I placed it in when I first encountered it. Can you comment on how you considered the work or how you placed it when you were making it?

CSR It's interesting – during that time, ten years ago, even though many important works of documentary poetry had been published and in circulation for a long time, and people like Mark Nowak, among others, were working in a documentary poetic mode, I thought about what I was doing as engaging information as a genre. I was more concerned with conceptualism and the writing strategies articulated in that discourse. Specifically, I was attracted to conceptual writing's political potential, which wasn't the real interest of many of the poets working in that modality. For them, the procedure was everything. Often, the procedure was more important than its outcomes. That wasn't necessarily my main interest – I love to work with procedures, but I think I found something important in developing procedures and not being faithful to them, tweaking them or moving in different directions in the process.

MN You have an earlier work, *Haikú minero*, which also experiments with incorporating different source materials into the poetic text.

CSR Yes, *Haikú minero*, which I published in 2007, is very much a work of documentary poetry, though again, I wasn't really aware of that as a field when I wrote the book. *Haikú minero* is a sort of introspective odyssey into the bowels of the earth. The poems reveal the tragedy of three miners who were trapped in a clandestine mine near Andacollo in 1999. This was years before the world-famous case of the thirty-three Chilean miners in 2010. In the text, the documentary impulse and reappropriated journalistic material are intertwined with a poetics of confinement and inner inquiry. I decided to take on the subject of the miners by intuition, and in doing so I started working closely with news headlines and other media representations of the accident. I hadn't yet read Rukeyser's *The Book of the Dead* or Nowak's *Coal Mountain Elementary*, so it was a surprise to me when I found these works and realized that *Haikú minero* was related to them not only in subject matter but also in style.

MN I believe you wrote *Chile Project* when you were living outside of Chile in the United States. Can you describe some of the context around the work?

CSR Yes, I had been living there for a few years when, in 2013, it was the fortieth anniversary of the coup d'état. It was fascinating to witness from abroad how the right-wing government in Chile tried to frame the anniversary. There still wasn't a lot of recognition of what had happened. There were gestures about asking for forgiveness and acknowledging the victims, but we were far from any serious examination or inquiry into the atrocities that had taken place. The politicians wanted to deny this memory. Having regained democracy in Chile, and since we were commemorating the coup's anniversary, there was still a strong sense of injustice, of not having the complete truth, of impunity. That animosity was very much in the climate there. It's been all these years, and we are still not able to put the perpetrators of the coup on trial. We still don't know how many people were killed, or where the corpses of the victims are located. Families are still looking for them. The relatives still don't know what happened to them, how they died, and they are not able to give them a proper burial or close the grieving process. We were, and are, still grieving as a country.

Folks on the left began to make documentary films about all the crimes that had been committed during the dictatorship, and books were beginning to be published on this as well. I had this feeling that I wanted to write something about it, but not in any kind of traditional way, not in the form of lyric poetry. I found inspiration in works of conceptualist poetry such as M.

NourbeSe Philip's *ZONG!* and Vanessa Place's *Statement of Facts*, for example, which was her project using trial records and testimonies, and also in the work of Caroline Bergvall. These books were present in my mind as I began to imagine writing something about the coup. Looking back, it's no surprise that I ended up resorting to these kinds of strategies. It came very naturally for me to start digging into archives. The first thing I came upon was the digital archive of the Museum of Memory and Human Rights. The digital archive mostly has documents – pictures, passports, images of personal items that people had donated to the museum, a lot of forms. It's full of forms, in fact, such as a document concerning a man who had been imprisoned in a facility that listed the kinds of interrogation and torture he was subjected to. These documents had a huge impact on me. When I saw them, I thought, "Why should I bother to write something about this when I could present these documents?" Addressing this history through the frame of traditional lyric poetry seemed like a waste of time. I don't want to be disrespectful, as I really admire what the first generation of poets under the dictatorship did. They were looking for new ways to express what was happening there. But I had a feeling that this modality, this way of telling things, was already done, and if I wanted to talk about this subject, I needed to find a different way of telling the story.

MN It's worth noting that you're thinking about this from the perspective of a Chilean living in the United States after the other 9/11. So there's a countermemorialization project that's going on here, one pushing against the upsurge of violent, jingoistic nationalism after September 11, 2001. Also, it's worth underscoring that the documents in *Chile Project* are all composed by US state officials.

CSR Yes, that's another relevant aspect of this work – me being a Chilean person working out of the United States. It was a strong motivation for me to work on these materials from the place where, in a way, everything began. The attempts to boycott Salvador Allende's government began in the United States before he was even elected president. Obviously, this occurred in the context of the Cold War, and the Nixon administration from the very beginning saw the rise of the left in Chile as a menace. They compared it to Cuba, even though in reality they were quite different projects. Allende's path to power was a popular one. It was a true democracy. He was democratically elected, even though there was strong and fierce opposition from the elite in Chile, who did everything they could to prevent his rise to power. And they did so with significant support from the United States.

MN In your presentation of the CIA documents, you removed the unredacted language – none of which had any real significance – and in doing that, you were able to foreground the manipulation of all the hands involved in the operation and its erasure.

CSR That's right. I left intact only the marginalia – the notes and stamps and all of the hands that signed off on the operation – the processing of the operation in its most banal, bureaucratic traces. What's present is the manipulation of the history.

The other thing that is important in *Chile Project* is the media or mediation of all the language. The book originates as a set of documents that were typewritten, and then, of course, several hands intervened in the processing of those documents – stamping them, signing them, writing in their margins – which then, of course, referred to or anticipated sets of all-too-real actions. Then, these documents became a set of scanned digital documents that were uploaded into the repository where I found them. With those documents printed out, I whited them all out by hand using liquid paper. Then I scanned each of the documents and uploaded them again as a book onto the publishing repository of Gauss PDF.

MN There's something I want to note here in your use of the word *procedure*, as it's an important word for you. I am thinking of your recent pamphlet *Alternative Set of Procedures*, and how much the concept of procedure more generally resonates through your work. For instance, in *Chile Project*, in documenting Operation Condor – the campaign initiated by the US Army School of the Americas to politically and militarily repress leftist governments in South America in favour of right-wing dictatorships – you cast light on the procedures that the US government has established into a practice for conducting terrorism and supporting antidemocratic regime change abroad. You present not only the government's protocols for conducting such operations, but also the protocols by which they alter and erase the documentation of their actions. Against these procedures, you deploy an "alternative set of procedures": an "alternative" for procedural writing, one that cuts against the purely aesthetic approaches of the conceptualist poetry we discussed earlier.

CSR It's true. All of these things animated my spirit and animosity and contributed to how I engaged with the materials from the CIA. At the time of writing *Chile Project*, the first testimonies of what was happening at the Guantánamo Bay prison were appearing, and this question of "enhanced interrogation methods" or "alternative set of procedures" became a fundamental aspect of the rhetorical strategy for publicly presenting modes of torture as something other than that. It didn't matter that the US was putting a fancy name on it. In *Chile Project*, it felt like I was able to relate the methods that were happening at Guantánamo and later at Abu Ghraib to the methods thought up by the School of the Americas and practised by the various dictatorships they supported throughout Latin America.

MN *Chile Project* is, as you said earlier, the second piece in the trilogy following *11*, which you published in Spanish in 2018 and is now published in English translation by Ugly Duckling Presse. I am thankful for Scott Weintraub's brilliant discussion of the book in *Asymptote*, as he concisely articulates how *11* narrates the coup through the appropriation, erasure, re-inscription, and excerption – perhaps the key word for the book's activity is *manipulation* – of documents related to the establishment of the dictatorship.[1] I'm wondering if you could discuss the various documents that you cite in the work and describe both how you manipulate them and what possibilities for reading are created by such textual manipulations.

CSR There are many types of sources included in *11*. First, there is the Chilean constitution of 1980, crafted by a special committee appointed by Augusto Pinochet to have a tailor-made set of laws to validate the dictatorship and ensure the privileges of the ruling class over time. Then we have the two official reports of the Commission on Truth and Reconciliation – the Rettig Report on forced disappearance and the Valech Report on torture. There are forms and letters and certificates from detention centres; text from interviews; testimonies from victims and perpetrators; explanatory texts for pictures that I incorporated within the work – but without the pictures; transcriptions from radio broadcasts; excerpts from the economic measures taken by the junta during its first year; excerpts from the Pinochet trials in London from the post-dictatorship era. A wide variety of sources trying to reconstruct in a partial and veiled way all the years of the dictatorship and some period of the post-dictatorship era. I applied several procedures to all of them, mostly erasure, reorganization, decontextualization, and recontextualization through montage. I treat every document in a different way, and I let the document choose the procedure. It was according to the material itself, to its content, that I chose one way or another to intervene, letting or at least trying to preserve, to make more evident, the essence of each one. The reading possibilities, I believe, are endless. It would be the task of the readers, of their own subjectivity, to fill the blanks in the history. I like to think of *11* as a radical exercise of memory, one where remembrance is challenging, and the reader is forced to enact a reconstruction.

The way I decided to work on these documents was mainly that I would compile a large number of materials, and with those I would establish a certain chronology. Early on, I realized that the arc of the project concerned the disappeared. The book begins with the disappearance of two GAP agents, who were the bodyguards protecting President Allende. The last person documented in the work was a Mapuche kid the police kidnapped and disappeared. Even though the police car's license plate is well known, we still don't know what happened to the kid. So that's the arc of the work: the disappeared, the documentation of their disappearances. I tried to establish a chronology of events, but I'm not too faithful to it – the order of the documents is not necessarily chronological. But I wanted to narrate the dictatorship in a veiled way in order to force or push a subjective exercise of memory.

The procedure I decided to impose on each page I confronted was quite organic, responding to each document's materiality and visuality. I was simply working through each text and trying to figure out on the go what it was proposing in terms of a possible intervention. There was a lot of trial and error in the process, a lot of experimentation. I realized that erasure, blank pages, and gaps were becoming a central part of the work. In this, I was inspired by Heimrad Bäcker's book *transcript*, which was another piece of writing that influenced how I approached the documents of the Chilean dictatorship. I think *11* and *transcript* are similar, but if you read them closely, it becomes clear how they are separate and different projects. I say this not only because of the subject matter – since Bäcker's is composed with records from the Holocaust and mine is from the Chilean dictatorship, both of which are tremendous atrocities in the history of humankind. Even though they have similar approaches or strategies towards their corresponding subjects, they're very different books. I was, however, inspired by a couple of Bäcker's poems in *transcript*, and reinterpreted them or transposed some elements of them from his context to the Chilean context. I felt a certain permission to do this because, when you study the documentation of these regimes closely, you begin to see how, for instance, Pinochet borrowed elements of his own rule's iconography and the pompous style of its self-presentation from Nazi propaganda. I was interested in thinking through these connections as I made certain transpositions from Bäcker's text to my own. As one example, Bäcker has a poem that itemizes the music a band played for one of Hitler's birthday celebrations, which resonated with my research because I had come upon a list of Pinochet's requests for a marching band to play a specific list of songs to serenade him for one of his birthdays. In following Bäcker's poetic form for presenting such a list, I felt like it made the juxtaposition or disconnect between the pageantry of authoritarianism and the realities of state terrorism all the more palpable.

MN Reading through your series of writings on *Jacket2*, and also through commentaries on your work, I've become aware of the Chilean poetic tradition of the antibook or book-object. Lately, I've often been thinking about the Mexican poet Ulises Carrión and his "new art of poetry" for the way that it moves beyond the mere exploration of syntax or style in visual poetries and develops a model for an engaged mode of the publication and circulation of poetic texts. For Carrión, a poet must innovate at the level of the text as well as of the context of poetry. From your critical writings on the intersection of poetry and book arts, I have learned that this experimentation with the context and format of the publication has long been a vital tradition in Chile as well. So I'm wondering if you might discuss the contours of this textual-visual genealogy in Chile and your work's relation to it.

CSR Chile has a long tradition of visual poetry, or poetry that concerns itself with the visual aspects of its presentation or form. First, I'm thinking of *la lira popular,* which was a newspaper-like broadsheet publication composed of loose sheets of paper with poems printed on them. They often featured a title that was quite polemical or controversial, and they usually had an image as well. This practice has roots in the troubadours of medieval Europe, but in Chile it became a popular mode of poetry publication in the late 1800s and early 1900s. People called this kind of publication "string literature," because the poems were published on loose sheets of paper, and people would hang them on strings in town or in markets to sell in the streets. The poets who composed these poems were popular poets, and they composed their poems in décimas, a very particular metrical pattern that resembles a song, which helped them memorize and transmit significant amounts of language. This poetry circulated among a large number of people, many of whom were illiterate, so the visual element was important. Half of each page would be made up of the engraved image, usually depicting the event featured in the poem. The subjects of these poems were often assassinations or executions. These poems were the tabloids of their day. But it's interesting because it was poetry that worked alongside images. Often it was the poets themselves who made the images, or poets working together with artists to produce some kind of printed image. So I think *la lira popular* offers an interesting origin in Chile of the relation between poetry and image.

Then we have Vicente Huidobro, who came from a wealthy family and was able to travel extensively. He lived in Paris for a long time, and he became close friends with Apollinaire and with the Dada scene. He then became part of the avant-garde in Chile. Huidobro had a large set of visual poems that he called caligramas, after Apollinaire's *Calligrammes*. And he had an important impact on many subsequent poets who developed a strong visual element in their writing and the ways they organized language. For instance, there's Guillermo Deisler, who worked during the years of the dictatorship. Deisler went into exile and began to participate in mail art movements, so he was in conversation with poets and artists from Uruguay, Argentina, Mexico, and from all over Europe as well. You can think of him as a kind of Chilean Ulises Carrión, in that he's important for conjoining visual work, collage, and poetry. I mean, his work is fundamentally visual, but he always called it poetry. There is this link with the visual arts, but somehow it keeps being poetry. And then there's Enrique Lihn, who is associated with Nicanor Parra and Alejandro Jodorowsky. In the 1950s, these three developed a publication called *El Quebrantahuesos* (The Bone-Breaker), which they published on a public bulletin board outside a famous restaurant in downtown Santiago. It was a collage work that combined images with titles from newspaper headlines, and they would play, often in a very ironic way, with subjects in the news or that were popular in culture at the time. In *El Quebrantahuesos*, we can see perhaps the origins of Parra's "antipoetry," which fundamentally emphasized its visual element. I ought to mention Parra in this genealogy for the way he insisted on a visual poetry through his artifacts. Are you familiar with that element of his work?

MN We have a collection of Parra's antipoems in English that New Directions published in Liz Werner's translation, but I can't recall if that includes the artifacts.

CSR The artifacts are works combining language and image. In Chile, we sometimes joke that Nicanor Parra is the originator of memes. He would take an image of some kind and combine it with a comical poem or reference or title that would play in some fascinating way with the meaning of the image. So Parra belongs in that lineage as well.

But going back to your original question, I don't think I was thinking of this tradition when I began making works like *Chile Project* and *11*, though it does provide a context. I wasn't responding to any particular element in these writers' works, but they were present and were part of my poetic education in Chile. They had a strong influence on me in the way that they offer what I often refer to as the anomaly in poetry, meaning poetry that doesn't resemble in its form or presentation what we traditionally think of as poetry. Not lyric poetry, for instance. Yet, when we study these anomalies, when we look at their resources and communicative strategies, we begin to see how they are part of an extensive tradition of poetic practice through time. The anomaly is something that has been with me since I started to write poetry. It's this love or affection for, or fascination with, or inclination towards what is not normal in poetry. This tendency has been relevant to the way that I frame the task of each poem I write. Every time I'm confronted with an idea for a book or piece of writing, I'm always thinking about how it can be done differently.

MN I'm curious if you could say more about how poets from these earlier generations experimented with conceptualist practices and politically engaged poetics – with what the poetic text is, how it could be composed and function in the world, how it is materialized and disseminated.

CSR During the 1970s, the main form of art in Chile was folkloric and popular art. It had a particular aesthetic that was recognized as leftist or committed art. That disappeared after the coup because those expressions were censored and the artists were persecuted, incarcerated, and assassinated. We had, as in Germany, soldiers burning books in the streets during raids. There's a story of soldiers burning books about cubism because they thought it had something to do with Cuba. A lot of important and relevant work was buried at this time because it was deemed to be leftist or Marxist. It was thrown into the fire. Because of this, we had a series of years that were a total cultural shutdown. No one risked it. But during the 1980s, the Art Actions Collective, CADA, showed up and started doing performances and actions. They drove a truck full of milk in a kind of parade, stopping in villages or slums and giving milk to the people. It was an action carried out by poets and artists. This piece resonated with the policies of Salvador Allende, who had this initiative to fight malnutrition and hunger that assured a litre of milk for every child in the country. Allende established this measure during the first year of his government. So artists undertaking an action like this had significance. It was subtle. But CADA became more aggressive with their actions over time. Raúl Zurita was a member of this collective. So was Diamela Eltit, another writer, and Lotty Rosenfeld, a multidisciplinary artist. This overall scene of artists, writers, and their works responding to the military coup came to be known as La Escena de Avanzada, which is Spanish for the avant-garde.

So one of the ways that art could happen without government intervention or censorship was through this kind of conceptual practice. The military and the police couldn't understand what these poets and artists were doing. It didn't make sense to them, so it was less likely to be prohibited or censored. It was a strategy the artists developed in order to make works in that context, to get away with things while at the same time delivering a strong political message. This art and these kinds of actions are very present in the cultural memory. During the riots in Chile in 2019, these actions from the 1980s had a tremendous influence on how people organized themselves and responded to the government.

MN I think of leftist avant-gardism as a way of generating procedures or techniques or tactics that anticipate the contexts in which they might be deployed – often with the aim of protecting what is held in common. The forms and uses of language, embodiment, collective action, and collective modes of production, ways of organizing demonstrations and resistance – the leftist avant-garde becomes a place to theorize, experiment with, and instantiate such aesthetic and political strategies.

CSR *Avant-garde* is a military term. In a way, it's always about finding different and innovative ways of crossing enemy lines. That particular generation in the 1970s and 1980s turned to provocative humour as a tactic of resistance. The government was taking their friends and relatives, torturing them, killing them, exiling them. Life was dangerous. The popular dream embodied by Salvador Allende's government had been violently destroyed. Life lost meaning completely, and the only way to make sense out of it was to keep moving, keep resisting through art. Irony, for many of them, seemed to have a certain power in the face of all the terrible things that were happening. I think of Sergio Pesutic's book *La Hinteligencia militar* (The Military Hintelligence) – the misspelling of "intelligence" is intentional. There is not one word inside of it. It's composed of one hundred blank pages.

MN I want to ask about interrogation, the figure of the interrogator, the voice and diction and syntax of the interrogator, and, finally, the mark or trace of the interrogator over time. This figure is central to the two main works we've discussed – *Chile Project* and *11* – and it plays a central role in your more recent works in English, such as *Bluff, Common Sense,* and *The Exit Strategy.* Can you discuss your interest in the voice and position and language of the interrogator, and also how you've explored it in these works?

CSR This is an interesting and difficult question. The procedures and the language of interrogation were my field of inquiry while I was composing *11*. But the coincidence of working on these materials when the documents and testimonies from Guantánamo and Abu Ghraib appeared allowed me to tackle this topic from a different perspective. I decided to incorporate the voices of the perpetrators. This was something I was already doing, but I did so in a more subtle way through the documents and forms and laws and bureaucratic exchanges included in *11* and *Chile Project*. Those, too, are composed in the voice of the perpetrator. But in the context of something as violent and as direct as torture and interrogation ... I thought I could approach it by other means. I decided to explore other records to try to establish connections that would result in different ways of dealing with the topic. This is how I came to the *Spiritual Exercises of St. Ignatius of Loyola*, mainly the part on confession, the transcripts of the trial of Joan of Arc, and the interrogations carried out by the Inquisition. But I also resorted to other elements, such as tarot reading, divination, and fortune-telling as modes of inquiry. I was very attracted to the voice and methods of the interrogators, but always from an appropriate distance. This was something I was interested in recreating, rearticulating, but from the records, from the documents, collecting the traces of (in)humanity through the facts. It was not something I was interested in recreating from imagination.

I think of the poet and lawyer Bruno Vidal. He was a member of the communist party in Chile, and he wrote several books from the voice of the perpetrator. I don't often mention him, because in an important way I take a different path. He fictionalizes the voices of the perpetrators. He doesn't work with documents. They may be an inspiration, but he tends to work with histories that we all know, particularly from the dictatorship. His whole universe is the military world. His poetry is very controversial. In the beginning, many considered him to be a right-wing poet, but over time it became clear that he was performing a kind of operation on right-wing rhetoric, saying clearly what they think but refuse to say, attaching that perspective to them, in a way exposing them. It was a kind of Hegelian play of mirrors where you see the reflection of something and it looks even more real than reality. I think it's important to cite Vidal and his work. I don't recognize him as a central influence, though, because when I use the voice of the perpetrator, I don't want to make things up. I don't want to fictionalize. I'm interested in the sources, in their attempt to frame real voices and actions.

MN There is something particularly potent today in exploring fact and facticity in poetic language. I think of this in our own Trumpian moment, where both the fascist and liberal factions of the US are committed to cultivating the Bush-era disdain for "reality-based communities."[2] When I think back to confronting *Chile Project* for the first time, what struck me was the refusal of metaphor, the refusal of any kind of heightened language, against the rhetorical background of the language of the times – language that continues today. Forensic fact in language felt like an antidote that poetry could offer.

CSR That's very interesting. Truth has been, in these times, dissolved into subjectivity. It seems to me that there are multiple truths going on, and they're all conflicting with each other. More than fact, though, what interests me is the representation or registration of facts – both the process and the documentation of how facts become registered.

MN This discussion of the document and the interrogator leads me to think about biopolitics – the means by which individuals and institutions of power seek to regulate bodies through force, which is materialized in a diversity of actions, proceedings, and language. I would love to hear you discuss how your work as a pharmacist and as a student of bioethics has informed your poetry over the years. There is a quote from your book *Bluff* that provides an interesting conceptual window into your work, "The truth is always almost unbreakable." I love this quote for a number of reasons: there's the fact that the interrogator is always trying to "break" a "truth" he wants to hear from his subject; there's the resistance of the subject under torture to not utter the "truth" that the torturer seeks, and thus to maintain a higher order of truth; and there's the way the histories you document disrupt the convenient historical narratives cultivated by the perpetrator and interrogator, and open onto, again, a higher order of truth than those assembled by colonial and imperial forces.

CSR When I incorporated this quote into the text, I was thinking about the subjects that break down during an interrogation or torture session. But I have a feeling that there is another kind of truth that underlies it, which is of a higher order, as you mentioned, and which relates to the human condition itself – and that would be what really breaks down in these scenarios of such crude violence. That fragility, that transience, I believe, would be the only unbreakable truth. In fact, the basic definition of torture speaks of the torment of the body to obtain a truth; it is the search, the inquiry of truth through punishment.

Bioethics is a discipline that seeks to give answers to dilemmas related to life, and it is a valuable tool, not only through language but also through philosophy, to try to find poetic solutions to complex problems such as torture. I remember that at the beginning of my master's degree in bioethics, I attended a talk where a person who had held an important position at Amnesty International spoke about the importance of having medical personnel in interrogation and torture settings. I was stunned by this. My astonishment prevented me from intervening. I had newly arrived in the country, my English was not that good, and I was still not very comfortable speaking in front of an audience, but I think it was more the content of his argument that blocked me. In a room full of medical and nursing students, this person was defending and found morally justifiable the presence of medical personnel in torture scenarios. I understand that this is something that must have taken hold post-9/11, and that the speaker was arguing that medical personnel were there to assist the interrogee. But that is a fallacy. Doctors and nurses who are involved in torture contexts are not there to look after the interests of the interrogee. They are there to ensure that the subject does not die before revealing the desired information. They are there to advise the interrogators on what methods are suitable or not, according to the subject's condition – recommending, for example, not to use electricity but to continue with beatings. Coming from a country where torture was systematically implemented as a state terrorist policy, I could not believe what I was listening to. My inability to respond at the time turned into rage and into a driving force. In a way, I wrote the trilogy as a response to that. You could say that poetry was a way of avenging that affront and that use of the archive. The documents that registered such atrocities were the perfect weapon. Appropriating the language of the perpetrators – veiling, unveiling, censoring – I was able to use their own rhetoric against them.

ENDNOTES

1 Scott Weintraub, "Narrating (The Other 9/)*11*: The Poetics of Carlos Soto Román," *Asymptote* (website), January 3, 2019.

2 "Reality-based community" was, in the mid-2000s, a term to denigrate people who base their judgment on facts. The term first appeared in an article by journalist Ron Susskind, dated October 17, 2004, ("Faith, Certainty and the Presidency of George W. Bush") where he interviewed an unnamed official in the George W. Bush administration. I quote an extended excerpt here:

> In the summer of 2002, after I had written an article in *Esquire* that the White House didn't like about Bush's former communications director, Karen Hughes, I had a meeting with a senior adviser to Bush. He expressed the White House's displeasure, and then he told me something that at the time I didn't fully comprehend – but which I now believe gets to the very heart of the Bush presidency.
>
> The aide said that guys like me were "in what we call the reality-based community," which he defined as people who "believe that solutions emerge from your judicious study of discernible reality." I nodded and murmured something about enlightenment principles and empiricism. He cut me off. "That's not the way the world really works anymore," he continued. "We're an empire now, and when we act, we create our own reality. And while you're studying that reality – judiciously, as you will – we'll act again, creating other new realities, which you can study too, and that's how things will sort out. We're history's actors … and you, all of you, will be left to just study what we do."

Suskind has still never revealed the speaker's identity, but many have speculated it to be Bush's senior advisor Karl Rove.

Documenting Physical Investigations with Language

A Dialogue with Tanya Lukin Linklater

TANYA LUKIN LINKLATER'S PRACTICE AND WRITINGS CITE Indigenous dance and visual-art lineages, our structures of sustenance, and weather. She undertakes embodied inquiry and site-specific rehearsals. Her work reckons with histories that affect Indigenous peoples' lived experiences, (home)lands, and ideas. Her recent exhibitions include Aichi Triennale, Japan; Gwangju Biennale, South Korea; New Museum Triennial, New York; San Francisco Museum of Modern Art; and Toronto Biennial of Art. *Inner blades of grass (soft), inner blades of grass (cured), inner blades of grass (bruised by the weather)*, curated by Kelly Kivland, was presented by the Wexner Center for the Arts in 2024. She is represented by Catriona Jeffries, Vancouver. Her book, *Slow Scrape*, draws on documentary poetics, concrete-based installations, and event scores and can be read alongside her practice of choreography. She recently completed her PhD in Cultural Studies at Queen's University and is presently a Postdoctoral Fellow in Decolonial and Transformational Indigenous Art Practices in the Visual Arts Department at the University of Victoria. Her Alutiiq/Sugpiaq homelands are in southwestern Alaska, and she is based in Nbisiing Anishinaabeg aki.

Lukin Linklater's book *Slow Scrape* is, in the words of Layli Long Soldier, "neither wholly poem nor verbose prose and exposition, but reads as text in step – toe-to-floor, light and gentle or heel-to-earth, pounding; felt from the ground, up." Lukin Linklater draws upon documentary poetics, concrete-based installations, event scores, and other texts composed in relation to performances written between 2011 and 2018. Citing memory, Cree and Alutiiq languages, and embodiment as modes of relational being and knowledge, the book unfolds a poetics of relation and action to counter the settler colonial violences of erasure, extraction, and dispossession. *Slow Scrape* can be read alongside Lukin Linklater's practice as a visual artist and choreographer.

I had the great honour and pleasure of working as an editor with Lukin Linklater in the development of *Slow Scrape*. Our conversations and collaborations have been fundamental to thinking in many trajectories, from aesthetics and politics to issues regarding memory, materials, and relations.

The following dialogue documents this ongoing exchange in an interesting way: the first half is from 2020, written in correspondence, as Lukin Linklater and I worked through edits for *Slow Scrape*. Initially published in *Tripwire: a journal of poetics* following a series of Lukin Linklater's event scores that formulate an important poetics of relation and action to counter settler-colonial paradigms of appropriation and erasure, we then decided to republish the exchange as an afterword within *Slow Scrape*.

The second half of the dialogue emerges from the context of Lukin Linklater's and my public conversation held at Catriona Jeffries Gallery, co-organized with the Contemporary Art Gallery, in Vancouver on April 4, 2024. Within Duane Linklater's installation *cache*, Lukin Linklater and I celebrated the launch of a newly published monograph on her visual and performing arts works, *My mind is with the weather* (2024), to think together through a number of issues prominent in her work, from land and landscape, cultural belongings, the many modes of settler-colonial appropriation, and issues of resistance and Indigenous sovereignty. Together, we prepared an edited transcript of this exchange to best present it within the context of this book.

MN When I first encountered your writings, it was in a visual arts context: you had printed excerpts from your poem sequence "The Harvest Sturdies" on canvas tarps that were installed throughout Open Space, the artist-run centre in Victoria, BC. Close to the works were stunning videos of these tarp-texts also installed out on the land, in northern Ontario. Can you discuss the journey of these texts towards *Slow Scrape*, your writing of them, and the various forms of their publication prior to this book?

TLL I hadn't intended on writing a book. I worked on each of these texts at different times within different contexts from 2011 to 2018. The poem "In Memoriam" was written in 2011 and was published in a special issue of *Drunken Boat* guest edited by Layli Long Soldier. I had met Layli at Bard College, where she was studying and I was visiting one summer. "In Memoriam" is a text in relation to a series of works: performance, choreography for three dancers, and video I had developed during that time, centred on specific histories on my island that were violent and resulted in intergenerational grief, displacement, and loss of language and Alutiiq ways of being. I was interested partly in the ways in which memory lives in the body beyond an event or a series of events, and possibly how it manifests for generations. I suppose I was also interested in how we make sense of ourselves in this time, given the constraints of history that have produced our current context. I considered text as part of a larger process of this investigation of history, memory, and the body. I later asked Layli if she was open to a poetry mentorship in 2012–2013. We met weekly or biweekly via Skype. I lived on Nipissing First Nation in northern Ontario at the time, and she lived in Tsaile, Arizona. Across that distance, we read together. She encouraged me to write about what felt urgent.

There were political actions taking place that were very present for me as I watched them unfold on social media that fall and winter: Chief Theresa Spence's hunger strike, Idle No More, and round dance actions in shopping malls at Christmas time in Canada. I was also moved during this time by the attempted assassination of Malala Yousafzai, a girls' education activist, which I read partly in relation to discourses surrounding education within a Canadian context of the legacy of Indian residential schools and the Truth and Reconciliation Commission of Canada. I wrote

"Not like us," "The Harvest Sturdies," and "A girl" during this mentorship, as I worked through some of my thinking around education, treaty, and women's experiences and work in relation to both.

It was an intensive research process. I interviewed three of my Omaskêko Cree relatives for "The Harvest Sturdies," asking them about their lives. I wasn't exactly certain what I was asking them when I first began visiting with them on the phone. I thought I was asking about who taught them to tan hides, sew, and bead, and when they began to take up this learning and work. As the interviews unfolded, it became clear that my request extended to a remembering of relations with family and relations with the land in ways I could not have anticipated. They also shared about the very private cultivation of their inner lives. These works were a form of documentary poetics, in that I directly quote my relatives. I wanted to reflect their generosity and concision in the writing, and this was in alignment with a way of writing that I developed over this time.

MN What is the relationship between these compositions and your visual arts practice?

TLL I often attempt to make sense of the world through writing. Years ago, during a studio visit, Pablo de Ocampo described writing as the substrate of my arts practice.

Occasionally, I install text works in museums or galleries. In "The Harvest Sturdies," I've used visual poetry to reference a stretched hide, the repetition of beadwork, or smoke in a tipi that is colouring the hide. For this project, I chose to print on canvas or tarp-like material that we might use for a tipi or a temporary shelter on the land, citing the home and the land as the locations for intergenerational learning that Agnes Hunter, Marlene Kapashesit, and Lillian Trapper shared with me.

I've started bringing text into my video work in more pronounced ways in the last couple of years. I began to make text works, videos, and sculptures for exhibition partly as a way for the work to travel without me, to circulate beyond the live event. I was concerned that if my work only lived in performance, it might disappear or be erased. As an Alaska Native woman, I think about the history of discourse surrounding Native Americans in the United States – the ongoing trope of the vanishing Indian as well as the substantive efforts to erase our intellectual traditions, to marginalize our contributions to most fields, an epistemic violence. The live event, even the exhibition, disappears. Perhaps my practice shouldn't be remembered; others have to decide that. But moving towards the art object in small ways means that my work can have a life that extends into the future.

I've often thought of how contemporary dance is an abstract form. My videos, attentive to the body, communities, architecture, or landscape, might also be considered abstract for an everyday viewer to encounter in the museum. I consider text as a potential way for the viewer to enter into the work; however, I balance this access with strategies of refusal.

MN In situating the texts within your visual arts practice, perhaps I overemphasize the object itself, which is something you are of course interested in, but with that, throughout your work, there is, like you say, a refusal of it by means of a different emphasis on the live event, in movement, in choreography. So I'm curious if you could also discuss the relationship between your writings and this other element that is central to your work?

TLL I am perhaps best known for making performances or videos with dancers. An older Anishinaabe man where I live (the small city of North Bay, Ontario) recently told me that I make things happen. That was a significant comment, as it was a recognition by a community member of the live event, of the ways in which I labour to make an event happen. It's a kind of slow build over time that becomes visible in performance but takes ongoing daily investigations, reflection, reading, thinking, conversations with curators, etc. Writing is an important part of this process as a document of these moments. These are processes dependent upon a number of constraints or conditions that I've put into place and require a flexible responsiveness. So much of my practice is in relation and in response to histories, to the present moment, to the conditions of the museum, to the conversations I'm having with dancers, composers, curators, etc.

At times, I document physical investigations with language, distilling language from conversation with dancers. The dancers and I notate their dances in different ways. I keep my notes for future investigations or performances, building over time. It can be a kind of back and forth between languages, possibly a kind of continuous translation between the body (which comes to have its own series of languages initiated by the dancer), materials (including cultural belongings made by our Ancestors), and other forms. I tend to jot down key questions in journals that I later ask during the choreographic process. Or I document questions that come up during the performance-making process through conversation or connections I am thinking through. Often writing is a very unseen part of my practice. This writing may never be shared publicly. I consider my journal to be a working space, a studio of sorts.

In terms of the ways in which poems and event scores are visibly or audibly present in my practice, since 2013 I've been reading texts alongside dancers and / or my videos. I have allowed myself the space for these performances with dancers to fail; I consider them to be studies, experiments. In some cases, the poems are a score, structure, or script for the making of a dance within the museum or gallery. I work through an open rehearsal process to build these performances and have come to work with a group of five independent dancers, each of whom has different strengths, movement languages, and views that they bring to the process.

The readings with videos are configured differently each time: I choose different poems, event scores, and videos for each event. I'm particularly interested in these moments where my voice collides with the image in a way that may never happen again. I can't fully anticipate these moments. I leave that to chance and give myself the constraint of thirty minutes of video and thirty minutes of text. I time the performance at the live event but don't rehearse in advance. This means that the readings or interpretations of both the poems and videos might be infinite.

MN I see throughout *Slow Scrape* a movement between action ("making things happen") and memory (documentation), both thematically and formally in the design of the texts. I'd love to focus on the latter for a moment – memory, with all of its partialities, scars, gaps, richnesses, the ways of being these poems are constantly imagining and articulating, their possible futures and assembly of relations. Can you discuss how forms of memory materialize and are materialized within these writings?

TLL I don't think I'm unlike many Indigenous peoples in this commitment to remembering and continuous action. The idea that I make things *happen* reminded me that the liveness of the event in this moment is a part of a durational inheritance that extends to my Ancestors. What I mean to say in another way is that making things happen, organizing large-scale events for families and communities, was and continues to be an Alutiiq practice.

My work continuously considers orality, embodiment, our philosophical concerns, history, and the present moment. I wonder broadly about how we have continued to insist on our Indigeneity (Alutiiq-ness or Sugpiaq-ness in my case) even in the face of dominant structures and systems that have actively dismantled our languages, minds, and relationships to ourselves. I'm interested partly in memory embodied at the scale of felt structures that insist in the midst of the historical. Elsewhere, I've begun to write about insistence as an accumulation of quotidian, minor actions that in some moments become visible. I think my larger practice investigates the ways in which the relational, coded in orality (including embodiment) and connected to the material, allows for this insistence. This insistence is not only concerned with the past but allows for our peoples' ways of being and knowing in the present towards a continuance, our future, where possible.

My thinking is in alignment with discourses initiated in the late 1960s by Indigenous peoples – practitioners and theorists working in relation to their communities, to sovereignty, to justice, and to what has come to be described now as resurgence – that continue today. I situate my practice within these larger histories, yet I'm speaking from specific moments and experiences that I've encountered in my lifetime or that I've come to know about. I feel a deep responsibility to our Ancestors, to today, and to the future. I think that the real work is happening in communities – in my villages and across Alaska, in Nbisiing Anishinaabeg Territory where I live, and in Cree communities in Canada that I am in relation to as well. My artistic practice and writing gesture towards that.

MN When I first read your event scores, I immediately thought of them as reformulating Fluxus and other historical avant-garde practices in a newly engaged way. Here, I think of people like Allan Kaprow, Nam June Paik, George Brecht, Yoko Ono, among others. Were you drawing from this tradition, or if not, were there other artists or aesthetic tendencies that animated the possibility of these works for you?

TLL The event scores arose out of a graduate course with Dylan Robinson called "Indigenous and Settler Affect: Unsettling~Writing~Feeling" at Queen's University in the spring of 2016. Dylan shared a series of event scores with us, and we were encouraged to write in a range of ways. I was particularly moved by Yoko Ono's event scores. I also experienced what I perceived to be a live event score when Eber Hampton led an Indigenous conference delegation at the University of Alberta around the same time through verbal directions for a small series of physical actions that were intended to slow our sense of time, connect us to our breath, as a greeting of the sun. This small action was quite profound for me within that context, as it was unexpected. Even though I had experienced these kinds of directions within dance and performance-studio classes over decades and have also led these kinds of exercises in various spaces, it was quite striking to listen, breathe, visualize, and move within this other space. It helped to create a shared experience among the group.

I found it quite easy to rest into this way of writing. It was generative to me in its concision (which is a form of refusal), the almost plain language, and its intentionality.

I connected this idea directly to my experience of performance. Yet I also considered that the event score could function solely as a text. I have performed the event scores at times, but not as a set of directions for an audience, instead as a distilled, concise text that I've spoken, sometimes accompanied by video. A number of works in this book were written initially for that course and went on to be published, performed, or integrated into video works.

MN Another element that stands out for me in *Slow Scrape* is the practices of listening that are at its core – something that is deeply allied with my own interests in poetry and artistic practices. And perhaps, in the frame of listening, this is where memory and action come together in a fruitful way. I can see a few different forms of listening that take place throughout this work: intergenerational listening, translinguistic listening (Alutiiq, Cree, English), mediated listening (through global and national news and also through one's personal relations), terrestrial or land-based listening (topological). Are there other forms that you see? Can you discuss if or how these forms of listening inform your practices?

TLL I appreciate your analysis across these different contexts. Mostly, I consider listening an integral part of being Indigenous. I've come to call it deep listening. My early training in listening came as a youth at the kitchen table, where my dad visited with aunties, uncles, and other relatives, neighbours, and community members. He also spent considerable time with my sisters and me on the land and waters near my village hunting and fishing. I have not attained my father's ability to discern weather, the tides, or the messages left by animals, birds, and fish at home. This discernment takes a lifetime of experience, and I left my village as a young person to attend university. Yet this early training, listening to relatives visit or my father teach us about gillnetting salmon and when the different species run annually, allowed me to later spend time with Anishinaabe and Cree Elders and knowledge holders in Alberta as a young adult, listening, attuning myself to their way of speaking and communicating. This time in Alberta within these invisible networks was quite formative for me.

I've continued this practice of listening in my adult life. Listening is connected to learning, which means synthesizing knowledge – integrating ideas into what we already know or upending what we think we know in order to apply that knowledge to our lives, to change our practices, a process that may take years. However it also means that when we listen, we learn a level of discernment and responsibility in this listening. I might also mention that I listen to the voice, to conversation, to sound, to the body, to the multiple ways we communicate in everyday life and in the performances I organize. This listening is multisensorial. Elwood Jimmy speaks about an enlivened and expanded listening; I think a great deal about listening with the full body.

MN In reading through the book, I wonder if part of this listening practice is situated within a concept of mentorship, in intentional acts of accumulating and transmitting cultural knowledge. Perhaps "mentorship" isn't the right word, but what I mean to gesture towards are the thoughtful ways you foreground your relations with others, which is both an acknowledgment of indebtedness as well as a commitment to give back.

TLL I look to people in my life who have provided moments of guidance over time. Our grandmother in Peawanuck, Agnes Hunter, my late auntie Sue Lukin, auntie Marlene Kapashesit in Québec, auntie Irene Isheroff Linklater, and my father, Ivan Lukin, to name a few. Often I connect with my peers, and we are learning from one another. Here I think of Layli Long Soldier, Wendy Red Star, Elwood Jimmy, Duane Linklater, Raven Chacon, Laura Ortman, and Jennifer Wabano. I also look to the work of artists, writers, and thinkers who came before me, learning from their cultural production. A few of these are Maria Tallchief, Rita Letendre, Sonya Kelliher-Combs, Ralph Lemon, Senga Nengudi, Karen Pheasant-Neganigwane, and Rebecca Belmore. I look to cultural belongings found in museum collections as information left by my Ancestors. Yet I learn from the youth as well, from my children, from the Anishinaabeg and Cree youth in North Bay. The transmission of knowledge isn't only from the older generations to the youth; this transmission of knowledge is multidirectional. I think of Ivanie Aubin-Malo, who has deep knowledge of contemporary and fancy shawl dance; I think of Billy-Ray Belcourt's incisive writing; these young Indigenous folks teach me.

• • •

MN Tanya, we are meeting again here at Catriona Jeffries Gallery in Vancouver – a few years after our first dialogue on *Slow Scrape*, and for the first time in person since the book was published – to celebrate your new exhibition catalogue, *My mind is with the weather*. Since we first began to develop *Slow Scrape*, you've often referred to our meeting as "a visit." It's a very casual term, but in the way you use it, it's come to have a certain significance for me. *A visit* is a time where we get to connect as people, as writers and artists who are doing work and want to talk about that work or some specific outcome of work, but also want to talk about our families or what's happening in our lives and what we are thinking about and what books we are reading that we are drawing inspiration from and what we might plan to do together in some sort of collaboration. I'm really thankful for these visits, because each one is situated in a commonplace context of making work and being a person, while also being a place where it feels like a lot of discovery occurs.

I wanted to begin our visit this afternoon by picking up on a theme that we've often discussed over these years, regarding relations and relationality. You are an artist and thinker who is exploring and opening up meaningful ways to consider relationality. It occurs in the site specificity of your works and in the developing of contexts and your sense of citation and attribution that is prominent in your writings. Perhaps we can also think about this relationality through the theme of weather. The concept and the figure of weather plays an important role in thinking of our relations to others, to the land. There is a concept that you articulate in *My mind is with the weather*, the word is *lla* – can you give some context to this term and how you think with it?

TLL *Lla* is a concept word that is translated to mean *weather*, so there is a physiological aspect to lla. I think a great deal about how lla has organized our daily life for multiple millennia. I'm from two villages on Kodiak Island. Our Ancestral village was destroyed by the 1964 Good Friday earthquake and a series of tidal waves. I've been thinking about lla, or weather, for a long time, but in my writing, thinking, and making I've started to coalesce these ideas or bring some clarity to them.

In *Slow Scrape*, in a poem, "They fall the ground beneath you," I visit the oral histories that are held in the tribal library of the Native Village of Afognak. In these oral histories, the people of Afognak, including my relatives, describe their experiences of the earthquake and tidal waves. I think that's partly where this sustained interest with weather comes from. I'm also trying to think about it in an expansive way, as a kind of event, or as a series of ongoing events. In the everyday life of my villages today, the weather decides whether we will travel to fish, hunt, be outside working on the boat, or inside drinking tea. A remote village, we have to fly or boat in. If there are high winds, we are stuck on the island. There is no mail for periods of time. Sometimes the weather is so bad there is no television or phone service. Weather is so present in the ways that we live on the land and the water at home.

There's a book by Angayuqaq Oscar Kawagley, who is Yup'ik from Alaska, that I read when I was young. In it, he writes about lla, or ella in his language, in Yup'ik, the closest language to ours, which is Sugcestun. (In fact, the Elders or fluent speakers in both communities can converse with one other.) He describes how lla takes different forms. Lla is the weather, sky, consciousness, the Creator of the universe, the universe itself. Lla is a feeling, a tone, an atmosphere. It's about lived experience on the land.

We're in a moment where the climate crisis is ever present. I didn't know how to address it in my work. I take time to arrive at a response to political or cultural events or other histories that are happening in real time. In the project "An amplification through many minds," which is documented in *My mind is with the weather*, I visited Ancestral and cultural belongings in Berkeley, California. During these visits, the Sonoma County wildfire was happening. That wildfire altered the entire trajectory of the project. There were rolling blackouts through the Bay Area. The electrical infrastructure was failing. There was deep concern about the electrical grid continuing to spark, and because the region was in a drought, this was a frightening possibility. Everything was very, very dry. Strong winds come through at certain times of the year. All of that came together and altered the path of the work that I was undertaking with these belongings. I addressed weather in the form of the wildfire. The weather did not allow me to ignore it. It was unfolding in real time.

Weather, for me, is complex and real, lived, felt, physiological, but also metaphorical and conceptual – an idea that is rooted in old ideas in my homelands. It's a complex and open term.

MN In your contribution to *My mind is with the weather* and in several of the artworks that are documented, you talk about weather systems and the navigation of land and Territory and the interpersonal dynamics of weather as a shared ambient sphere. But then there is this figure of weather that is the "ongoing storms of colonialisms." I thought this was an important and necessary way to come at ecological crisis – citing there the settler-colonial histories that are at the core of the ecological crisis. Here, I'm thinking of the essay in which Zoe Todd and Heather Davis argue that the dating of the Anthropocene should not be anchored to the Industrial Revolution but to settler colonialism, its histories.[1]

Then there's another interesting engagement with weather in what I found to be an unexpected place, in Berkeley, at the Hearst Museum of Anthropology. You mentioned the fires raging to the north of there, but there is a weather that you cite in the collection itself. It's a lack of weather, or "weathering" as you sometimes put it, a settler-colonial weather that is imposed upon the cultural belongings.

TLL The "ongoing storms of colonialisms" is a phrase that arises from a quote by the late Barbara Shangin, an Alutiiq Elder from the mainland. She says of Sugpiaq people something to the extent of: ever since the Russians came, it's been one bad storm after another. But within this idea is the hope that the storms will eventually pass. The anthropologist James Clifford discusses this quote in one of his books. He really belabours it, which I found quite irritating. This is what typically happens – Alutiiq or Sugpiaq people, what we say is not listened to; it is discarded, dismissed. This feels like a common experience.

I took up the idea of "the ongoing storms of colonialisms" and extended it. In conversation with Beth Piatote, who is also a contributor to *My mind is with the weather*, she says this is not a natural disaster. These are human constructed, white supremacist, extractive, settler colonial, patriarchal (ongoing) events. They are a specific set of activities that were intended to create disaster for Indigenous peoples. With the "ongoing storms of colonialisms," we acknowledge that we're not out of colonization. For me, weather has been a way to think from different positions.

Jordan Wilson, who is here, has spent time thinking and writing about cultural belongings. Ancestral or cultural belongings are placed in weatherproof spaces – the museum with its constant measurements of humidity, darkness, loud sound coming from ventilation systems, an incessant noise. Previously, belongings were held close to the body; perhaps they were garments, or were made of gut, which has this ability to swell and change form depending on its use. Gut needs water and to be with or near the body to warm it in order for it to shift its form – when those belongings enter the collection's storage spaces, they begin to brittle, to ossify, tear, rip. They no longer have a relationship to human beings, to the land, to the weather, to community, to songs, to everyday life, to conversation.

Emelie Chhangur tells me that I bring weather to the museum. What does that mean? For me, it has to do with embodiment, with our sweat and our breath; the water vapour, our tears; how, when we touch belongings, we alter them; how the sound of our voices enters into those belongings; and how they greet us and we greet them. There's this way of visiting with them that hopefully replenishes them, even for a short time. This is the weather of the body, body weather.

MN I'm wondering if we might move from cultural belongings to the body, a move that is also from archive to repertoire. I'm someone who has a kind of archival imagination. I'm thankful for archives. It's where we learn about the possible through a charting of past practices. I am indebted to archives and repositories, but that does not mean they are beyond scrutiny. I'm thankful to your work for putting these spaces of collecting, as well as their practices of collecting, under scrutiny. And this is where repertoire comes in. As you say, you are bringing breath, bringing sweat, bringing voice to these belongings. You're also bringing embodied movement. Can you talk about these choreographies you've been exploring and their relation to collecting institutions, galleries, museums? And can you address specifically how you engage with the idea of rehearsal in these spaces?

TLL Dance is not just a physical practice. It's an intellectual practice. So much of it for me is about being open, proposing ideas, listening, connecting with other kinds of lived experience or research, and then allowing for bodily research to happen in real time, to unfold between the dance artists and me. I'm always working with folks in a way that's not typical for the stage, where we might have three weeks or six weeks of rehearsal to present a finished or polished performance that may then tour, be repeated many times in different places. I have a limited amount of time within gallery spaces and a set number of days (perhaps five, seven, or ten) of rehearsal with the dancers. I've been choosing not to culminate the work in performance but to show the process of rehearsal.

If we believe that dance does something in the world, then it's already doing it as soon as we begin. If folks want to come and be in relation to that process, they can witness it through open rehearsal.

I've also worked with dancers over a long period of time, and so they have embodied memories of our work together. Each project often develops into another one. I don't perform works multiple times. I have documented work that lives in the world in other forms, such as video. In the project, "An amplification through many minds," I visited with belongings, orating my experience. The viewer reads text on screen and cannot hear my voice. Subsequently, in the sections with the dance artists, I ask them: what does it mean to be in dark, stale cupboards as a belonging that has withered? I remember dancer Ivanie Aubin-Malo described trying to move the seams of the belonging, to expand, and how, without the water that we smooth onto the gut, it's not possible. We then asked, what does it mean when we, as a relative, pick up belongings and interact with them? That caused the dancers to gently pick one another up and place each other down softly.

How we work through a project depends on the place that we're in and who we're with, but overall, embodiment is central to this exploration. I think that weather and embodiment are crucial to my practice right now. Site specificity and research are also core aspects of rehearsal.

MN There's also this element that you call the "short form," which is a discrete unit of production of some kind. To be clear, when you use "short form," you don't mean it to be simply a mode of writing – I say this because there is often discussion in prose circles about "the short form." In the way that you've developed this idea of the short form, its media, in practice, shifts; the inscriptive mode is open to interpretation from iteration to iteration, form to form. Will you discuss what you mean by "short form" in terms of your practice?

TLL First and foremost, I've experienced "short form," in relation to Inupiaq dance in Alaska. Inupiaq dancers undertake amazing and beautiful ninety-second dances. The dancers mark the dance in the first sequence. The singers will gently hit their sticks on the side of the drum and sing quietly. This is a preparation for what we will experience. A quiet preparation with the dancers' small gestural movements. Then, all of a sudden, in the second sequence, it's full out – full voice, full dancing, incredible athleticism. It's so powerful. I love to watch Inupiaq dance.

The dance is ninety seconds in length, but underneath is a lifetime or a long duration of practice. Anyone might say of the short form, well, it's a painting, it's a sculpture, and of course a lifelong artistic practice surrounds it, but I think it's also about ethics and a way of being in the world. You talked about how when we visit, we visit holistically. We talk about our kids and what projects we are up to, and we have this conversation as people who embody ways of being in the world. For me, short form is connected to that. It's also connected to longer considerations of, in my case, Alutiiq or Sugpiaq knowledge.

The short form of *lla* might be a rainstorm or a northwesterly wind, but amid those shorter durations, the long form of *lla* is vast and cannot be encapsulated. Only in a moment it becomes visible. Much of practice that happens is unseen and only in specific moments becomes visible.

I also think about it in relation to makers of traditional art forms from Alaska. I have a deep love and respect for them as well as our Omaskêko Cree relatives who make the profoundly beautiful mitts and mukluks I write about in *Slow Scrape*. The unseen labour that's only experienced in the space of the home, with community. I've been thinking lately about how a garment doesn't tell us where to find the materials or what time of year to harvest, how to harvest, how to process. This beautiful work happens in the community and in family. That work embodies a kind of opacity or refusal, because it doesn't tell one how to do it or what it's doing. It withholds that knowledge and that experience. It's only for people who have the right to that knowledge, who have inherited it, who have lived it with their family, who have learned it. They enact it in the short form.

But I will say that, speaking about the complex relationships we have with museum collections, it's significant that we visit belongings in order to learn from them. Many of our people have gone to see masks, regalia, or other material culture to learn from our Ancestors. For me, the short form is about concision, it's about refusal. So that I don't drain something of its power by overinterpreting it. It's what becomes visible.

MN We've discussed one particular aspect of the short form that you practise, which is the event score. One element of those scores that I think is important is you cite, attribute, and dedicate those scores to certain people. There's Eber Hampton, Dylan Robinson, Sherry Farrell Racette, Maria Tallchief, Eve Tuck, Helen Simeonoff, Edgar Heap of Birds. Each score both thinks with and is directed towards each of these thinkers or cultural workers, and through these citations, these scores articulate an important constellation.

To perhaps bring this back to *lla*, to weather, and relations, you also cite traditions of thinking, specific people who might be known as speakers or artists, nonhuman relations such as tides and weather and guts and hide – all of these things are cited as authors or composers or holders of knowledge. Can you discuss this form of relation-building in your work?

TLL I do consider it a citational practice, a form of building a community around a work not only of thinkers, but practitioners and folks who influence my thinking. We don't make work in isolation. We're part of discourse, of conversations. I think it's disingenuous to assert that we are making work in isolation. I'm often trying to insert myself into specific lineages. When I respond to Maria Tallchief's or Rita Letendre's work – that's a kind of citational gesture. It's a way to think about myself in relation to those artists.

I'm working on a project now about women on my island who are cultural workers. I consider myself a cultural worker as well. There are many Sugpiaq folks on my island who are doing this work. I'm just one of many. It's important to acknowledge them, to cite them, and to say their names: Dora Aga, Feodosia Inga Kahutak, and Nadia Mullan, in this instance.

MN I have maybe one more question. One of the people you cite – in your essay, but also in a poem you composed for the book *Breaking Protocol* – is Zitkála-Šá.[2] She's a figure that I want to bring more attention to, because I've seen her cited by you, by Layli Long Soldier, by Raven Chacon in artistic works over these last years, and I find her to be a compelling figure to think about in these times. So I'm curious if you might be able to offer some context on how you engage with her and her writings.

TLL Beth Piatote suggested I return to her while I was writing my dissertation. I was already familiar with her – I had read her writings as an undergrad – but it had been a long time since I had thought about her. Beth encouraged me to remember her, in a sense. While reading I thought about the complexity of her: as someone who writes about her early life, about living the old way with her grandmother and her family, then being taken to boarding school, and becoming a teacher in boarding schools. This is a complicated history. The history of boarding schools and residential schools in Canada is just so present, I think for all of us as people who have survivors in our family.

Zitkála-Šá writes about riding the train from west to east, and we understand how it is a tool of colonial expansion. She looks at telegraph poles and thinks about how they have electricity pulsing through them; how these poles were trees that had been shorn and put to purpose in the project of colonial expansion. She makes the comparison to herself and all of the kids that go through these systems – these schools – that it's as if they've been shorn and pumped with this electricity. And yet, she says she still feels or senses the life force of the original tree. She's reflecting on her own life. She became an activist later, after she was a teacher. When you read these passages in her writing, you can feel that transition in her thought.

I want to mention – because it is looming large here in the gallery – this work of Duane Linklater's and acknowledge his address of these histories, which has been significant for my practice. I've watched the continuous resistance of the federal government to adequately respond to the abuse that happened at St. Anne's residential school. We had family who attended that school, which is referenced in this work that I'm looking at – *immolations_of_saint_anne_*. Three times they burned down the school. I think about that action as another kind of poem, an important kind of poem or score – the repeated burning down of the residential school. I think of it as the kind of action that Layli Long Soldier would see as a poem.

MN "Grasses grasses grasses." From her poem "38" – how the poem ends with the action of the colonizer's mouth stuffed with grass.

TLL Yes, "grasses grasses grasses." It's that kind of active resistance that she would identify as a kind of poem. So when I think of Zitkála-Šá, I grapple with these difficult and complex histories – of her being forced to attend these schools, of her becoming a teacher in these schools, of her resistance later in life, and how her resistance – materialized in particular moments, in succinct gestures – can be a poem.

ENDNOTES

1 Heather Davis and Zoe Todd, "On the Importance of a Date, Or, Decolonizing the Anthropocene," *ACME: An International Journal for Critical Geographies* 16, no. 4 (2017): 761–780.

2 Maria Hupfield, ed., *Breaking Protocol* (Inventory Press, 2023).

Permanent [Upside Down] Revolution

A Dialogue with Gail Scott

"IF WRITING IS THE ACT OF ALWAYS SEEKING MORE UNDERstanding, more lucidity," Gail Scott writes in *Permanent Revolution: Essays*, "prescriptive directives have no place in our trajectory towards the delightfully mysterious edge of language." [1] She is a writer working perpetually at this mysterious edge of language throughout her prose works, essays, and translations experimenting with the limits of how language and its composition reflect, refract, and resituate the writing subject at the overlapping vectors of political contestation, gendered expression, linguistic inquiry, and desire's promiscuity.

Gail Scott is the author of six narrative works: *Spare Parts, Heroine, Main Brides, My Paris, Spare Parts Plus Two,* and *The Obituary.* Her essays are collected in *Permanent Revolution: Essays, Spaces Like Stairs,* and *La théorie, un Dimanche,* which was translated into English as *Theory, A Sunday* (2013). She is co-editor of the New Narrative anthology *Biting the Error: Writers Explore Narrative.* In 2023, Wave Books published her memoir, *Furniture Music,* winner of the 2024 Québec Writers Federation Mavis Gallant Prize for Non-Fiction. After fifteen years of teaching creative writing at the Université de Montréal, she is now a full-time writer.

Scott and I first crossed paths not long after I moved to Montréal in 2011. Her position within the city's literary terrain fascinates me. As a native anglophone, she has been an active agent in the francophone cultural and political contexts of Québec since the avant arts scenes of Montréal in the 1970s and 1980s. Working within radical leftist and feminist circles during this time, she was part of a first generation to engage with the emerging body of theoretical texts arriving from France and to consider their implications for what writing might mean and do in the contemporary. In this extended engagement, she has produced a singular corpus of narrative works. They are daring and sensual, swift and oblique, robust with living. There is a particular pleasure a reader experiences in navigating the contours of her works – a sense of existing with careful attention in the uncertain, always unfolding presence of the world. Over the decades, she has maintained a fiercely internationalist engagement with writers and artists around the world, while at the same time asserting the importance of the unique cultural dynamics that compose the specificity of Montréal.

In September 2021, Scott and I met at a corner café in our Mile End neighbourhood of Montréal to discuss her recent collection of essays, the contexts of her writing through the years, and the particular additive "+" that features throughout the work, a signal of her perpetual movement beyond container and category. From that exchange we've arranged the following dialogue.

MN Perhaps we can start with the overlapping contexts – the fractal of milieux – that exist and are articulated in *Permanent Revolution*? One of the many things I admire in these essays is the way you approach them through a robust conviviality and exchange with other writers and thinkers, with various networks of political and literary experimentation, in an open-ended dialogue. Can you discuss the various contexts and communities of writing you are engaged with in these essays?

GS Fractal of milieux ... *Fractal* seems to be a word of late + I can see how it might resonate with regards to travels undertaken throughout *Permanent* [upside down] *Revolution* in relation to the home base of Montréal. That my writing life germinated in post-Quiet Revolution francophone Québec – *a scintillating anything-goes period when the Independence Movement was left-leaning + the air full of utopian dreams* – no doubt pushed me towards other sites + practitioners of poetic resistance. By happenstance, my multiple-decade continental zigzag recounted in *Permanent* [upside down] *Revolution* began in a period when the Québec independence movement was headed towards more middle-class aspirations – as per many movements of resistance against colonization or semicolonization. Of course moving on inevitably involves recursion; past trajectories continue to thread present encounters + present creation. The writing of the early Québec years has been coloured by the allure of poets met on these travels. For one, poets around New York's St. Mark's Poetry Project, Belladonna, + the Bowery Poetry Club in the early Obama years. These New York extended visits were the Harper years in Canada; it was freeing to travel, to find myself in a progressive community offering varied + bold approaches to the relative freedom of the poetic line, in conjunction with aspects of social resistance at a time when I was feeling a little psychically tamped down at home. Ditto for an earlier San Francisco encounter with several terrific New Narrative writers; it has also been – + remains – crucial. It was such a relief to find queer + feminist fiction writers *working in English* who sought as I do, experimental + intersectional forms of narrative, forms more *intégrale* [to use a Nicole Brossard term] to who we – lefties, queers, feminists – are in the world. But if, as Carla Harryman has suggested, my prose sits a little on the fringes of New Narrative, a fundamental factor continues to be the slippy-slidy syntax encountered in the streets of Montréal – where languages interpenetrate in a manner shocking to l'Office de la langue française. I will speculate [since I seem to be falling into the role of critic of my own work here] that uncertainty of utterance encountered daily – whatever languages are involved – fosters a desire in writing for the open possibilities of the poetic line. As for my perpetual need to both stay + go, when possible – the path between Montréal + New York has been well trodden over time by Montréal anglophone artists: Leonard Cohen, Moyra Davey, + Julie Doucet, to name three.

MN In looking through various groups or tendencies you've been involved with or in conversation with – *La théorie, un dimanche*, language writing, New Narrative, and the various conversations you've been involved in with Vancouver and New York writers and artists these last decades – you often bring to these conversations a fascinating outsider perspective: as an anglophone working in a francophone milieu, as a Québécoise in a primarily US-centred context, as a prose writer working among poets. Can you talk about this experience of writing and thinking from the margins even amid these marginal tendencies and group formations? (As Lisa Robertson stated at your launch for *Permanent Revolution*, you are very much a writer "keeping the intransigence of the margins alive.") How do think this positioning has impacted the reception of your works? Do you feel that you and the position from which you are writing have been recognized in your involvement and exchanges in these various circles?

GS Certainly, one conscious reason for travelling to nonfrancophone regions of Canada + the US was the hope that my prose experiments – some call it my difficult writing – might receive more nuanced readings in English that I was frankly not getting enough of in late-twentieth-century Québec. In Canada, the main destination has been British Columbia; I am drawn to the West Coast poets, whose work, I feel, is most akin to my own in the Canadian context. I have often thought a literary causeway exists between Vancouver + Montréal. But if it goes without saying that I feel fortunate to be based north of the forty-ninth – I'm afraid I do not feel entirely like I come from a country, but from a city. Or even a city state. My audience outside of Québec, at least for my later, more experimental work, seems less Canadian than part of a welcoming continental prose network. [I do try not take as a sign of my fortunes in Canada that the Canada Council, the envy of so many non-Canadian artists, has not seen fit to give me a grant since 2004.] Yet my Québec baggage comes with me, wherever I go. My desire to cull what I can from poetry to structure the relations between sentences [no mean trick] may also be attributable to the experience of l'écriture à la Duras, Barthes, etc., filtered through a Québécois cultural lens. My sentences are somewhat Gallicized, destabilizing meaning. As well, the habit of "fiction/theory" practised in the eighties *La théorie, un dimanche* group has helped foster a rhetorical note in my novels. Rhetorical gestures sit more comfortably in French sentences than in English; I have done a great deal of playing around to find ways of deploying such gestures in a poetic fashion in my English sentences. Does this mean writers doing this kind of work are forever stuck in the periphery? For my part, I am not in love with the word *intransigent* to describe us. The margins or periphery, in my opinion, are ever threatening to engulf the centre; our work is therefore treated as troubling, a hard sell. This is not helped by the appalling state of criticism, contemporaneously, in so much media. Indeed, artists of the so-called margins, in my experience, display tremendous fluidity in their creative works. The point is not to improve marketing options, but rather to respond to a continual state of emergency that seems to underwrite so much of the human condition. One would stop, if feeling without hope, this perpetual rise + fall of fortunes which is the price of the radical writer's commitment to change. For my purposes, + I think, for those around me, Lenin's question *Que faire?* is eternally viewed in a microscope of doubt + desire. In that, it's true, we are intransigent.

MN Throughout *Permanent Revolution* the "+" sign takes on a particular linguistic and political urgency, as a connector, but also a signalling towards a certain sense of excess or movement beyond containment that has been a central theme in your prose. I'm wondering if you might discuss what this "+" means critically to you – linguistically, politically, and (interrelated with both fields) in terms of gender.

GS Michael, you have almost answered your own question! I suppose it is a kind of algorithmic device, inasmuch as it allows the exponential + differential – a short form for the multiplication of instances + exceptions, immanently apropos in writing about gender on the queer spectrum, for example. For on that particular scale, any degree of masculinity or féminine – and what do these terms mean, anyway? – may easily eclipse into a degree of the next. But the reach towards opens the door to far more than an accumulation of gender postures. It implies that the grammatical period – the closure that represents – can be endlessly deferred, depriving sentencing of its lean towards closure. You see this "+" pattern in toddler speech; for me toddlers, whose language is not yet trimmed by grammar + syntax, are master linguists: the little boy who told me, "When I am a teenager, I am going to dye my hair + maybe some sparkles + wear makeup + a nice dress + red stockings + LOTS of jewellery." Before running off, decked in his extravagant imagination, to add playing at monsters [ergo, the uncanny] to his repertoire. Another means I use for expressing multiple + inchoate possibilities without burdening the phrase [always my prayer] is the square bracket. Which, for me, is like an aside in speech, a device that women, for one, use immoderately in everyday conversation. To move beyond containment in the phrase + in literary form – here I refer again to the strictures of a certain type of narrative scaffolding – is to aspire towards a thought-altering gesture. Sometimes it lands upside down.

MN I am particularly smitten with your concept of "writing over the top" that you discuss in "Paragraphs Blowing on a Line": "This is the real meaning of *writing over the top*: The text, the writing becomes a kind of third voice, not the author or the narrator, but the voice of the author/narrator subsumed (as opposed to commenting from a distance as in a more traditional narrative) into the object of narration."[2] This passage articulates an integral aspect of the poetics of your works – in terms of style, genre, gender, and the presence of narration. I want to bring this concept in relation to another phrase you've used to describe your narrative modes, which you've described as a "sharding effect" (in the essay "The Sutured Subject"). Can you discuss the relation of these two terms in your writing?

GS "Writing over the top" is a precious notion for me. And I suppose with every project, the idea is to see how well I can pull it off without sacrificing the underpinnings, particularly the procedural thought process. There is "story," there is history, there is a certain amount of philosophizing [this word embarrasses me], linked to trying to unpack gleanings from the language of contemporary theoreticians + politicos, in relation to the language of everyday life. Which is the stuff of fiction. But this inclination towards language transmorphs in my prose into figures like the flaneur in *My Paris,* or the unconscious reveries of the mysterious Rosine in *The Obituary*'s Settler-Nun flat. To name two. Thus, in early drafts of my novels I am confronted with glittering piles of language detritus gleaned + noted from readings, conversations, graffiti, demos, sex, family life, neighbours, love, etc. Then, somehow, I have to find a trope, a moment or figure that can stand in vaguely for the whole spread, + operate some kind of wash, in the watercolour-painting sense of the word, over the whole. I'm looking less for transparency here than for a trajectory of language that is engaging + that actively engages with its interlocutors, the readers. The ultimate arbiter of what happens is the reader. Furthermore, each novel or prose work is very different because of how it engages with the context of a given moment in time ... A former student recently asked me a question that actually shocked me: "Did I know any good books about writing a novel?" Well, I thought, there is *Permanent* [upside down] *Revolution.* Because I have never taught writing prose as an exercise in character or plot development, which, I think, leads us straight into a conventional mindset, a posture of déjà vu. My "characters" are composed of their parts. And they are fractalled, sometimes [*The Obituary*], or parading about as avatars [the Chaplinesque flaneur in *My Paris,* for example].

MN In our conversation, you mentioned an affinity you felt with the artist and writer Moyra Davey. I wanted to bring her into the frame in our dialogue, because I think it's a fascinating affinity. I'm wondering if you'd like to discuss what it is that you find affinity with in her works.

GS The first time I met Moyra, she was sitting in a café in the Lux building, a former twenty-four-hour site on the Main, a bar, restaurant, magazine store, etc., one of the high spots of Montréal eighties nightlife. But it was daytime + there were several women there, including my then partner Erín, who had just lost a manuscript off the back of her bike. She had taken a few aspirins + some coffee to calm down. "That sounds about right," said Moyra, thoughtfully. After that Moyra moved to New York + I occasionally found myself in front of her art in a gallery somewhere in Manhattan. What I love about Moyra Davey's work is the combination of small gestures, put together in a way that makes profound statements, statements deceptively transparent on the surface covering + triggering a dizzying cornucopia of *matters* that we often ignore. Recently she published *Index Cards*, a collection of essays about her work that finishes with a text on Pierre Vallières, + a book he wrote in a New York prison where he was serving a term for sedition. The book has a famously ignoble title, using the N-word in his attempt to align the Black struggles of the sixties with those of French Canada. Moyra's essay recounts making a video called *I Confess* about the whole complicated question of how to talk about Vallières when looking back at that turbulent moment in Québécois history. It includes a conversation with the political philosopher Dalie Giroux, who writes brilliantly about the colonial ladder in Québec: top-rung colonials being the Anglos; middle position, the French, both colonized + colonizers of the Indigenous population. Giroux warns against the danger of being too soft on Vallières, for arguably appropriating in his writing the Black struggle for his own ends. I love the way Moyra Davey exposes her own procedures, even when they head off in erroneous directions. In this + other work, she has not forgotten in her thinking, in her art, to allow the kind of complex contradictory frankness that I associate with wading through the dichotomies of a diverse + often conflicted society.

MN Through our discussions, I am beginning to sense the extent to which your occupying of a subject position that is always multiple – your refusal of a singular framing, and this embracing of complexity and excess – is itself a form of anticolonial and anticapitalist resistance in writing and as a writer. It is one that involves, I gather, a serious commitment to questioning and embracing the uncertainty of where the process of (self-)

composition might lead. Can I ask you to reflect on what it has meant to occupy such a space over these decades?

GS These things are determined by a combination of luck + background. I have already spoken here of a trajectory of luck, really, in terms of my encounters. It is dicier to speak of background, given the human propensity to idealize or dramatize the formative years. You know a couple of my Dene nephews from your years of living in the Northwest Territories. So you may know as well, that question of recent ancestry has provided little in the way of a paper trail. On top of which – my mother's family were masters of what I like to call *tall tales + true*. I have little faith in a notion of stable self-composition. Even if my héroïne in *Heroine* tried – by *Main Brides* she was already falling apart. Consequently, the figure of self is generally unstable + often enough the butt of jokes. As in this excerpt from *Permanent* [upside down] *Revolution* about the problems with mixing up or trying to mix up settler + Indigenous culture.

It's lifted from the essay "Corpus Delicti" and mocks a certain idealization of the possibilities of translation:

> EXHIBIT D: INDIFFERENCE. BETRAYAL [...]
>
> In the abyss between the very ancient + the recent colonizing cultures are also found those whose origins have been in part obfuscated by the assimilate-or-die legacy of settler culture. And who can no longer assert a belonging on paper, or culturally, in the sense of tribal connections? If heritage is knowledge, such lacking of knowledge / experience of an ancestral culture may amount to a situation of little relevance. Certainly some, being lost, try to make exaggerated claims; others pronounce profound embarrassment vis-à-vis those claiming some degree of Indigeneity on the basis of a distant ancestor:
>
> *No matter what I say I feel a liar. After my maternal grandmother died, Grandpa told my brother our Grandma was Métis. Other relatives deny it. During her lifetime nary a word. I have a single memory of a neighbour calling her a squaw. Grandpa, while not in the closet about his mixed background, foregrounded his being American (from Kansas). We were left with threads: he was born to a family of horse people. They moved north + raised horses for the Crowsnest Pass coal*

mines. But the history of their origins has disappeared in the dust. How many grow up like this? Does it matter? One could also ask: When does a language cease to be written on the body?

It is worth recalling that the impact of cultural cannibalization works in two directions. A number of no-longer-spoken or little-spoken suppressed Indigenous tongues infuse / alter or add another layer of matter to plundering English. And those who would have spoken these violently suppressed languages, or who do, yet have no option but to write in the language of the colonizer, bring via their persons, their values, their heartbeats, lines, sentences, cadences, compositions that are other. And beautiful. I am wont to praise the beauty of such texts. But is not that, in itself, a colonial comportment? Wanting to be a good fellow traveller, the translator tries to calm her doubt by pointing out that there is a fundamental difference between writing by Indigenous authors in English who are rooted in their culture. And that of individuals with dubious claims. A difference that shows up, among others, in language cadence. Recently, for instance, I have been blown away by the genial dialoguing in Haisla + Heiltsuk Eden Robinson's *Son of a Trickster,* a masterful representation of [translated] speech in the realm of text.

For me writing is a matter of ear: it is what one hears in words on a page that takes the work out of the straitjacket of commodifying literary conventions. Words work differently on the page – sometimes a little differently, sometimes a lot – when translated from oral culture, or from writing in one language to other languages impacting it [a lesson I have learned writing in Montréal] – even in cases where these languages are no longer widely spoken. Attention to words sitting differently in the English language is what I hear in the work of so many Indigenous writers. Louise Bernice Halfe, to mention only one, because she is a trailblazer, + uses nêhiyawewin in her English-language work to great effect, + is a woman + one of the most amazing poets. Also, it is from her that I heard the expression of words sitting differently in language. It has happened that writers with weak claims of Indigenous belonging, be they authors of accomplished novels, but who lack a deep bodily sense of language / culture, become laureates of the critical literary establishment. Indeed, tokenism vis-à-vis minorities has often resulted in privileging that which most resembles the Canadian mainstream. *History belongs to the victors,* Walter Benjamin was fond of saying. It took the current waves of resistance headed by the Idle No More movement + a simultaneous cohort of dazzling Indigenous writers to see more clearly that values are communicated in the scaffolding of a novel; in how one moves through space + notions of time. In the relations between sentences + in the meaning of "individual" or person. Writers rooted in non-European language backgrounds sound different in English. And this is beautiful. The best critics – and the best translators – have ears.

Speaking of ears, good intentions can run afoul: our translator, in her novel *The Obituary*, which is precisely about buried roots + assimilation, shamefully misspells the book's sole Indigenous word, *Oligawi* (dream well), as *Ogigawa,* mistaking in translating the oral [from a conversation with an Abenaki woman] to the written. For one, hearing *L* as *G*. It is the critic Stan Dragland, in a kind text about this translator's "difficult" writing, who points out *Ogigawa* is in fact a Japanese word. Two things interest me about this:

1. How, in moving from one language to another, the ear, locked in its own cadences, mishears. An English speaker, for instance, tends to pronounce written *T*s at the end of certain French words, so that lentement (slowly, pronounced lɑ˜ t. mɑ˜) is erroneously pronounced *lant-mant.*

2. How small – albeit exponentially growing – the space is for Indigenous languages in the virtual information stream. At least relative to dominant languages with their residual strength of historical imperialism. The search was thus long for an Abenaki word for *goodbye* proximate to the word our translator thought she heard when speaking to the Abenaki woman. This involved a reconnoitring of prefixes + suffixes that might enlighten her error, even cross-referencing her search with the geographically neighbouring Algonquin, finally falling quite by accident on the Abenaki phrase *Oligawi* (dream well). So the woman with whom she had been in conversation on the way home from the grocer was saying not "goodbye" as she presumed but a form of "goodnight."

Thus one settler-culture ignorance piles upon another, ignorance in which the translator is often willingly complicit: *We rest our case.*

ENDNOTES

1 Gail Scott, *Permanent Revolution: Essays* (Book*hug, 2021), 121–122.

2 Gail Scott, *Spaces Like Stairs: Essays* (Women's Press, 1989), 94.

The Mystery of Indexicals

A Dialogue with Kevin Davies

I THINK OF KEVIN DAVIES AS A POET WHO IS EVERYWHERE and nowhere at once. I mean this in two ways: in terms of the topography articulated throughout his works, the perpetually shifting sites and scenes of his poems, and the location of poetic voice in relation to these scenes; then, in the reception of and critical attention to his books – *Pause Button*, *Comp.*, *The Golden Age of Paraphernalia*, and *FPO*. In the first, within a compact space a poem often flows "pole to pole" – from a worker flipping "flapjacks / in the trailer camp / of a Yellowknife gold mine" to finding oneself inside "the intestinal lining of a sea turtle off Ecuador." In the poem "Floater," Davies writes, "I AM THE / GLOBAL POSITIONING SYSTEM, / ME." One element I find so compelling in this embodied-technical rendering of the poet (who is both ubiquitous and imperceptible) is how Davies is able to track and trace such a system, while also incorporating elements of the infrastructures (technical, financial, and logistical) that uphold such a system of detection and inscription. When Chris Nealon writes that "Davies has written the most powerful account of – and argument against – contemporary capitalism in English-language poetry," I agree because of Davies's astonishing capability to circulate back and forth between scene and infrastructure, both in content and in the formal register of the poems.

Regarding his reception, I'll begin with a personal note: over the past fifteen years since I began reading his books, the name "Kevin Davies" has operated almost like a password to some of the most important conversations I've had with other poets and critics about what writing can be and do in the present era. Matters of language and representation, of perspective and parataxis, of describing the social, of articulating the presence and profuse mediation of contemporary capitalism in all of our relations, of how the poetic text might relate to and operate against this profuse mediation – these concerns become paramount in considering the experience of reading a Kevin

Davies poem. I remember thinking, on first encountering *The Golden Age of Paraphernalia,* that it was somehow both the perfect mirror of our times (the neoliberal order of the Information Age rife with the neolithic barbarism of the United States' imperial decline) while also being the future of poetry. I know I am one of many who felt this: I can recall reading Jasper Bernes in *Aufgabe* and Drew Gardner in *The Poetry Project Newsletter* essentially stating that Davies's poetics and sense of surfaces and time and voice offered something vitally important not only for the poetry to be written but also for registering the scenario of twenty-first century capitalism in which we live.

Despite the centrality of Davies's work for a particular cluster of poets and critics, his sporadic small-press publications and even rarer public appearances for readings and other such literary events have meant his work has remained undetectable to many. Even within that cluster who share the password of his name, Davies perhaps remains a mysterious figure. The opportunity to enter into dialogue with him emerged out of conversations with Catriona Strang and Jeff Derksen, both active in the Kootenay School of Writing with him.

In our exchange, which took place through correspondence between New York City and Montréal during the summer of 2024, Davies and I discuss the contexts of his writings, his influences, the absence of "control" in his sense of composition, and the mystery of the little voices that erupt throughout the contours of his poems.

MN I'm curious about the context of your earliest work. Tsunami Editions published *Pause Button* in 1992, but long before this first book Peter Culley, in his wonderful "Because I Am Always Talking" essay, writes of you in 1983 – "a Vancouver Island poet then in his early twenties" – as already having a certain reputation in the Vancouver scene of the time. In his description of you, he captures a kind of intensity, mystique, and singularity in your poems and in your presence that, in my mind, continue to this day. Where and how did you begin composing poems? Who were the folks you found as community in the movement from Vancouver Island to Vancouver?

KD I met Peter Culley in high school in Nanaimo, and that was the beginning of poetic community for me. I was writing stories in those days, and actually published three of them in my teens, but I was more interested in poetry, and Pete was already a seventeen-year-old poet. The year after high school I worked in the local pulp mill, where I met the poet Ken Cathers. I read his work along with that of another terrific local poet of about Ken's age, John Marshall. Ken also turned me on to Larry Eigner. In high school I'd already encountered work by Jack Spicer (early work for *One Night Stand* published in *The Capilano Review*), George Bowering, Fred Wah, Phyllis Webb, bpNichol, Christopher Dewdney, Brian Fawcett, etc. After a year at the pulp mill, I quit and travelled to California, where I bought a copy of *The Collected Books of Jack Spicer*, which changed my life. Pete sent some poems to Pierre Coupey, who invited him over to North Vancouver to talk things over. Through Pete's connection, I met David Phillips, Hope Anderson, Bill Little, Scott Watson, Barry McKinnon, and (crucially) George Stanley. At about the same time, Pete got invited by Robert Creeley to read at a conference in Buffalo. He met Victor Coleman, Steve McCaffery, and (again crucially) Gerry Gilbert, who subsequently became a close friend of both of ours. Pete also brought back a copy of *Legend* by Andrews, Bernstein, DiPalma, McCaffery, and Silliman. Woof.

Or a shorter version:

Peter Culley and I met in high school. We read like maniacs: modernists/historical avant-garde, the New American Poetry, the Canadian avant-garde of the sixties and seventies, and eventually (me more than Pete) the so-called Language poets. The books were the community, the scene. I was always moving back and forth between Nanaimo and Vancouver. Eventually we made contacts there among the so-called downtown avant-garde (exemplified by Gerry Gilbert) and started doing readings. Pete started publishing. I mostly didn't, but did a lot of readings, some of them pretty gratifying, some of them terrible. I wrote all the time, never having any idea of what it would be about (and that is still the case, though I write much less now). In 1984, the Kootenay School of Writing formed in Vancouver after the closing of David Thompson University Centre. That upped the size of the "community" considerably. I became informally involved, especially when Dorothy Trujillo Lusk and I returned to town after a couple of years in Italy and Toronto.

MN May I propose we keep both versions? I like what they share and state differently. And will you say more about Nanaimo? I ask because I imagine it at this time as a kind of hinterland, a place for extracting raw materials for the metropole. (In this it is perhaps similar to the anthracite coal country where I grew up.) I'm curious how reading modernist and historical avant-garde works in this context shaped your sense of the poem?

KD Nanaimo seemed like a place to get away from, though I never achieved this permanently till 1983. The "world" presented by the poetry I was reading seemed much more real, in some sense. Nanaimo was where I worked and tried to make sense of things, but it was being ravaged by land developers, its city centre even then being destroyed by anarchic sprawl and fast-buck hucksterism. In what sense was I experiencing this in conjunction with the reading of, say, Pound? Of John Wieners? I can't say, from this distance. It's clear that my reactions to the devastations of capital are represented in my work at that time, but I don't know in what way that might have "shaped my sense of the poem."

Nanaimo was then still a going concern as a resource-extraction centre (logging, milling, fishing), though its days as a mining centre were long gone. My relation to all this was, I think, never more than half-conscious, even when I was a mill worker. Certainly, reading Williams as an ephebe must have altered or enhanced my perceptions of the local arrangements.

MN How did reading *The Collected Books of Jack Spicer* change your life?

KD I'm wary of turning so-called biographical facts into narrative, which as far as I can tell is mostly bullshit. But:

After I'd worked in the pulp mill for a year after high school, I went travelling (by bus and hitched rides) around the western US. In City Lights Bookstore I found *The Collected Books* (and actually bought it rather than stealing it). I was already aware of Spicer because of the early poems published in Pierre Coupey's *Capilano Review*, which I'd discovered in Jack Hodgins's high-school English class. I subsequently spent three days in a Butte hotel room reading and rereading the book. I'm aware of having told myself, at various stages, that this "changed my life," but then what doesn't? Spicer's work proposed a different way of thinking and living? Probably.

Subsequently, I became interested in many Spicer-adjacent works – by Blaser, Chris Dewdney, Bowering's *Allophanes*, Victor Coleman's serial poems, etc. This was all before I became aware of the Language poets, some of whom have their own complicated relations to Spicer.

One thing comes to mind. I was still attempting to write short stories in those days, but it wasn't going well. I'd be trying to describe something or move the narrative along through a cunning mid-paragraph transition when suddenly I'd write down a preposterous non sequitur completely unrelated to the story at hand. Eventually the non sequiturs seemed more interesting than the narratives, so I paid attention. Spicer says something about trying to write a love poem and then writing that the loved one's eyes should fall out, or whatever, beyond any discernible intention. I don't want to sound superstitious about this. I don't think ghosts or Martians speak through us, as Spicer sometimes proposed with varying levels of seriousness. No one wants to hear about negative capability. But since about then I've never been able to *intend* to write a poem and then write it. I do mean never. I wish I could!

Peter Culley was much more attuned than I was to the discipline of the serial poem as laid out by Spicer and discussed by Blaser. He waited for the Spicerian radio to speak, and then wrote it down. My own practice, from then on, was much more chaotic.

MN I expected some wariness of "biography" and narration – "your life has no plot so stop narrating" and "I don't have a biography, I'm lower / middle class" being two passages of yours often in my mind – so thank you for indulging me.

Part of the reason I ask about raw materials (in asking about Nanaimo) was perhaps to shift away from autobiography. I'm intrigued how the array of objects in your poems – however specific they may be, from "the mightiest Portuguese bell tower to / the intestinal lining of a sea turtle off Ecuador" – often function as raw materials, in the sense that you charge them with the potential to be processed or repurposed for all kinds of outcomes and uses.

I'm compelled by the way in which you've created structures for poems where it seems possible for any object or surface in contemporary capitalism to be called in to make an appearance. And with this array of things and surfaces, it seems as though any rhetoric or mode of address to interact with them is also possible. Is this something you've considered in the composition of your poems?

KD Not consciously, but the *considerations* of what makes up a poem are no doubt different from what the poem might ultimately *do*. I've never had the sense of "control" that many poets and critics might insist on.

MN Or perhaps a better way of making this observation into a question: Can you say something about how you position the utterer of these poems, or how you construct a kind of personhood through the assemblage of all these things, surfaces, voices?

KD If I ever constructed a personhood, I apologize. But "voices" seems right – insert obligatory Rimbaud quote here. The mystery of indexicals seems something that has always propelled my work. Hundreds of little wars of position. I don't often reread my work – haven't read my first two books in years – but I have the sense that the number of positions from which voices appear to come has increased with time. But I would have trouble articulating any sort of intention here. I have always worked almost exclusively by intuition – not by choice but by basic makeup.

MN I'm interested in picking up on your earlier point about your interest in the non sequitur to discuss the methods for composing poems. I'm thankful for your PhillyTalk with Diane Ward for the way in which you discuss being an "occasional poet," and also how you hint at the kind of method of accruing particles and fragments of texts – here in drawing an affinity with and also a difference from Bruce Andrews and his modes of composition – on slips of paper that are then deployed in some momentary order for either a reading or a publication.[1] Has this mode of composition changed over the years for you? How has your thinking on composing – revising – redacting – redeploying in this way shifted through time?

Here, I'll note I'm including "revising – redacting – redeploying" in my sense of "composing" as I review the differences in your poem "Extraneous Detail" from its publication in Gerry Gilbert's *B.C. Monthly* (February 1986) and how it appears in *Pause Button*. In the first iteration you've organized the language in these kind of quatrains, and in the latter articulation, the lines are far more dispersed, placed across pages, interrupted by other fragments, with bracketed elisions – gaps, censorings, refusals – that delete the previous contents.

KD I had forgotten about the PhillyTalks with Diane. Yes, my way of "composing" has necessarily changed since then. I seem now unable to perform the kind of extreme collage evidenced in my four published books. The three currently unpublished manuscripts that I'm still working on comprise sections written in one sitting. They look a little like old-school lyric poems, which makes me suspicious of my own unconscious motives.

And I'd completely forgotten about "Extraneous Detail." It was a long series, only part of which was published by Gerry Gilbert. I think it's fairly typical of the way I would take extant sequences and repurpose them. I no longer have the original (or the issue in which part of it was published), so I can't compare.

I seem to recall discussing this with Diane Ward. I would write, write, write, usually early morning before work, sometimes pausing to shuffle phrases next to others, often trying to make the least sense, and when someone would ask me to do a reading, I'd "close" on a body of writing, arranging a sequence that takes, say, twenty-three minutes to read. After that, this sequence would join others previously stored, and I'd look for resonances and connections between them, making new constructions. This is absolutely the opposite both of Spicerian dictation and conceptual writing, even though I'm a fan of both.

MN I'm curious if you might describe your experience of the Kootenay School of Writing. I'm asking because perhaps the histories of these collective formations are best addressed through multiple perspectives. I'm deeply interested in the interpersonal dynamics of KSW, the affinities and antagonisms, the modes of working and thinking together and the problems of collective forms. I'm also interested in writers navigating these contours through questions of class and writing – a concern that seems all too absent in present discourse.

KD When KSW hit town in 1984, I was already deeply involved with the "downtown," "non-academic" poetry scene in Vancouver. Peter Culley and I were, I think, the youngest members of what was not any kind of organization but rather a jungle of viny affinities. Of the Kootenay crew, I first got to know Jeff Derksen, and through him the rest of the new people. I'm not sure that I was ever a member of the collective. I manned the office (light duty) for a couple of months after Dorothy Trujillo Lusk and I moved back from Toronto, and I did attend a few collective meetings, but I don't know that I was ever an official voting member. I set out chairs and stacked them, sold beer and returned the empties, performed a couple of introductions, read there several times.

Artspeak Gallery was an offshoot of KSW, and the Or Gallery soon became somewhat affiliated as well. So there was a strong back-and-forth between writers and visual artists, crucial to the scene I came to know. Lary Timewell/Bremner's Tsunami Editions was also closely connected. I typeset Lisa Robertson's first chapbook on a computer owned by the Or Gallery and situated then in the KSW space as the editorial work on Stan Douglas's *Vancouver Anthology* went forward.

I was also at that time involved in a study group called The Grinning Rictus of Late Capital. The core members were me, Nancy Shaw, Stan Douglas, and Hillary Pimlott. This was heavy on Frankfurt School and art discourse – Nancy and Hillary both ended up with communications PhDs. I got a lot out of the group, but I don't think I was able to get the others to read Sebastiano Timpanaro, then a hero of mine.

Re KSW, I was aware of but not a participant in the main contention: between the so-called work poets and the younger pod significantly influenced by the Language poets. This, I guess, played out in the duelling conferences, summers of 1985 and 1986. I was absent from both, being first in Italy and then Toronto with Dorothy. While in those days I didn't have any particular interest in the supposed lyric-anecdotal work of the work poets, their politics certainly overlapped with mine to a significant degree. I don't know much about Tom Wayman's subsequent iteration of KSW in the Kootenays, but the split was absolute. I also don't know much about how the Vancouver KSW played out after I left in 1992.

For me, KSW represented the appearance of same-age colleagues rather than a radical new aesthetic. I was already fully invested in the so-called radical poetries of the New Americans and the Language poets. To me, they were the baseline. The supposedly traditional poetries simply didn't exist, or I wasn't interested.

Because I worked evenings, I didn't usually get to attend the seminars run by visiting poets, though I got to know them by later catching up in the bar or whatever. So: Charles Bernstein, Lyn Hejinian, Clark Coolidge, Alan Davies, Abigail Child, Bruce Andrews; Stephen Rodefer and Ben Friedlander arrived together for a particularly debauched residency. Younger poets such as Melanie Neilson, Jessica Grim, Lee Ann Brown, and Andrew Levy also turned up.

The issue of class is interesting because a strangely large percentage of the KSW cadre hailed from the working class – at a minimum, Jeff Derksen, Deanna Ferguson, Dorothy Trujillo Lusk, Peter Culley, and Gerald Creede (though not all of them would approve of being lumped in as "KSW" writers). I think this is evident at the bare level of content in the works these and other poets produced over the years, but I don't have anything in particular to say about it. I wavered between armchair Trotskyism and anarcho-communism, so class struggle was never far from my mind.

One thing I did have in those days was a very specific sense of audience, this thanks to KSW and associated entities. At any given reading, you'd know almost exactly who'd be listening. I no longer have any such sense.

MN Your departure from Vancouver to New York City, did it happen not long after *Pause Button* came out? Why NYC? Did you land into some sense of poetry community there, like with the KSW? I'm curious if you can discuss settling in NYC and the writing of your next book, *Comp.*

KD I moved to New York City in 1992, before *Pause Button* came out. I remember seeing the book for the first time in 1993 when my then partner and I returned from two months in Russia. I already knew most of the people listed above, many of them NYC residents, so there was a sort of built-in community when I arrived. And I soon got to know many poets my age or younger, so it wasn't all that different from Vancouver – except that the constant interaction with visual artists was largely absent.

A fair number of the younger poets I met in the USA thought of language poetry as old-fashioned – the puzzling or garish remnants of a bygone generation. I certainly didn't feel this way.

As for *Comp.*: In addition to working as a copyeditor and proofreader, I also began teaching first-year English composition in the General Studies Program (since defunct, absorbed by the College of Arts and Science) at New York University – this through the kind intervention of the poet Robert Fitterman. I was not well prepared for this work, and I consequently took a deep dive into classical rhetoric, modern rhetorical theory, and the extensive literature of composition studies, all to get a basic sense of what I was being paid to do. This had a large effect on my own writing, at the level of content and otherwise. I last taught composition at the University of Maine in 2007, the same semester I taught my one and only class in creative writing.

MN I can imagine it having a large impact on your writing. Representations of labour and the management of language in various modes of circulation are, in my mind, such a central part of both *Comp.* and *Golden Age*. Just thinking of it makes me want to quote the frontispieces of *Comp.*:

What gets *me* is

the robots are doing
my job, but I don't get
the *money*,
some extrapolated node
of expansion-contraction gets
my money, which I need
for *time travel*.

Without asking you to connect it to your writing, could you say something about how you experienced or witnessed the cultures of jobs and work at that time? Thinking about the era from your arrival in NYC to the publication of *Comp.* in 2000, it seems the time of the great ascent of the financialized world, with NYC being the heart of the heart of that geography.

KD I need to think about this. My first job in New York involved renovations in a SoHo loft. I inhaled a lot of solvents while stripping the old paint off heirloom window sashes. I remember working on the roof of that six-storey building on the afternoon of the first World Trade Center attack, 1993? Lots of helicopters! My next job, my first official Green Card job, was as an evening-shift proofreader at a large printing concern, mostly involving the requirement for businesses to submit financial records to the Securities and Exchange Commission using the new EDGAR system (Electronic Data Gathering, Analysis, and Retrieval). So: a lot of numbers cascading in columns. Next came work at NYU: teaching ten writing-intensive credits a semester, tutoring twenty hours a week, and also doing academic advisement, amounting to three part-time jobs, no benefits. Towards the end of my NYU career (1995–2004), I cut down on the tutoring and advising and also worked, again, in a financial services firm that did EDGAR filings.

I consider most work stupid, but the teaching and tutoring I found somewhat less stupid, and I enjoyed the people. Later, when I returned from Maine, I was copy chief at a boutique financial marketing firm. Ask me about contango and backwardation, etc.

MN How did your conversation with Edge Books begin, and can you describe your editorial relationship with them has developed over the years? Rod Smith is a fascinating reader and thinker of poetry (as well as being a wonderful poet) and I'm curious about how you two began making books together.

KD I first became aware of Rod Smith when *Writing* magazine published sections from Rod's "CIA Sentences," and I finally met him in New York, 1993. We were interested in a lot of the same things in writing, music, politics. He came to New York to do readings every so often, and I went to Washington, DC, to read in events he set up. Rod was producing *Aerial*, his magazine, and Edge Books. I don't remember how my second book, *Comp.*, came to be published there, but maybe it was just understood? I don't recall pursuing any alternative. Parts of that book had been published in various places (many of which I'd forgotten till I looked up the acknowledgments just now), including a small chapbook by Joe Elliot's Situations press that I no longer have. Rod had good ideas for the arrangement of the book, and I'd already had very useful feedback from Bruce Andrews.

I recently saw a posting in which a poet announced signing a contract for a chapbook. I was astounded! People sign contracts for chapbooks? The only time I've ever signed a contract was for the French translation of *Comp.* by Le Quartanier in Montréal in 2007 (for some reason the place of publication is given as "France" in Edge's second printing of *Comp.*). I assume they had to use contracts for Canada Council reasons? I'm disgracefully unilingual, but I'm told the translation by Xandaire Sélène is excellent. None of my books with Edge have ever involved a contract.

Rod has done an astounding job keeping the press going all these years. Publishing with Edge seemed like being part of an ongoing writing experiment with many moving parts, one work seeming to respond to another, which is kind of what early KSW was like.

MN Can you describe the writing of *The Golden Age of Paraphernalia*? Looking through your works, the organization of the poems feels like a certain achievement in that the dispersed and discrete fragments and voices seem to find, in my mind, their ideal form and register. Can you talk about the development of this interlocked organization – the three floating interwoven poems marked by their grammatical mark or typographical layout, with the two long poems set within their movement? Were there models for this work you had in mind, perhaps even in other artistic fields?

KD The writing took place from about 2001 to 2007, but the arrangement of the book came together in a monthlong frenzy in the latter year, my last of three years in Bangor, Maine. The earliest piece is "Lateral Argument," which was published as a chapbook in 2003 and had earlier been published online. The other intact sequence, "Duckwalking a Perimeter," was written in Bangor. One of the other three sequences, ""Floater,""" was published intact in a University of Maine magazine and was ridiculed by a local reviewer.

I wish I could say something smart about the schemes and arrangement of this book. It represents, I think, the apex of my compositional tomfoolery, so I would like to be able to claim a plain strategy. But: whatever retrospective intention I might ascribe to it, the truth is that *I have never really known what I am doing*. Was doing. Did.

MN I want to stay with *Golden Age* for a moment longer though, as the work left such an impression on my sense of poetry when I encountered it. I recall feeling as though I were being taken on a kind of Virgilian tour where you, as the poet, allow the reader to witness or overhear the spectacle of "hundreds of little wars of position," as you write above, taking place around the globe. The experience of (lateral) movement and the shifting between scales (of observation) continues to be enthralling to read. I note that the dates you cite for the writing of *Golden Age*, 2001 to 2007, mark the destruction of the World Trade Center towers to the start of the global financial crisis, which feel like a fitting frame for the book. Can you share any reflections you might have regarding how you experienced or were marked by the language of the era?

KD The languages of colonial state terrorism and financialization were certainly in the air. I think the ongoing bullshit from the fiendish mayor and his racist cronies provoked a lot of counterlanguage from me. I was three blocks from the towers when they got hit. I remember pausing on the Brooklyn Bridge during the (surprisingly orderly) exodus from downtown and a VP of the company I was working for asking me if I thought the towers, which were on fire, could come down. Nah, I said. By the time I got home, they had collapsed, and charred bits of corporate language were floating in the air.

MN I want to ask about how you think of the space of the poem. Why do you think you were drawn to these kind of interlocked structures – both the poems in *Golden Age*, but also, in *FPO*, how the poem "Period Verse" bookends the long poem "FPO" – composed of discrete, potentially interchangeable, units? And I'm curious if you might have anything to say about how that literary form interacts with cultural or social forms beyond the poem?

KD "Period Verse" was originally one sixty-page stanza. Pretty much everything I wrote from November 2013 to November 2014. After extensive feedback from Thomas Evans, it got broken up into its currently fragmentary and bisected form.

As to whether I have anything to say about how "literary form interacts with cultural or social forms beyond the poem," it's possible I once had something to say about this. I don't doubt that forms make arguments, in a sense, but my only real interest in new or adapted forms is how they might provoke new content. Or, let's say, *material.*

MN I recall seeing a description of *Pause Button, Comp.*, and *Golden Age* as a trilogy, a "trilogy of error." Can you describe what you mean by that? How does *FPO* relate to these works?

KD The great Karen Black starred in the film *Trilogy of Terror*, which came out when I was in high school. "Trilogy of Error" was really just a joke riffing on that, I think originally in correspondence with Kevin Killian. There is no sense in which the three books compose a trilogy, but note that Black played three different characters in the film, so I suppose the three books could be thought of as "characters." Or monsters. From this vantage, I see less and less connection between the three books. And I see little connection between them and *FPO*.

But there may have been something else hiding in that joke. I used to have trouble rereading my published work and had dreams, nightmares, about it being riddled with embarrassing errors. There is thankfully now a pill for that.

MN You mentioned having three currently unpublished manuscripts that you're still working on – "lyriclike" poems with sections written in one sitting. Can you say more about these works and what, perhaps, you might like to do with them? Could you ever imagine a collected or selected edition of your work, a kind of *Collected Books*?

KD Since we started this discussion, one of them has been accepted for publication – in 2028, if we survive that long. All three are made up of writing I did between 2014 and early 2019, after which I had trouble just sitting down and writing. It's only recently that I seem to have acquired a new way of working after a few years of frustration.

As to selections or collections: my last three books are in print and my first one is available, with only a few typos, on *UbuWeb*, thanks to Brian Kim Stefans, so there's no need to collect. I think the trend is towards collecting things online, but I wouldn't want to do that either, because it would involve retaining a lot of things that should just disappear. "Selection" would have the advantage of cutting out a lot of stuff that has lost its purpose, if it ever had any. Thomas Evans has expressed an interest in this, particularly, as I mention above, so that the original version of "Floater" could be regathered and set forth on its own career.

In fact, a "selected poems" is in the process of being published by Disastra Publishing in Poland, under the title (in Polish) *Early Computer Music*, translated by Małgorzata Myk. I see this more a collaboration between Goska and my earlier work rather than as a standard selected.

But to get to the unpublished stuff: I probably exaggerate when I call the works "lyriclike." What I mean, I guess, is that they tend to be improvisations that are left as such rather than being poked and prodded into alliance with other improvisations and proposed as series. James Sherry once asked me what *FPO* was about, and I answered that I didn't think that was any of my business. But I was wrong. It is my business, and it is about – *something*. I'm just not quite sure what.

What I now seem to be engaged in, at this seemingly late date, is different. Spicer would probably call it pushing wood.

ENDNOTE

1 A recording of this exchange is available on *PennSound* at writing.upenn.edu/pennsound/x/phillytalks/Philly-Talks-Episode15.php.

Sensate Sovereignty

A Dialogue with The Culture and Technology Discussion and Working Group: Sadie Couture, Jonathan Sterne, Mehak Sawhney, Shirley Roburn, Andy Kelleher Stuhl, Burç Köstem, Hannah Tollefson, Randolph Jordan, Landon Morrison, and Allyson Rogers

ON MAY 13 AND 20, 2020, MEMBERS OF THE CULTURE AND Technology Discussion and Working Group – an informal collective of students, postdocs, and visitors working across several disciplines who have some affiliation with the McGill University professor Jonathan Sterne – met online to discuss an advance copy of Dylan Robinson's *Hungry Listening: Resonant Theory for Indigenous Sound Studies*. As a group of researchers working on an array of issues in media studies, communications, and sound and music studies, with a particular bias towards approaches and perspectives cultivated in cultural studies and media history, we considered Robinson's monograph a significant contribution to the field and were keen to engage with the work and consider how it could impact our own various undertakings. Inspired by the dialogical spirit of *Hungry Listening*, some of those present decided to extend our discussions in writing, in part to flesh them out further, and in part as a thank you to Robinson, who so generously shared his book with us before it was released.

Hungry Listening emerges from encounters between Indigenous sound performance and Western art music. It takes aim at the pernicious tendency for the latter to insist upon aesthetic assimilation as the end goal of these encounters, which far too often means derogating the former's ontologies and protocols of song. The book complicates settler audition by introducing what "settling" means from an Indigenous perspective in the first place. "Hungry listening" is one among many Indigenous perceptions of settler colonialism, and Robinson details multiple decolonial and resurgent approaches to listening throughout the book.

One of his major formulations is the idea of "sensate sovereignty," where artistic and sensory forms act both as obstructions to hungry listening and "provide a structure of knowledge sharing for Indigenous folks to enter into."[1] He weaves it into the form and writing of the book. Building on Indigenous theorizations of refusal and resurgence, Robinson's concept of sensate sovereignty "seek[s] to effect an epistemic shift in where and how we perceive Indigenous sovereignty."[2]

JS There is no dearth of writing on Indigenous modes of music-making or listening, but *Hungry Listening* is unique in my reading for several reasons. First, it engages at great length with academic new music from an Indigenous perspective. Most of the accounts I was familiar with before *Hungry Listening* focused on academic composition and music education, simply rejecting Indigenous forms of musical practice and knowledge. While that's certainly part of Robinson's account, he goes much, much further. Second, there is an engagement with sound studies to theorize and thematize listening as a political and cultural act. Robinson's titular concept names a behaviour in a way that goes far beyond simply saying, "settler colonial listening practices are settler colonial in their orientation." Rather, he treats hungry listening as a set of orientations and even techniques, and one thing I particularly like about it is that it is explicitly framed as an Indigenous reading of settler audition. In this, it reminds me of bell hooks's essay on Black representations of whiteness as terror in *Black Looks*. That and his discussion of critical listening positionality will be very useful to me in lots of work to come.

There are now two decades of work in sound studies on settler colonial listening,[i] starting in the late 1990s and early 2000s with Philip J. Deloria's *Playing Indian,* Erika Brady's *A Spiral Way,* Richard Cullen Rath's *How Early America Sounded,* the last chapter of my *The Audible Past* and moving forward into books like Gary Tomlinson's *The Singing of the New World* and Ana María Ochoa Gauthier's *Aurality*. But apart from Deloria's work, none of these books articulate a fully Indigenous perspective, though many give glimpses here and there from Indigenous sources. *Hungry Listening* represents something different, because it begins with an Indigenous perspective and articulates it throughout.[ii]

---

i SC: By Robinson's account, isn't a lot or even most sound studies work about settler colonial listening? In the conclusion, Deborah Wong writes, "While reading your book, Dylan, I had a world-shifting moment when I realized that the word *listening* should really have the word *settler* in front of it much of the time, in much scholarship. Outsiders know that the unmarked categories are the ones of which we should be most wary" (251). Maybe we ought to mark sound studies work produced by settlers in settler colonial contexts similarly.

ii JS: For decades now, I have been complaining about the racism in white Canadian sound theory – R. Murray Schafer, Marshall McLuhan, etc. – and have

I think *Hungry Listening* will be the first book in what will be a stream of writing in the coming years that will define a range of Indigenous perspectives in direct dialogue with sound studies and the more critical stand of interdisciplinary music studies: Jessica Bissett Perea's work on performing Indigeneity and Trevor Reed's scholarship on sound in Indigenous law (and their co-edited *Sovereign Aesthetics: Indigenous Approaches to Sound Studies* volume); Dustin Tahmahkera's research on Indigenous well-being and Ancestral acoustics; Kate Galloway's work on Indigenous sound art. What I would hope is that, in a few years, Indigenous scholars will find more spaces of their own within the university to discuss sound and music in ways that make sense to them; that Indigenous ideas are more fully integrated into interdisciplinary writing and thinking on sound and music; and that Indigenous scholars feel more welcome in those spaces than they may now (Robinson provides no stories about sound studies events, but he probably could have). This is the final major thread of the book that I appreciate: it's both within and without. Positionality is complex, compromised, negotiated. There's no "pure" stance for an academic writer to take, and Robinson treats that as a basic methodological tenet for how he describes the world. The job of non-Indigenous scholars in the field is to take up what he has to say, without making him solely responsible for educating us.

MS I fully share Jonathan's perspective about *Hungry Listening* being a critique of settler colonial perceptual orders through Indigenous sensory orientations and the potential it holds for scholars of sound, music, and perception. In the acknowledgments section at the end of the book, Robinson says, "I hope this book and my work here might contribute in some small way to opening space for future generations to challenge normative and settler colonial paradigms of perception and to affirm resurgent forms of attention."[3] If I were to describe my own experience of reading the book, it felt like recognizing and reverse engineering several settler colonial

---

received responses ranging from "Sure, but their other ideas are so important" to "But it's *science*" to "But *everyone* was racist in the 1960s." Arguments like Robinson's will, I hope, help to get settler scholars out of this rut, but I think honestly it's probably having more people like Robinson *in the room* (whether physically or metaphorically) which will force some more accountability around the presumptive whiteness in much sound theory.

perceptual orders followed by thinking through Indigenous cosmologies of sensing and being. The book is replete with powerful decolonial neologisms and offers multiple conceptual paradigms to decolonize perception and listening, some of which I list:

1. Hungry Listening and Indigenous Cosmologies: The title and primary conceptual lens of the book – "hungry listening" – emerges from Indigenous cosmologies and ways of knowing and naming. In addition to the two Halq̓eméylem words from which the idea is derived,[iii] Robinson gives us a glimpse into other adjectives used for settlers in Chapter 1. He quotes Cherokee scholar Jeff Ganohalidoh Corntassel to provide instances of Indigenous terms for newcomers – yonega is a Cherokee term for white settlers which means "foam of the water, without a direction," and wasicu is a Dakota term for settlers that means a "taker of fat." Indigenous terms for settlers describe not only historical relationships but also settler states of being which can be significant frameworks for decolonizing perception.[4] In order to decolonize settler colonial listening formations, what "settling" meant or means must be understood in the first place. Not only "hungry listening," but all of Robinson's theoretical insights emerge from Indigenous epistemic and affective ways of being.[iv]

---

iii HT: What is powerful about the concept of "hungry listening," to me, is not only that it names a set of settler orientations and techniques, but that it develops this analytic from an Indigenous perspective. The concept is "derived from two Halq̓eméylem words: shxwelítemelh (the adjective for settler or white person's methods / things) and xwélalà:m (the word for listening)" (2). Shxwelítemelh describes the ways of xwelítem – the Stó:lō term for non-Indigenous people – which carries the meaning of "starving person." Robinson notes that xwelítem came into use to describe the first influx of settlers into Stó:lō Territories, who arrived in "two states of starvation": both bodily, for sustenance, and greedily, for gold. "From the xwélmexw [Stó:lō people] perspective," Robinson explains, "settler subjectivity emerges out of a state of consumption" (47). As Robinson describes, "xwelítem hunger may have begun with gold, but it quickly extended to forests, the water, and of course the land itself" (49). Throughout the book, he develops the analysis of hungry listening by demonstrating its continuity through time. This drive was not only foundational to settler colonialism in Stó:lō Territory during the gold rush, and present throughout colonial policy, but remains palpably present in more recent paradigms of recognition and reconciliation.

iv JS: I think it's important that the hungry listening concept is a translation into English. A de- or anticolonial sound studies would need to depend much more

2. Positionality versus Identity: Robinson argues for a listening positionality that is disentangled from identity. He argues that positionalities change with where, when, and how one is located. For Robinson, "Identity is a cohesive fact, while positionality is a 'shifty' state."[5] This idea of positionality as fluctuating in addition to being complex and specific stems from Indigenous modes of being in a relation: "Shifting contexts of inclusion and exclusion are Indigenous modes of being in relation that are not predicated on an epistemology of relationship as a static state. Resurgence and decolonization do not exist as completed work but instead as ongoing processes in flux."[6]

3. Multi-Sensory Listening and Subjective Sound: Robinson challenges the idea of listening as purely aural and of sonic stimulus as something objective. Against the Western models of sensory divisions, he introduces listening as an embodied multi-sensory experience in Indigenous cultures. He also argues against any specific definition of listening – "Decolonizing musical practice involves becoming no longer sure what LISTENING is."[7] He understands sound (and other media to express sound) as subjects that beget an affective and/or responsible response. He introduces a third subject in the pairs listener and music, writer and reader – space, whether it be the space of performance or the space of the medium (page, screen) in which listening is carried out. This also explains his formal choices, which emerge from what he calls apposite methodologies, performative writing methodologies which take the form of "writing with" rather than "writing about."[8]

4. Functional versus Aesthetic: In opposition to Western notions of music as aesthetic, Robinson introduces Indigenous understandings of music as functional – music and songs are "more than representational" and are experienced as law, medicine, teachings, embodied history, and "forms of doing."[9] While the Western aesthetic state is that of contemplation, the Indigenous functional state might vary.[v] Since Indigenous songs cannot fit the

---

on language learning outside of English, especially non-European languages, and the epistemologies and cosmologies that come from those languages.

v AR: *Hungry Listening* brings into relief just how inconceivable it can be for listeners socialized into the Western tradition (in formal music education and philosophy) to conceptualize music as anything other than aesthetic objects and experiences, even in contexts where music is considered functional. What

Western idea of being a "thing," Robinson suggests "Indigenous + art music" as a model of collaboration which denotes conjoining rather than merging two fields of musical practice.[10] The logogram "+" becomes a structural means to assert Indigenous sovereignty and refuse the epistemic violence that occurs in Indigenous-Western collaborations in a settler-colonial context.

5. Sensate Sovereignty and Structural Refusal: Robinson expands the ideas of sovereignty and refusal at the heart of decolonial theory to the domain of perception by proposing concepts such as *sensate sovereignty* and *structural refusal*. While the former includes the "potential of written, visual and aural obstructions,"[11] the latter includes a refusal of "aesthetic strategies that impede Indigenous knowledge extraction and instrumentalization."[12] Both these ideas alter perceptual orders structurally for sharing Indigenous epistemic-affective-aesthetic modalities of being.

SR What I appreciate most about Robinson's book is his textual embodiment of Mehak's fifth point on "sensate sovereignty and structural refusal," which could also be described, in Peter Kulchyski's terms, as enacting a politics of form. There is a long tradition, from Hugh Brody in the 1980s, through to Kulchyski, Stephanie Irlbacher-Fox, Peter Van Wyck, and Julia Christensen more recently, of northern scholars interspersing academic texts with narratives, testimonials, photographs, and creative pieces in an effort to break the hegemony of Western academic forms and create spaces for Indigenous experiences and politics. However, Robinson takes this to a new level, actually demonstrating how an Indigenous relational politics can structure the relationship between a text and an audience. Robinson includes between the chapters a series of "event scores" that function variously as examples, nudges, challenges, and instructions compelling readers to reconsider their modes of listening to Indigenous cultural property.[vi] The first of these sections, "Writing Indigenous Space," is

---

if Indigenous protocols – not just content – formed the basis of collaborative performances between Indigenous and Western art music? What if these performances followed Indigenous rather than Western logics? How can Indigenous and non-Indigenous artists enter into truly reciprocal relations?

vi LM: A good example of one of these event scores can be found at the end of Chapter 4, where Robinson presents his "Event Score for Responsibility:

exclusively for Indigenous readers and explicitly so. The reader is thus invited, from the outset, to enter into an Indigenous politics of form, in this instance by governing their reading behaviour to respect proprietary knowledge.

As a form of address, *Hungry Listening* is profoundly conscious of its multiple audiences and enacts ethics of appropriate relationship, modelling to readers how musical scholarship can approach Indigenous creators, performers, and music in ways that respect Indigenous sovereignty and value Indigenous creations on their own terms. At the same time, this respect is reciprocal: mirroring the gesture to Indigenous readers at the book's outset, Robinson gives over space in his conclusion to two non-Indigenous scholars. This is a remarkably generous gesture and at the same time a demanding one: Robinson gently but firmly demurs when the scholars ask for a protocol – coming to terms

---

qimmit katajjaq / sqwélqwel tl' sqwmá:y" as a critical-affective response to Alexina Louie's *Take the Dog Sled*, a piece for two Inuit throat singers and seven musicians that was commissioned by the Montréal Symphony for a 2008 tour of Nunavik (and which, in a painful irony, premiered alongside Schafer's "North/White" [1973], a piece for snowmobile and orchestra commemorating the machine that decimated dogsledding). Against Louie's description of the music as a lighthearted "snapshot of the North" (184) – in marketing for the piece, she exclaims to the would-be listener, "I wanted to put you on a dogsled. Enjoy the ride!" – Robinson throws light on the horrendous history of sled dog slaughtering (or qimmiijaqtauniq) between 1950 and 1975. His event score consists of stage directions for the realization of a decolonizing work where Louie's music is brought into close contact with a disturbing colonial past that it otherwise obfuscates. Robinson intervenes here in several key ways, beginning with his plans for funding the new project, which involve employing an Inuit filmmaker to spend one month helping Inuit youth document daily life in their communities. From there, eight short films are to be created which correspond to the lengths of eight movements of *Take the Dog Sled*. These films are to be played in parallel with a performance of Louie's piece, but in a neighbouring hall, forcing audience members to choose which event they wish to experience. In both events, prior to the eighth movement/film, documentary footage is to be shown that confronts the audiences with mid-century scenes from the slaughter of sled dogs, as well as testimony given by Inuit people involved in the Qikiqtani Truth Commission (2013) and interviews with Royal Canadian Mounted Police. In this way, by alternating "between explicit political critique and poetic gesture, between Brechtian distancing and subtle openings to reorienting perception" (199), Robinson challenges Louie's unexamined portrayal of dogsledding in the North and opens a space for sovereign Indigenous perspectives to emerge within the context of new music performance.

with how to respond, how to be in respectful relationship to Robinson's text, is exactly the work they must do.

Kulchyski describes that for Indigenous self-government, "The politics of form is of considerable importance … the form in which power is deployed not only reflects the cultural values of those who deploy it, but it embodies, enacts, and perpetuates those cultural values."[12] How things are done shapes what can arise out of any interaction. Indigenous governance is not restricted to rules that might structure a government body but encompasses everyday life: social forms and protocols; storytelling and means of narration; the community as a "form" of social being. *Hungry Listening* enacts its politics of form to confront the often-unspoken norms and protocols that govern musicology and discipline its listening, challenging readers to both think and listen differently.

AS I found this work profoundly useful from a vantage point of interest in sonic arts and media politics. In chapters three through five, Robinson critiques specific musical events in order to draw out the myriad ways that hungry listening and Indigenous resurgence interfere with one another in moments of performance and audition. Centrally, he asks, "to what degree composers should be held responsible for an ethics of *formal* musical choices (in addition to narrative and representational choices)."[14] Robinson makes a strong case for music as a site where critics should begin dissolving the supposed – and politically limiting – barriers between form and content or structure and representation.

In critical media analysis, a large body of work examines texts for the *representations* that surface in their authorship, their performer casting, or their tropes. A responding stream counters that representation is not enough – that critique must focus on the political economic *structures* that determine the representable, or on the standards and protocols, materialized in *infrastructures,* that determine how content travels. This discourse across academic, artistic, and informal spheres can, for all its liveliness, feel like a dialectic without a third term. Robinson's critical stance manages to cut across all these concerns, in part through a fresh approach to sound in performance, and also by dislodging the question from a rigidly Western-humanist framework. *Hungry Listening*'s case studies pass through and out of standard musical vocabularies, pulling them into a context of cultural, institutional, and epistemic incommensurability. An extractivist composition doesn't merely select a tempo but imposes Western temporality on its Indigenous participants. A choice to employ consonance might not so much balance dissonance as avert the alienating potential of the encounter between opera stage and unfamiliar audience – an alienation and a dissonance that might have called forth Indigenous trauma without making it digestible for settler audiences. At each point, concerns of form draw a continuous line from sonic vibration itself out to the enclosing concert hall and society and back; prior to imposing Western ontologies of song and excluding Indigenous ones, there was no break in musical performance between aesthetic object and political context.

Asking composers and critics to attend to "the formal encounters between musical languages and epistemologies" forbids the attitude that representational elements can be simply spliced and recombined into intercultural works – an attitude that, Robinson shows, can readily transduce inclusionary intent into a flurry of extraction.[15] Structures and protocols, in other words, cannot be arranged in the way that Western composers have become used to arranging voices and notes. To think about performance (and therefore mediation, I'd argue) from a standpoint of affirming Indigenous sovereignty will mean refusing the notion that there can be voice without protocol or protocol without voice.

SR Deborah Wong and Ellen Waterman's conclusion section is sure to provoke a strong affective reaction in many readers; in contrast to Robinson's more polished arguments, this section documents an awkward muddling through, a dialog seeking but not settling on clear answers. The section is effective in modelling the "working through" through which settler audiences can encounter and adopt more decolonial listening practices. At the same time, I found it frustrating, echoing a frustration I felt throughout the book: there is a lack of nuance in the depictions of settler listening. It is certainly fair to argue that Robinson does not owe such nuance when Indigenous people and knowledges have been stereotyped, minimized, and degraded in settler scholarship for centuries. Additionally, a clear message of the book is that settler scholars need to do some more work to deconstruct the settler ear, just as film scholarship has deconstructed the male gaze.[vii] Yet I still found that the particular historical moments

---

vii MN: In our group dialogues on the book, the conclusion provoked a lot of discussion. Opening up the end of the book to two non-Indigenous scholars to respond created an uneasy and uncertain space following the clarity of Robinson's arguments, histories, and descriptions. Wong and Waterman want protocols from Robinson for how they might respond, and, in that wanting, they realize, as Shirley states above, that "coming to terms with how to respond, how to be in respectful relationship to Robinson's text, is exactly the work they must do." I see this engagement as a valuable example of the "apposite methodology" Robinson describes earlier in the book, "processes for conveying experience alongside subjectivity and alterity," a form of "'writing with' a subject in contrast to 'writing about,'" one that envisions "possibilities for how writing might not just take the form of words inscribed on the page but also forms that share space alongside or move in relationship with another subjectivity" (81). In creating a polyvocal and multi-positional dialogue on the work as its conclusion, Wong, Waterman, and Robinson model an instance of the book's reception. Their questions, like ours, are: How is this book useful and what are we going to do with the discussions it catalyzes moving forward? They are working it out together. There are no smooth, easy conclusions.

SR: Michael, your provocation "How is this book useful?" brought to mind the interventions in the 1980s by another Stó:lō scholar, Lee Maracle, who took a leading role in raising parallel questions in the CanLit sphere about the telling of Indigenous stories. Her approach very powerfully foregrounded the issues; however many of the reactions, particularly from white writers, were defensive. Debates often centred around whether an individual writer could write stories and characters outside of their own experience, when the goal of Maracle and many of her contemporaries had been for the CanLit community to confront issues of structural racism that privileged white writers telling stories over BIPOC writers telling their own. In contrast, thinking of your own comments later about diversity of tactics, Robinson is taking another tack here, one that mirrors how Nacho Nyak Dän master storyteller Louise Profeit-Leblanc has broached bringing the pedagogical values of traditional storytelling to the page. In "Stories Have Their Way with Us," Profeit-Leblanc sets the text up with a story-within-a-story. A traditional story told by revered Yukon Elder Kitty Smith resonates powerfully with her own life experience: it is implied that the heroine's transcendence, taking a difficult healing path and recovering from very painful circumstances to find a happy life, had inspired Kitty's own resilience and recovery in the face of devastating challenges. The text shows, rather than tells: the traditional story acts as a container, a safe space, for a listener (in this case, a young Kitty Smith) to do the work they need to do to explore other ways of tackling difficulty and to grow from their circumstances. Robinson creates a similar container for Wong and Waterman. As readers, we are witnesses to their "working through" of what concepts of hungry listening mean for their own practice. By including space in his conclusion for Wong and Waterman's process, in all its messiness, Robinson is not only showing the reader what a decolonizing practice of "working through" might look like. He is that Robinson chose as originary to his conceptions of "hungry listening" presented settler logics rather one-dimensionally. These moments – the Delgamuukw trial, the Fraser River gold rush of 1858 – live for me as rich crystallizations of the multiple facets that led to them. There is not one settler logic of extractive listening, and to reduce the various drives to one simple greedy acquisitiveness makes it easier for the reader to associate these moments with distance rather than continuity, with difference rather than with complicity. If the challenge is to evolve politics of decolonial listening that include settler "decomplicity," it requires non-Indigenous Canadians to grapple with such moments in all their complexity, to work not only with their darkness but with the struggle, hope, and oppositionality that they also contain.

SC Two related concepts Robinson develops which are central to these conversations on listening are *listening positionality* and *critical listening positionality*. He introduces the terms as part of an overarching framework informing the work, and as central to "this book's larger questions around the ontological and epistemological stakes of what listening is."[16] For Robinson, "listening positionality" describes the ways in which our individual and collective experiences, backgrounds, and ways of being in the world influence how we listen. In the context of settler colonialism in North America, such listening positionalities influence how many of us (Indigenous and settler both) encounter music and other sonic experiences. In Robinson's account, hungry listening is a settler colonial listening positionality (possibly among others) and "must be understood on a continuum."[17] Subjects will have

---

validating and foregrounding the need for non-Indigenous people to undertake such reckonings in a vulnerable and open-hearted way.

JS: I had a very split reaction to the conclusion. Stylistically, it is a brilliant move, and in a subgenre of academic writing that receives almost no attention (quick: name three academic books with memorable conclusions!), Robinson does something entirely original and entirely in keeping with the methodology and argument of the rest of the book. But in watching Wong and Waterman struggle with their own positions with respect to the text, I had a negative reaction. Those of us with one or another kind of privilege have to stay with the discomfort of understanding the unpayable debt behind that privilege, and I read them as trying to do that, trying to model an ethical reception of the book. It's just not the particular ethical reception I had (or wanted).

a varied relationship to settler colonial listening positionalities and will have "their own specific forms of hunger, starvation, and drive towards knowledge fixity."[18]

One of the main prescriptive calls in the work is to engage in a process that Robinson calls "critical listening positionality" (CLP). CLP is the practice of interrogating our listening positionalities in order to "listen otherwise."[19] CLP is a reflexive questioning of how our experiences, identity markers, and backgrounds influence our listening, as well as on a more structural level, "how perception is acquired over time through ideological state apparatuses at the heart of subjectivation."[20] Robinson specifically offers a vision of CLP as varying on an individual basis, but which "might begin through detailing specific aspects of one's positionality and then identifying the ways in which those aspects allow or foreclose upon certain ways of looking, kinds of touch, or listening hunger/fixity" (60–61). Exactly how this process will play out is an open question, but Robinson floats the idea of engaging in CLP with Indigenous + art music as a guest on "Indigenous sound territories."[21] As a guest, one must be open to hearing new things, as well open to the idea that listening otherwise might not involve hearing anything at all. As Robinson notes, guest listeners "may always be unable to hear these specific assertions of Indigenous sovereignty, which is not to be understood as lack that needs to be remedied but merely an incommensurability that needs to be recognized."[22] CLP and listening otherwise may not be wholly the responsibility of the listener when it comes to cultural events and sonic encounters. As touched on by Shirley and Andy, Robinson argues for formal and structural interventions into spaces, performances, and procedures to facilitate such perceptual shifts.[23]

Robinson's use of the concept of listening positionality forcefully counters any notion readers may have about universality of listening, the ability of sound to uniquely overcome difference or link listeners together. For some, this insight will be clear and nicely builds on generations of intersectional feminist and critical race theory. For others with different theoretical and intellectual backgrounds, this will be an important reckoning and moment of tension. There is no essentialized listening experience in Robinson's account, and while he may not explicitly outline the various settler listening positionalities that Shirley was hoping for, he repeatedly allows for and acknowledges the different relationships to hungry listening and that many of us have been raised with. Another useful aspect of *Hungry Listening* was, to me, the incisive linkage Robinson makes between settler extractivist orientations in general, and the specific instances of this logic which ground his analysis and are his central concerns throughout the work. Drawing on scholars Leanne Betasamosake Simpson and Naomi Klein, Robinson notes that from this extractivist orientation, Indigenous land, people, culture, and, importantly, music are seen as resources to be taken, stolen, and used for settler ends.[24] Robinson's naming of this behaviour and logic immediately makes clear the stakes of his argument, even for those not currently engaged with or interested in the Canadian classical/Western new music scene.

BK Robinson performs a kind of structural refusal in the book itself. Besides a refusal of specific content, structural refusal seems to explore what forms of writing and knowledge practices impede extraction, consumption, and epistemic violence.[25] This refusal beyond the level of content is important, since it gets to the crux of his refusal of the politics of recognition. Whereas Indigenous art is consumed as content, structural refusal forces us to attend to the "deeply normative infrastructure of art music production and presentation."[26] Overall, I found the implicit distinction between a refusal at the level of content and structure very useful in thinking through the political stakes of aesthetics.

Additionally, structural refusal also seems to shape how the book is written, meant to not be consumed so easily by settler publics. In the middle of his introduction, Robinson explicitly addresses his settler, ally, and non-Indigenous readers, inviting them to stop reading the introduction from this page forward, as the rest of the introduction is written exclusively for Indigenous readers.[27] I found this move incredibly powerful in relation to the concepts Robinson introduces in the book, both because it calls for the reader to practise critical positionality and invites them to participate in Robinson's structural refusal.[28]

I did find myself wondering how all of this fits into the discussion of sensate or perceptual sovereignty. In our discussion, Jonathan pointed out how Robinson's request that settlers not read the first chapter seems in tension with contemporary big-data practices where every chapter of the book will be rendered machine readable and searchable. On the one hand, this provides a critique of big-data practices. On the other hand, thinking through how one practices structural refusal under conditions of big data seems like an interesting question.[viii]

HT Along with Sadie and Burç, I also appreciated the way Robinson theorizes extraction and extractivism. Significant contemporary scholarship is devoted to expanding these concepts and tracing their expression through aesthetic and cultural forms. While there is a tendency in some of this work to base conceptions of extraction in abstract economic forces, *Hungry Listening*'s analysis is grounded in a deeply embedded set of historical and ongoing relationships and sensory orientations, making it a unique and important contribution to this literature. Robinson powerfully articulates how forms of aesthetic extraction and sensory extractivism operate, as well as their political stakes. Building on Leanne Betasamosake Simpson's articulation of extractivism and assimilation and Wolfe's foundational notion that settler colonialism is a structure rather than an event,[29] he names and articulates settler colonialism as a set of perceptual logics. In this formulation,

---

viii JS: Specifically, no big-data system can honour Robinson's request without someone going in and modifying his text or the way the system displays search results. And if settler scholars use these systems to do a search that includes *Hungry Listening*, it will effectively invite them to violate his wishes.

HT: Robinson's notion of sensate sovereignty seems distinct yet resonant with notions of Indigenous digital sovereignty – where self-determination over information collection, storage, and access is articulated in similar terms to how jurisdiction is asserted over territory. Both articulate what Shirley previously describes as a kind of politics of form, where Indigenous protocols set the terms of knowledge keeping and knowledge sharing.

AS: Indigenous-led and otherwise anticolonial infrastructure for digital knowledge exchange is of course a larger field of thinking and building than we can fully address here, and not one that *Hungry Listening* engages directly. (For one example, see the Mukurtu project and discussion in Kimberly Christen, "Does Information Really Want to be Free? Indigenous Knowledge Systems and the Question of Openness," *International Journal of Communication* 6 (2012): 2870–2893; for another, Roopika Risam, *New Digital Worlds: Postcolonial Digital Humanities in Theory, Praxis, and Pedagogy* [Northwestern University Press, 2018]). Even so, the inevitability that the book will become the object of datafication, and the linkages and frictions that result in considering that scenario, return us to the necessary and multiply sited relation between structure/format/protocol and sovereignty.

Robinson demonstrates how settler colonial structures not only manifest in external institutions but, importantly, through forms of subjectivity and orientation that are taught and enacted by variously positioned people.[30]

As a response to sensory extractivism, Robinson proposes and practises strategies of sensate sovereignty, one of which is the blockade. "If Indigenous knowledge and culture is mined and extracted," he writes, "then it would follow that a key intervention for disrupting the flow of extraction and consumption would be the blockade."[31] Expanding on the work of Yellowknives Dene scholar Glen Coulthard,[32] for whom the blockade is a key political tactic and form of negation, Robinson considers how the blockade could and does operate as an obstruction to epistemic violence through various politico-aesthetic forms.[33] Here, sensate sovereignty operates as a kind of refusal via aesthetic strategies that impede the extraction and instrumentalization of Indigenous knowledge and culture. Robinson shows how blockade, as tactic of sensate sovereignty, not only negates or impedes hungry listening but also, drawing on Métis artist and scholar David Garneau's "irreconcilable spaces of Aboriginality,"[34] affirms Indigenous sovereignty and enables resurgent work. This idea is echoed in recent reflections on the solidarity actions in support of the Wet'suwet'en Hereditary Chiefs and Land Defenders, where Leanne Betasamosake Simpson argues that blockades are not only "a negation of destruction," but an "affirmation of life."[35]

RJ We in academia are locked in a race to stake our territorial claims, our quest for proof of originality the substance of our mimetic rivalry: to coin a term, to claim our corner of the knowledge market, to make something useful for the knowledge production of others while requiring acknowledgment of our role in that production. Like patent holders. Robinson's coining of the term "hungry listening" functions differently. His contribution to my own academic development is to lay my own hunger bare. To explain why I am unsatisfied in having failed, for example, to "discover" the "meaning" of a totem pole positioned next to Vancouver's Burrard Bridge, an area that I have been making work about for the better part of the last decade. The pole is silent, to me, while the sound of the bridge traffic is loaded with signification. That the pole should remain silent, to me, seems intolerable in light of academia's claim to freedom of information in all contexts and in perpetuity. Lack of access feels unconstitutional. Isn't there a government form for that? I grew up on that land, after all. Shouldn't all its secrets be my birthright? So the thinking goes. I am listening hard, but my ears are not calibrated for this kind of hearing. Striving to think of these poles in my own work as necessarily intersecting, they become entwined with my position as settler. My preference for ambiguity in art is rendered contradictory by my desire to know everything there is to know about that which informs my work. I become intolerant of ambiguity on the land so that I may shape the land according to my own selective ambiguity under the guise of artistic license, a license stamped by the same governing body that grants researchers our right to information. Reading what it means to be a "hungry listener" has revealed what my next step should be, a prompt to rethink what it means to be satiated as both researcher and creator. In the service of better digestion, it is time for me to fast.

LM Like Shirley, Burç, and Hannah, I appreciated the book's theorization of defamiliarizing strategies in the form of structural refusals and blockades. Robinson appeals to defamiliarization as a way to foil sensory extractivism and decolonize listener subjectivity because, "like Brechtian *Verfremdungseffekt*, the listening impasse sends perception off in other directions and slows hungry ... listening habits, privilege, and biases."[36] From this commitment follows an imperative for "artists, composers, curators, and musicians to impose new listening impasses through their work,"[37] creating music that is "indigestible" for hungry listeners. For Robinson this is more than theoretical, as he makes clear with his own distancing manoeuvers in the arena of new music, reframing the work of Canadian composers like R. Murray Schafer, Harry Somers, and Ernest MacMillan in light of their complicity in a violent history of extractivism that appropriated Indigenous cultures as a kind of national inheritance.

Interestingly, it is from within the same new music institutions that Robinson seeks to change that I have previously encountered defamiliarizing rhetoric. The concept is fundamental to modernist aesthetics, with Russian formalist Viktor Shklovsky articulating an early plea for artists to "remove objects from the automatism of perception ... pricking the conscience ... so that one may recover the sensation of life."[38] Echoing this sentiment, mid-century composers often used some form of aesthetic distancing to explain why their music was regarded as impenetrable and frustratingly resistant to listener expectations. And still today, composers like Georg Friedrich Haas are framed in relation to an "ethics of defamiliarization," with his use of overtone chords (i.e., harmonies based on the harmonic series) described as a "tool for encouraging utopian hearing, confronting listeners with sound that refines their appreciation of intonation and forces them to question their received listening categories."[39] While there are political aspects to this discourse, the emphasis remains largely aesthetic and is far removed from the kind of decolonizing project Robinson has in mind. What are we to make of the double valence of defamiliarizing tropes in these different contexts?

Elsewhere, I thought Robinson's distinctions of "inclusionary / intercultural music" versus "Indigenous + art music" were useful in drawing out the inequities in Canada's new music community. Indeed, the book's specificity to a Canadian context is one of its key strengths, and for that reason, it is certain to make a strong impression on music departments across the country. But the implications of Robinson's work should also strike a chord in new music circles abroad, resonating for instance with the recent Defragmentation – Curating Contemporary Music project in Europe. Funded by the German Kulturstiftung des Bundes (Federal Cultural Foundation), this initiative examined issues of race and gender diversity in relation to four new music festivals (MaerzMusik, Darmstadt, Donaueschingen, and Ultima), mapping out proposals for ameliorating what continues to be an entrenched, white-male-dominated cultural milieu.[40] Building on the conclusions of this study, George E. Lewis recently proposed introducing Spivak's concept of "creolité" into new music discourse as a way to move past the "gate-keeping, border-policing, and kinship-enforcing functions of genre." [41] On the one hand, this idea parallels Robinson's discussion of intersectional identity and listening as a "practice of oscillation (moving between layers of positionality),"[42] but on the other, it rubs against the ideal of Indigenous sovereignty with its call for a "creolized, cosmopolitan new music for the twenty-first century."[43] Going forward, it will be interesting to see if these perspectives can be brought into dialogue to redraw existing maps of the new music scene on both local and global scales.

Last, and along similar lines, I am confident that Robinson's discussion of listener positionalities holds significance for a "disciplinary redress" currently underway in my home field of music theory. Like musicology (which Robinson addresses in relation to a controversy that resulted in the hashtag #AMSSOWHITE), music theory as a discipline has been slow to reflect on its complicity in perpetuating settler colonial practices, mindsets, and institutions, and it is only now beginning to seriously wrestle with many of the fundamental questions Robinson poses in his book – i.e., who gets to study music, what kinds of music can be studied, in which cultural and institutional contexts, and towards what ends. These questions demand real, structural change, which *Hungry Listening* embodies in its creative interventions and critiques of settler-colonial listening positionality, offering important lessons to those who will listen.

AR Robinson's thorough critique of how inclusionary/intercultural performances extract and "fit" Indigenous music and performers into Western structures, thereby reasserting colonial dominance, is a much-needed framework for understanding the Canadian musical context and will undoubtedly resonate further afield. The combination of Indigenous and Western art music has become normative at major nation-building events and on prestigious stages across the country as evidence of Canada's "progressive values." By examining this intersection, Robinson is able to strike at the core of the settler Canadian conceit whereby the politics of recognition, accommodation, and multiculturalism adopted by the federal government are deemed sufficient in addressing Canada's colonial history and ongoing colonial violence. Drawing on Sara Ahmed, Robinson exposes these inclusionary performances as utopian and nonperformative in that they fail to accomplish reconciliation or decolonization in any real sense. Instead, a fantasy of reconciliation through friendly dialogue is enacted on stage, creating a powerful affective atmosphere that encourages audiences to feel like they are taking part in reconciliation when no substantial or lasting political work has taken place: "A utopian nonperformative, inclusionary music may here stand in for more significant forms of action and redress, ones that involve taking up a greater degree of intergenerational responsibility in the acknowledgment of Canada's history of colonization and the reverberations of intergenerational trauma as they play out in Aboriginal communities across Canada."[44] Contemporary inclusionary performances continue to treat Indigenous artists as "content" that enriches Western performance traditions. Western structures and protocols – including the performance space, audience-performer relationship, and rituals – remain intact, and therefore continue to dictate the terms on which Indigenous performances take place: "Inclusionary music, which on the surface *sounds* like a socially progressive act, performs the very opposite of its enunciation."[45] Inclusionary performances do little if anything to destabilize listeners' normative modes of perception, which Robinson is calling readers to question and investigate.[ix]

The alternative Robinson puts forward is "Indigenous + art music" where aspects of musical practices that are irreconcilable would be kept intact. Indigenous + art music avoids the fusion and hybridity that characterizes many intercultural performances and acts as a metaphor for the friendly reconciling of cultural differences through ongoing dialogue. Robinson's critique offers the potential for presenting organizations to radically unsettle the rigid protocols of Western art music and destabilize settler modes of perception. Robinson's call to reflect on the scopophilic drive that characterizes colonial attitudes seems particularly relevant for musicians and musicologists schooled in the Western tradition who are encouraged to be voracious listeners and to develop a range of specialized listening abilities throughout their training and careers: "a drive to look, but also ... an urge to penetrate, to

---

ix HT: This is powerfully articulated in Chapter 5, "Feeling Reconciliation," where Robinson illustrates the continuity of hungry listening by tracing the ways that inclusionary liberal politics of recognition orient hungry listening and shape "affective atmospheres of reconciliation" (17). In these spaces, audiences encounter and are affected by "reconciliation's sensate qualities: its textures, its materiality, its atmospheres, and particularly its resonance" (204). The chapter traces how certain friendly and nonagonistic "inclusionary" musical and theatrical performances are constitutive of what Mushkegowuk geographer Michelle Daigle describes as the "spectacle of reconciliation," where Indigenous knowledge and culture are consumed. The stakes of these accessible and affirmative performances and aesthetics are made clear: the "equilibrium of colonialism is maintained", foreclosing meaningful redress and enabling settlers to remain settled (Michelle Daigle, "The Spectacle of Reconciliation: On [the] Unsettling Responsibilities to Indigenous Peoples in the Academy," *Society and Space* 37, no. 4, [2019]: 703–721).

traverse, to know, to translate, to own and exploit."[46] This attitude assumes that everything should be accessible to those with the means and will to access them; everything is ultimately comprehensible, a potential commodity, resource, or salvage. Again, decolonizing music studies is not simply including Indigenous content and histories in curricula. Robinson's work asks us to examine the methodologies and infrastructures that are built on settler colonial and patriarchal forms of thought[47] and be open to having these spaces and relationships transformed, as they would have to be to enter into reciprocal relationships with Indigenous communities. New protocols would undoubtedly involve refraining from listening and from studying certain music under certain circumstances. It would mean finding ways of being "together-apart" and respecting sovereign Indigenous spaces.

MN I am thankful for Robinson's book – thankful for its core conceptual concerns; thankful for the work's "writing with" and "writing aloud" that give form to the rich intersection where Robinson is researching; thankful for its histories, personal and social, its citational substructure, and for the attention it gives to artists like Tanya Lukin Linklater, David Garneau, Peter Morin, Laura Ortman, and Raven Chacon, among others, who are doing some of the most exciting and necessary artistic work in North America; and thankful for the book's generosity, its vital negations and affirmations. I know that what I've encountered in *Hungry Listening* will resonate through my future research, writing, and dialogues.

The monolithic quality of settler listening, as Robinson portrays it, has been another point of rich discussion. While reading, I thought of potential counterexamples to such a firmly defined mode of extractivist settler listening. I thought of Thomas Berger, for instance, working in Sahtu Dene, Gwich'in, and Inuvialuit communities in the mid-1970s to hear testimonies against the construction of the Mackenzie Valley Pipeline, and the documentation of that listening in his report arguing against the pipeline's construction. I thought of Keith Basso using his decades of experience working as a linguistic anthropologist in Western Apache communities to provide expert analysis in legal cases so as to protect cultural places and materials from further settler plunder. And yet, both examples sustain the overarching dominance of the imperial juridical system and uphold a reconciliatory perspective that Indigenous nations not only *fit* within the imperial nation-state, but also *enrich* it with their difference (as Allyson discusses above). The more I reflect on it, finding singular instances that present or parse out difference in settler colonial listening is beside the point of Robinson's argument. As a force, through its effects, settler colonial listening is, indeed, monolithic. It extracts, and in its extraction, it materializes the conditions that perpetuate its regime of the audible. Here, I admire Sadie's emphasis above on hungry listening being "*a* settler colonial listening positionality (*possibly among others*)" (emphasis added): it *may* be one of others, but before parsing differences, it seems necessary to address the extent to which it is an absorptive and totalizing mode of perception.

This leads me to a final point, which is more of a question and concern I have moving forward from the book: beginning from a belief in the necessity of a diversity of tactics, what are ways to further materialize blockades, obstacles, and perceptual impasses to obstruct and resist settler colonial listening? Above, Hannah outlines the way in which Robinson draws upon Coulthard and Garneau to think through forms of *structural refusal* and negation that are an integral part of instantiating a sensate sovereignty.[48] Robinson offers examples of what such structural refusals and perceptual impasses look like in the form of the book (the section intended only for Indigenous readers) and in his discussion of Jin-me Yoon's "work of lateral exploration" in urban spaces.[49] Following from Robinson's discussions, I see a need to discuss in greater depth the array of historical precedents and social compositional strategies for developing such impasses on numerous fronts, specifically with regard to the sonic. Thinking of the major social movements of these last years in Canada and the United States – from Occupy to the student protests in Montréal, from Idle No More to Black Lives Matter, from Standing Rock to Wet'suwet'en – I note the extent to which an important element of these struggles has involved diminishing/muting/undermining specific sonic-auditory regimes and the articulation/(re)production of countersonic-auditory spaces. What are ways to resist the inclusionary muzak of settler colonialism? How to halt its petrocapital ambient soundtrack? Robinson's research offers an invaluable framework and set of approaches for addressing such questions.

ENDNOTES

1 Dylan Robinson, *Hungry Listening: Resonant Theory for Indigenous Sound Studies* (University of Minnesota Press, 2020), 24.
2 Robinson, 24.
3 Robinson, 259.
4 Robinson, 47.
5 Robinson, 248.
6 Robinson, 237.
7 Robinson, 47.
8 Robinson, 81.
9 Robinson, 45–46.
10 Robinson, 9.
11 Robinson, 24.
12 Robinson, 23.
13 Peter Kulchyski, *Like the Sound of a Drum: Aboriginal Cultural Politics in Denendeh and Nunavut* (University of Manitoba Press, 2005), 15–16.
14 Robinson, 132.
15 Robinson, 140.
16 Robinson, 2.
17 Robinson, 3.
18 Robinson, 60.
19 Robinson, 11–12.
20 Robinson, 10.
21 Robinson, 53.
22 Robinson, 53.
23 As Robinson notes, "Whether the white cube of the gallery, the proscenium stage–concert hall, the outdoor festival stage, or the black box, each site urges us to think and listen to music in particular ways that may not be conducive to the kinds of listening otherwise we might hope to advance. What happens when we change these sites of listening to include intimate spaces of one-on-one listening, spaces in relation with the land, spaces where audience members are not bound by the particular kinds of attention these spaces assert?" (61).
24 Robinson, 13–14.
25 Robinson, 23–24.
26 Robinson, 180.
27 Robinson, 25.
28 Robinson writes, "If you are a non-Indigenous, settler, ally, or xwelítem reader, I ask that you stop reading by the end of this page. I hope you will rejoin us for chapter 1, "Hungry Listening," which sets out to understand forms of

Indigenous and settler colonial listening. The next section of the book, however, is written exclusively for Indigenous readers" (25).

29 Leanne Betasamosake Simpson, "Dancing the World into Being: A Conversation with Idle No More's Leanne Simpson," interview by Naomi Klein, *Yes!*, March 6, 2013; Patrick Wolfe, *Settler Colonialism and the Transformation of Anthropology* (Bloomsbury Press, 1999).

30 Robinson, 18.

31 Robinson, 23.

32 Glen Coulthard, *Red Skin, White Masks: Rejecting the Colonial Politics of Recognition* (University of Minnesota Press, 2014).

33 Robinson, 24.

34 Robinson, 24.

35 Leanne Betasamosake Simpson, "Being with the Land, Protects the Land," *Abolition Journal*, February 21, 2020.

36 Robinson, 73.

37 Robinson, 72.

38 Viktor Sklovsky, "Art as Technique," in *Russian Formalist Criticism: Four Essays*, eds. Lee T. Lemon and Marion J. Reis (University of Nebraska Press, 1965 [1917]), 12–13.

39 Max Silva, "Heard Utopia vs. Utopian Hearing: Haas's *in vain* and Political Ambivalence in New Music," *Twentieth-Century Music* 15, no. 1 (2018): 86.

40 For example, between 1946 and 2014, only 334 out of 4,750 pieces performed at Darmstadt were composed by women, and only two were by non-white Afrodiasporic composers.

41 George Lewis, "A Small Act of Curation," *On Curating* 44 (January 2020).

42 Robinson, 60.

43 George Lewis, "Lifting the Cone of Silence from Black Composers," *The New York Times*, July 3, 2020.

44 Robinson, 230.

45 Robinson, 6.

46 Robinson, 34, quoting David Garneau, "Imaginary Spaces of Conciliation and Reconciliation: Art, Curation, and Healing," in *Arts of Engagement: Taking Aesthetic Action In and Beyond Canada's Truth and Reconciliation Commission*, ed. Dylan Robinson and Keavy Martin (Wilfrid Laurier University Press, 2016), 23.

47 Robinson, 268n8.

48 Robinson, 23, 72–73, 257–258.

49 Robinson, 254–258.

A Sediment Diversion for the Audible World

A Dialogue with Ryan C. Clarke

A TONAL GEOLOGIST FROM THE NORTHERN RIM OF THE Gulf of Mexico, Ryan C. Clarke notices the passage of time as both a trained coastal sedimentologist and artist-researcher as an editor and Director of Educational Programming at Dweller Electronics, a group dedicated to providing Afrological counterpoint within an otherwise Eurologically dominated music industry. His individual works investigate local cultural objects and their metaphysical communications with their proximal geological landscape. Knowing intimately the ways his home is at great risk of physical and social loss, he develops methods to not only document this loss quantitatively in scientific research as a trained coastal sedimentologist, but qualitatively with works that aim to articulate the vernacular knowledges his people share with the Mississippi River Delta and its distributaries. By interpreting the various articulations of Black music as a depositional record, he views the progression of technology and culture at large as being downstream of Black innovation in dialogue with its surrounding environment under the proposition of geologizing Blackness.

As an ethnomusicologist and coastal geologist, Clarke studies surface processes, focusing particularly on sedimentation and stratification. These ever-shifting landscapes, according to Clarke, exist in a feedback loop with their sonic regimes. He theorizes how a territory's sonic repertoires exist as part of its topsoil, and how these repertoires contribute significantly to the formation of its geological strata, which in turn impacts what is sonorously and audibly possible on those grounds. With meticulousness and a fascinating capacity for drawing connections, Clarke studies these dynamics in the effort to comprehend the social-ecological composition of the present.

I first came upon his work through the essay "Reverse Hallucinations in the Lower Delta" and its accompanying audiovisual mixtape *Care Forgot: A Southern Electronics Visual Mixtape*. These vital works articulate the historical palimpsest of the present and offer up future pathways for cultures of thriving difference, resistance, and conviviality.

As a starting point for our exchange, I proposed that we read Tiffany Lethabo King's *The Black Shoals: Offshore Formations of Black and Native Studies* as a way to propel our thinking on the imbrication of coastal geologies and cultural discourses. Our discussion moves swiftly from this initial point to consider delta processes, procedures of avulsion and extraction, the anti-imperial rhythm systems that Clarke calls "unleveed musics," and his remarkable, important conceptualization of the sediment diversion as a way to resist those forces that conspire to claim, contain, and foreclose the world.

The following exchange took place in conversation and in correspondence between New Orleans and Montréal during the winter of 2022 and the autumn of 2024.

MN In *The Black Shoals,* Tiffany Lethabo King thinks with the shifting geologic and oceanic formation of the shoal in order to situate and spatialize a methodological approach. The shoal is, according to King, "an accumulation of granular materials ... that through sedimentation create a bar or barrier that is difficult to pass and, in fact, a 'danger to navigation.'" The shoal is a "shifty formation" that can "erode over time, drift, and eventually accumulate in another location," and due to this perpetual errantry and unpredictability, it "exceeds full knowability / mappability." "Materially," she writes, the shoal is "a site where movement as usual cannot proceed."[1] Beginning from this terrain and the careful navigation it calls for, King then approaches her particular subject of inquiry: a theoretical conceptualization of the relationship and dialogic traffic between Black and Indigenous studies in the Americas through a series of points-of-encounter just offshore.

In resonance with King's offering, I wonder if you might discuss the relation of the shoal to the delta, describe what a delta is, geologically, and what this physical formation might offer up as we begin to think about the acoustics and the territory of the Lower Mississippi Delta?

RCC In the most basic of terms, a delta is a discrete bulge of the shoreline formed at the point a river enters an ocean, sea, lake, lagoon, or other standing body of water. The bulge is an accumulation of sediment as it is depositing more quickly than it can be redistributed via waves or tides. A paper from Jaap Nienhuis *et al.*[2] acknowledged that there are more than 11,000 deltas around the world, but for the sake of simplicity, I'll be imagining large rivers that in turn form the deltas that most people would acknowledge as such. This all happens, of course, if there is enough sediment in the river (a source) for a delta to form (a sink).

A delta follows a life cycle of around one thousand to two thousand years with a clear growth phase and deterioration phase. In the growth phase, a river has been "captured" into a stable place of deposition. As a result, the delta rapidly grows towards its own relative stability. But, as this bulge at the end of the river gets higher and higher, the river finds itself working harder to deposit the sediment at the top or even around this vertically accumulated earthen structure. So the river shifts laterally towards another part of the shoreline, or avulses to another delta lobe. This begins the growth process for another area nearby to start its own new delta, but it also begins the death of the previously mentioned delta.

Shoals are dependent on deltas: a shoal is an abandoned outer structure that forms from detachment from a waning delta. When a delta is active, it spreads, or progrades, out into whichever body of water it's depositing into. During the abandonment stage of a previously active delta, tides and waves, once powerless against the mighty river flow, now have enough force to rework the nearby deposits. This leads to an erosional headland that quickly gets detached into what is known as a barrier island. With later submergence under sea level, this drowned or subaqueous barrier island is now understood as a sand shoal.

As a site of speculative understanding, deltas and their cycles are rich in knowledge reworked as Black methodology and logics: the nonlinearity of a delta is evident in its inherent procedure of avulsion (sorrowful songs avulse to gospel avulses to blues avulses to R & B avulses to jazz avulses to rock avulses to techno and rap, all producing their own discrete but interconnected lobes), both expanding but stacking beside. But what happens when structure denies avulsion, such as, for example, mass construction of levees along the Mississippi River after the Great Flood of 1927 or capitalism commodifying what it once thought of as noise (field songs) into extractive resource (modern music industry)? Understanding modern Black infrastructure as having antecedent geologies, underground forms that inform what happens on the surface, can lead to many questions: how extraction of rich soils leads to physical degradation, how capitalism can be understood as a colonial mapping project and the inherent ephemerality of a delta refusing to carry permanence and to impose such upon it is violence (through delusion), how shoal production and its processes can be viewed through another production, Black cultural production, each with their own internal and industrial stressors reworking itself within the tension of external forces.

An example: Cubit was an oyster fisherman in 1862 whose two daughters didn't want to take the Mississippi River all the way down to its terminus to get into an adjacent bay, Bay Rondo, so he cut a bank of the river and incidentally made what geologists now understand as "sediment diversions," a procedure used in the replenishment of a deteriorating wetland. His cut, now called Cubits Gap, was a mistake that ended up building a fully formed subdelta in less than fifty years. Cubits Gap can be seen as a knot of memory where, woven into its process of existence, we can elucidate further Black methodologies. Where can we find our next Cubits Gap?

All of this assumes Blackness as an inherently ephemeral (fleeting) depositional / erosional process and any violence enacted upon it is something akin to weathering (American South, in situ) or erosional (weathering involving transport, i.e., the great migration). What is gained and lost in these processes?

Acoustically, sound plays a pivotal role in this speculative coastal geology. As the shoal ruptures a framework of previously thought binaries between Blackness and Indigeneity, so do Black cities of the Delta. Mardi Gras season can be seen as a shoal, a tarrying or procession – a wading in the water. The opaqueness of a second line comes to mind, another bulge that avulses from Orleans Street to Canal Street between hurricane seasons and river years.[3] How the humid sea-surface temperature of the Gulf waters lends itself to fog signals, often in lieu of lighthouses. To hear is to see down here. Sound is also a discrete bulge, not with hard lines but with felt ranges. The geology of the space informs those navigating and building on top, an antecedent geology of Blackness.

MN Thank you, Ryan, for establishing a profound ground for engaging this active terrain. You've introduced a number of possible directions to move in – sediments and lobes, procedures of avulsion and extraction, antecedent geology, mapping and the colonizing delusion of enforcing permanence, Cubits Gap, as well as an epistemology and acoustemology of the landscape – and I want to take up each of these points in turn.

I'm thrilled by your smooth linking of the delta's geological processes to its ecology of musicking. It's folded within your sentences, and I'm wondering if you can make more explicit how you understand this interrelation. And can you elaborate specifically with the example of the Mississippi Delta as to what forces or perspectives or incorporated structures (in both the geological and sonic-cultural senses that we are developing here) attempt to deny avulsion, to control the deposition of sediments, and to extract its rich soils?

RCC For those who feel the Black Atlantic is a sturdy lens for viewing diasporic cultural movement and production, the Mississippi River is both a useful and proximal example (or a proximal being? partner? elder?) to find a through line between colonial and neocolonial stress mutation on a landscape. Nineteenth-century Czech classical composer Antonín Dvořák celebrated negro spirituals as "product of the soil." In his overconfidence that the spiritual was truly American music of the land and not of state, he also hints at a metalanguage I find personally insightful in understanding music as a result of a physical, tilling process as much as it is an aural one. Field songs: a term giving equal weight to the land as the shouts given in, to, and of.

To veer away from Dvořák's Americentricity towards a more Mississippian understanding of Black cultural production, we can look to sorrow songs, spirituals, gospel, and predominantly something I'm broadly calling first-wave Black genres as *unleveed musics*. This is a genre where styles of song were pulsating responses overbanked into the southern plain with relatively minimal constraint or interferences on the music-making outside of the socioeconomic pressures for Black folks. This is to say the music industry wasn't signposting desire for Black musicians, these were folkloric tools that had more function than marketability. Both the pre-industrial engagement of Black music of the time and the relative freedom of the river to flood as it wished were obviously not wholly positive, but the understanding that these floods were needed to continue a fertile and healthy wetland was well known. It wasn't until the Great Flood of 1927 that some form of externally controlled infrastructure was instituted where, in two decades' time, the majority of the Mississippi would be leveed and dammed (damned), resulting in a riverine Catch-22: those living on its banks indeed now found annual safety from overbanking floods, but the land was effectively disconnected from the renourishing soil of the river itself, now rendered vulnerable by their newfound dependence on fallible structures. Such a structure also begins the era of modern Louisiana wetland loss, with the general consensus on it beginning in 1932.

To keep listening to the Mississippi River and understand its history as a knowledge system, not as a playful metaphor, one must consider Black cultural production alongside Western riverine control structures. For the Mississippi, it was Fort Randall Dam where, in 1952, the single largest decrease of suspended sediment load in the Mississippi River was recorded. For Black folk, it was the ratification of the race record in 1920 with Okeh Records releasing Mamie Smith's "Crazy Blues / It's Right Here for You," further transmuting the mass commodification of Blackness into the form of something manuel arturo abreu considers the "financilization of affect."[4] This moment is tangible evidence of epistemological bifurcations between Black people, their work, and the manufactured inherence of alienation with one's own labor. As an extension of their ontological fungibility through chattel slavery, the music industry pantomimes this series of colonial relations with incentivization the race record in the twenties, later with the Telecommunications Act in 1996, and with the Digital Millennium Copyright Act in 1998. Through governmental regulation, bending the material capacity for Black expression to be broadcasted writ large on its own accord. These structures contained what I'm calling second-wave or leveed Black musics: rap, Detroit techno, Chicago house, and jazz. Such sweet thunder proved too enticingly extractive to let be. Now, ever-new levees continue to restrict new topographies to be deposited. Spotify playlist algorithms not-so-quietly inform musicians what their music should sound like and how often it should be played. Silicon rhythm has no swing, too optimized and too quantized – not the metre soil people know. Manuel De Landa spoke to this in 1996 with respect to cultures attuned to the rhythm of the tropical cyclone:

> It is a perfectly rhythmic creature: it blows in one direction for six months of the year, blows in the other direction for another six months, and every seafaring people in Asia that made a living from the sea had to live with the rhythm of the monsoon. The monsoon gave those cultures their rhythm. If you want to go that way, well, you have to go that way in the summer, then you get there and you have to wait for the winter to come back. You have to plan your life to that rhythm.[5]

From another conceptual perspective, the Mississippi lends itself to a framework built by George E. Lewis of the Association for the Advancement of Creative Musicians and professor at Columbia University – Afrological and Eurological systems. The Mississippi and the American South's geology is clearly interested in horizontality as a means to build and to sustain itself. Other concepts the Mississippi is interested in are ephemerality and movement, as noted within shoals or barrier islands discussed above. Delta waning and avulsion could be seen as geological kin to burning cultures in various Native American tribes, the understanding that life and death both sit in the same circle. The Mississippi, with its simultaneous avulsions and lobe building, understands this as a survival practice as well and to impose a delusion of permanence (levees) is to kill it (not a death, murder) – something so clearly seen in southern Louisiana wetland's trilemma of oil withdrawal, subsidence, and sea-level rise. Without the banks consistently flooding, there are no means to combat these unnatural adversaries. Leveeing, extraction, and their ilk impose a verticality or hegemony into an environment that is unconcerned with height.

The flatness of a second line, where there's no clear understanding of who's the dominant performer in a procession (possession), or a ring shout in Congo Square, or other Afrologics like call-and-response, repetition within a drum circle, the importance of improvisation as a cosmology (a position beyond music), or Black dance music where the end of a song is less resolution and more extended hand, only asking for the next song to continue to be in communion beside. These horizontal Afrologics are reflections between the music and the environment. But who's looking at who?

This deltaic understanding is close to Deleuzian rhizomes but not synonymous with them: a bunch of tributaries depositing roaming lobes connected through a shifting source network where the cyclical nature of the river channel captures results in multiple depositional centres. Interconnected like the rhizome, yes, but not interdependent nor centralized. Instead, an emphasis on shifting sites of dominant deposition as needed for the system's health. Something akin to what techno producer and NON Worldwide cofounder Melika Ngombe Kolongo, a.k.a. Nkisi, calls in DeForrest Brown Jr.'s podcast series *Techno at the End of the Future,* "a decentralized rhythm strategy,"[6] where as one rhythm gets subsumed by the mainstream or fades away, another rhythm is already popping up somewhere else, ready to continue the goal of getting people together.

There's something more direct going on in the term *strategy*. To speak explicitly, it's a literal life-saving pattern. A pattern of life no different than a drum-framed African cosmology.

Music, and a lot of the information inside of music, have been really worthwhile to Black people. I think it's what drew us together through most of colonialism. It's what held us together during the Civil Rights era. Encoded theories of liberation inside songcraft. Hymnals performing as camouflaged text to better understand what it meant to fight for our lives. Notes to pass on and remember. Even now, Katrina, and memories of Katrina, are embedded in songs still. How did we survive? The archive is woven by and between the tones.

How can we contribute to a counterarchitecture while engaging in traditional knowledge systems? Trying to inform the perils of human-induced collapse into nonvocal forms of understanding is incredibly important. We must learn to respond appropriately to the tones of life. This quickly becomes a matter of: How do we better value ourselves? How do we better hear each other? How do we take care of each other?

MN I'm pausing to think with this phrase of yours, *unleveed musics*: music made by those who negotiate the modernizing imperial fantasy of control over nature and natural (rhythmic) systems, who know the protection promised with such "control" is not and will not be extended to them in the duration of social crisis (*when the levee breaks*, via Kansas Joe McCoy and Memphis Minnie, they will *have no place to stay*), who adapt their lives in the face of recurring floods and the resulting social crises and thereby imagine a mode of existence in their expectation so as to survive and thrive beyond them. And to continue your connection of topography to music-making: the word *levee* comes from the colonial French of the Mississippi Delta, from *lever, to rise*; so an *unleveed music* is one that sits below, *with* and *in* the shifting conditions of soils and sediments. Such musics – in the perspectives and (horizontal) forms of composition they articulate – bear the traces of these negotiations, imaginings, tactics.

In thinking about a "decentralized rhythm strategy," your question from above, "Where can we find our next Cubits Gap?" begins to resonate more resolutely in my mind now. The sediment diversion is an act in rhythmic listening with the Delta and its cycles. It is a way of perpetuating horizontality – a horizontality against the militarized will of the petrocapitalist state and its proponents, its desire for a verticality sustained only on its own terms, and the settler-colonial modes of appropriation and accumulation that are its premise as well as its ongoing effect.

So in thinking about these "horizontal Afrologics" – the uncertain, shifting lead in an ad hoc ensemble and the ethics of improvisation, to name only two of the facets you state above – and how they are reflections between an environment and its musics, I'm wondering if you might speculate how these praxes in the music of the lower Delta might reflect back to thinking with the geological and ecological? Is it too much to ask of an unleveed music that it might cultivate some mode of resistance against that trilemma you name above of extraction, subsidence, and sea-level rise?

RCC I'm unsure if unleveed music can *do* anything outside of getting people together. It's like asking water to do anything other than flow. It's the structures that surround the music that are its refusal, preventing it from doing much of anything other than being a manipulated vector towards unsustainable accumulation of wealth and power.

Two proposals after the Great Flood of 1927 – the Mississippi River and Tributaries Project (1928) and The Flood Control Act of 1936, respectively – brought about an almost complete leveeing of the Mississippi River, with every theoretical drop ending at the mouths of the river. With this confinement, any pollutant that finds its way into the river is there until it reaches the Gulf of Mexico. Because we've assumed levees as an inarguable fact of life, there's a subconscious cultural understanding that it's no emergency that a metric ton of nitrogen makes its way into the river annually. And because there's no floodplain to distribute such sediments, the Gulf of Mexico now carries an oxygen-depleted (hypoxia) zone of 6,952 square miles, mapped as of 2019. Modern industry – of which I've named southern music and the engineering of the Mississippi as two examples that are spatiotemporal kin – has attempted to lead us to the conclusion that we have created at a scale that we can no longer destroy. Modern industry has produced a sort of atomized pseudorelationship with a prerequisite for consumption (for example, the performer-audience, desired object-buyer, artist-critic, river-land, nature-extractor) when, in reality, relation and its sustainability are where we should begin and end. For the modern music industry, relationality barely exists outside of the "related artist" tab, for ads to be placed in front of us, as long as they're keeping us busy with the nice sounds we seem to like so much. There is no more nature, meaning relation, in music writ large, outside of the usual controversy and mutual followers. Maybe the issue starts with "writ large" before "music"?

As an in situ example of a historical response to the then-budding musical infrastructure we're grappling with today, in 1931 Louis Armstrong cultivated an oft-forgotten baseball team in New Orleans that was nicknamed the Raggedy 9 because of their tattered uniforms. He gave them fresh clothes and called them the Secret 9. Outside of the revitalized jerseys, he also taught many of them how to play in a band and incorporated them into the jazz circuit In "Decentering 'Race' and (Re)presenting 'Black' Performance in Sport History," S.W. Pope describes the relational benefit of unifying teams with musical ensembles: it provided a professional platform for all to hone their craft as well as to perform on a much larger scale for much bigger audiences.[7] This cross-pollination was happening throughout the southern jazz circuit, with Count Basie and Benny Goodman soon following suit. Another feature of this team was that every member was allegedly also a member of the now-famous Zulu Social Aid and Pleasure Club, a club of which Armstrong was also considered a member. This example is a short but illuminating understanding of what New Orleanians know as benevolent association. Local benevolent societies were a response to a massive uptick in the mortality rate in Louisiana in the late nineteenth century, with New Orleanians organizing institutions for their own benefit. As Claude F. Jacobs notes in "Benevolent Societies of New Orleans Blacks During the Late Nineteenth and Early Twentieth Centuries," these societies, rather than the Black hospitals and centres, were the dominant forms of health care, with a mission "to socialize and help each other in illness and death, especially during the recurring epidemics in New Orleans,"[8] covering costs for funerals, second lines, and even procurement of the tomb and plot in many of the city's aboveground cemeteries. Founded in 1844, the Dieu Nous Protège Benevolent and Mutual Aid Association "actively helped slaves purchase their freedom."[9] More recently, these benevolent societies are predominately a cultural preservation project, with many of the social clubs now most prominent during Mardi Gras, although they continue to operate year-round to organize social care.

What Armstrong and jazz performers in that era were doing with opera houses, lounge rooms, and pitching mounds follows the same logic as the marshland does when reacting to sea-level rise through a process known as hysteresis. Hysteresis is a concept some of us feel every day in our homes. Air conditioners use hysteresis: if you set the desired temperature to seventy-one degrees Fahrenheit, the air conditioner will never actually stay at seventy-one. It will cool down to seventy degrees and then turn back on once it heats up past seventy-two. Stability is not static but is constant dynamism in response to the world around you. The American South is an embodied tome of almost hysteric hysteresis. To live there is to constantly respond with the dynamism of the earth underneath, where the social and geological often feel like they are emitting from the same source. And such deltaic sociality, discrete but interconnected, can carry neotectonic change.

These are Cubits Gaps to me. In 1862, Cubit's daughters saw the amount of resistance it would take to travel into Bay Rondo, and so they thought beyond a concept they *knew* worked and imagined something that *might* work. It was this imagining that led to the main way geologists fight wetland loss over a century later. Cubits Gap as a historical moment for modern sedimentologists to then engineer sediment diversion might find its analog in jazz's benevolent associations. And this is not to say halftime shows are the goal, but the horizontal intermixing between audience-performer-club member-neighbour could be a useful and wieldy tool to find our own gaps in the infrastructure, which cannot be dismantled on its own terms. Why would it allow itself to be? Hopefully we can produce enough gaps in the infrastructure to start to grow land. In Louisiana, that's only happening in one place. The Atchafalaya Delta, about 135 miles from the mouth of the Mississippi, is building soft wetlands at a rate of one square mile per year. The Atchafalaya Delta, sourced by a river of the same name, is an offshoot of the Mississippi but was given thirty percent of the Mississippi waters for it to claim as its own. Less leveed than its much larger sibling, it has found stability between its own deposition and human induced wetland loss effort previously mentioned above. A square mile a year may not seem like a lot, but for a place where the law of the land is decay, growth is hope. And since nature is one of the few things we can learn from that isn't each other, finding reflection in the world around us might be worth our while. For me, it's here.

MN Your articulation of "benevolent associations" – as a particular cultural form that arises in the cultural-geologic specificity of the Lower Delta, but also more generally as a social concept, a practice or a mode of relations that can extend from there – is stunning. It returns me to your work *Care Forgot,* which documents a conviviality that I see as a kind of Cubits Gap, as you theorize it, in the way that it charts a path towards different forms of being together that seem all too foreclosed in our present moment.

So I'm curious if you might describe what you see as happening in all that you've assembled in *Care Forgot*? What are the "benevolent associations" there, and how are they a kind of Cubits Gap?

RCC Watching the film after editing it about five years ago, I see a sort of mathematics at play. A geometry happening. I think there's a resonance going on with what predicates the event that produced Cubits Gap and what predicates the event of a second line or Mardi Gras that might be understood as a reaction to spiritual-historical confinement. Confinement of alternate culture, confinement of alternate life similar to a confinement of riverine systems. These phenomena can be seen as breaks – whether it's in Black life emerging through slavery with the Code Noir, which then brings the ring shout and the drum circle to return, like cosmological stowaways, which then allows the ring shout to straighten out into the procession. Or to reference Cubits Gap – which would initially be determined as a crevasse splay – a bursting out into a new channel, a new subdelta. Both insist on the recognition and the acknowledgment of the spatial relationship among themselves and the world of various objects around them. Rather than assuming architectural solipsism of the levee and city, these are the architectures of the Earth we are insisting on. New Orleans specifically is a place of paradox, as the city has been built into a casket constructed by levees, it's important to continue to see what ideas emerge from a place that has had a superimposition of life and death upon it for almost a hundred years. And has dealt with Western epistemology longer than the land around it, as it predates the United States as a thought.

Over time, the levee as a gesture of control has begun to signify disillusionment with the Western world for many of us down here. We see the inherent ecological collapse these structures facilitate – this short-term environmental amnesia, as we now have multiple moments in our history of how levees have failed us. Black and lower-class communities especially. St. Bernard Parish in 1927 and the Lower Ninth Ward in 2005 come to mind. And so when I see things like Carnival, or environmental engagement that is more about being in circulation (across time and space) rather than walling ourselves off from the reality of the locality, I recognize that as an affirmation or reaffirmation of nonhegemonic relations.

What does it mean to engage with something geometrically? It is to acknowledge the spatial relationship among various objects.

From there you begin to develop into self-organization, or self-adaptation. For instance, the way a delta develops is the spontaneous formation of a pattern. A dendritic, tree-like sprawling. But then, that pattern is already adapting to the pattern it's set out as it continues to develop. That's where you get self-organization. Pattern change in a complex system where the pattern is adapting to the very behaviour it created. This is how I'm seeing the development of New Orleans culture (and Black culture, more generally), where you can get Blues to aberrate into jazz, and jazz aberrating into R & B or rap or techno, as it continues to sprawl away from its initial region. Making a way out of no way might be perceived as simply chaotic; I think it's something I might understand as deterministic chaos. We're setting up a culture to find your own voice. Everyone is speaking and doing their own thing, which brings to mind another musical phrase, heterophony. Found in the Black church before it was a traditional jazz concept, before it was the foundation of free jazz. You can hear all three in Albert Ayler's music, for example. Going back to the congregation during hymns, where everyone would solo alongside the choir while the pastor led the tune. You could understand that as a group solo. Black music is, in essence, a continuous group solo. I think that's what all of these "Cubits Gaps" are tending towards. What's your own solo? What's your break?

MN These second lines and benevolent associations, this heterophony of the group solo that you describe so wonderfully – I think of them, as you stated it earlier, as a "counterarchitecture." You state it again: "This is the architecture we are proposing."

I can recall feeling this exact statement in my body in times of uncertain convergence with others. The first example that comes to mind is the 2012 student protests here in Québec, where it felt like – in being out on the streets together throughout the spring and summer – that we were redefining the city, how we interacted with it, how we cohabited it with one another. Those manifestations and actions felt like a proposal for the city, a kind of conviviality that we were enacting each night.

RCC I think counterarchitecture is often a counterproposition. How can we show you another way to be together? What's another way we can *be* each other *with* each other *for* each other *about* each other? How do we listen to one another?

This is why I really have so much love for the Black music continuum – the music is only possible through listening. We talk so much about improvisation as if it is this pure, exogenic heat release, as if all one is doing is releasing. Yet there's so much that is about taking in what's around. There's so much circulation, so much relation. It's not simply about spewing what you have to say. You only have something to say because of what you've heard and because of where you're from. If you refuse that, then you've gone mute. You're gonna be stuck.

I love parades insofar as they do rhyme with the strike, the uprising, the protest. They assume and enhance the form of embodied congregated resistance for when it's time to do so. They get your body primed for what it means to be in the streets and to speak up for yourself. I think the tradition of Black music is a sort of technology of a "generative grammar," to reference

Chomsky. Black musical structures and societies give you the tools and the parameters to learn how to speak for yourself. Like the twelve-bar blues or general song pattern in jazz of head, verse, chorus, verse, coda. People will say how musicologically rote a lot of jazz or popular blues is, but the magic is in how it prompts one to reach unbelievable degrees of freedom surrounding ornamentation and aberration. What's even more exciting is how you can see this formality in the material and immaterial cultures around Blackness, such as with the New Orleans shotgun homes. The same stakes are at play. In this way, I think New Orleans applies a question to all the inhabitants of the city: Where is yourself in all this chaos, and how can we find each other in this madness? Here lies a city of echolocation.

So to return to *Care Forgot*, what I really see is an encryption of collective meaning refusing the constraints of linearity, an inscription of a suppressed history of spatiality. Of togetherness, an ontological graffiti culture on a Western cityscape at play that tries to make sense of the questions above.

That's why in the video you get this flow of black-and-white imagery together with more modern day ones. The sounds are mostly from my own field recordings, sounds that I've collected from my friends, and clips that mean a lot to anyone who has lived in the city for the past twenty years, I'd say. They would send me these voice memos as they walked around the city during Mardi Gras. Listening back, the footage begins to showcase a sense of collective autonomy. I wanted to use the sounds that I was hearing. I don't think of it, necessarily, as "found footage," because there's always in my ear a kind of coloniality in that idea. I "found" it, I "discovered" it. There's something of the romantic and the journey of the individual hero in that idea. When in reality these are shared songs, shared voices, shared notes. I wanted *Care Forgot* to be a document of a series of spatial and temporal relations.

Which is why I'm saying it's mathematics, as that's all that mathematics is: a documentation of a series of relations. What I see in *Care Forgot* is the closest thing that we can do to modelling after nature, expressing unbounded life. Which is why I'm interested in the idea of Blackness being a sort of a geology. The piece is ultimately a moment showing an ongoing series of models of the generative capacity that nature performs and how we can embody that nature to share it between each other.

ENDNOTES

1 Tiffany Lethabo King, *The Black Shoals: Offshore Formations of Black and Native Studies* (Duke University Press, 2019), 17.

2 J. H. Nienhuis et al., "Global-Scale Human Impact on Delta Morphology Has Led to Net Land Area Gain," *Nature* 577 (January 2020): 514–518.

3 "*Second line* means the followers, or joiners, who fall in behind the 'first line,' composed of the brass band and the social club, which typically sponsors the parade. Second liners are a massive and heterogeneous group of individuals drawn from all walks of life. The distinctive interaction between the club members, musicians, and second liners produces a dynamic participatory event in which there is no distinction between audience and performer. In fact, watching such a parade is practically impossible, as the massive crowd surrounding club and band obscures the view, and any bystanders are insistently urged to join in the parade" (Helen A. Regis, "Blackness and the Politics of Memory in the New Orleans Second Line," *American Ethnologist*, 28, no. 4 (2001): 755.

4 manuel arturo abreu, "afterschool semester #1 manuel arturo abreu," *YouTube* video, October 18, 2019, 54 min., 45 sec.

5 Manuel De Landa, "An Interview with Manuel De Landa," by Konrad Becker and Miss M. at Virtual Futures, *Future Non Stop*, 1996.

6 DeForrest Brown Jr, host, *Techno at the End of the Future*, podcast, episode 1, "London," Camden Arts Centre and HKW Berlin, October 2021.

7 S.W. Pope, "Decentering 'Race' and (Re)presenting 'Black' Performance in Sport History: Basketball and Jazz in American Culture, 1920–1950," in *Deconstructing Sport History: A Postmodern Analysis*, ed. Murray G. Phillips (SUNY Press, 2006), 147–177.

8 Claude F. Jacobs, "Benevolent Societies of New Orleans Blacks during the Late Nineteenth and Early Twentieth Centuries," *Louisiana History: The Journal of the Louisiana Historical Association* 29, no. 1 (1988): 24.

9 Jacobs, 24.

Acknowledgments

Thank you to the interlocutors of these pages. Your works, your words, your ways of living and making are the inspiration for this book.

I am grateful to have published these dialogues, often in a different form, in: *Tripwire: a journal of poetics*, *Chicago Review*, *OEI*, *e-flux*'s You Can't Trust Music, *Amodern*, *The Capilano Review*, *032c magazine*, *Sound Stage Screen*, and *The Conversant*. My sincere thanks to the editors.

The Fonds de recherche du Québec – Société et Culture and the Canada Council for the Arts funded portions of this book's undertaking, and I'm thankful for their support.

A special thanks to Jeff Derksen for initiating the dialogue of this book, to David Buuck for making space for many of these dialogues in *Tripwire*, and to Jayne Wilkinson for her editorial feedback on several of these exchanges. Thank you to Catriona Strang for her meticulous editorial attention and support, and to Ryan Fitzpatrick for their clarity, labour, and generosity.

My love and gratitude to Juliette Bertoldo – for the dialogue that surrounds the making of this book, for our ever-expanding conviviality.

Works Cited and Further Reading

abreu, manuel arturo. "afterschool semester #1 manuel arturo abreu." *YouTube* video. October 18, 2019, 54 min., 45 sec.

Ashley, Robert, dir. *Music with Roots in the Aether: Opera for Television*. 1974, 14 hours.

Bäcker, Heimrad. *transcript*. Translated by Patrick Greaney and Vincent Kling. Dalkey Archive Press, 2010.

Berman, David. "North America's First Free Black Settlement in Our Neighbourhoods." *Village Preservation Blog* (website), May 25, 2022.

Bernes, Jasper. *Starsdown*. ingirimusnocteetconsumimurigni, 2007.

———. *We Are Nothing and So Can You*. Commune Editions, 2015.

———. *The Work of Art in the Age of Deindustrialization*. Stanford University Press, 2017.

Bersianik, Louky, Nicole Brossard, France Théoret, Gail Scott, Louise Cotnoir, and Louise Dupré. *Theory, A Sunday*. Belladonna* Collaborative, 2013.

Brathwaite, Kamau. *History of the Voice: The Development of Nation Language in Anglophone Caribbean Poetry*. New Beacon Books, 1984.

Brown, DeForrest Jr., host. *Techno at the End of the Future*. Podcast. Episode 1, "London." Camden Arts Centre and HKW Berlin, October 2021.

———. *Assembling a Black Counter Culture*. Primary Information, 2022.

Chomsky, Noam, and Morris Halle. *The Sound Pattern of English*. Harper & Row, 1968.

Christen, Kimberly. "Does Information Really Want to be Free? Indigenous Knowledge Systems and the Question of Openness," *International Journal of Communication* 6 (2012): 2870–2893.

Clarke, Ryan C. "Reverse Hallucinations in the Lower Delta." *Rhizome*, May 26, 2020.

———. *Care Forgot: A Southern Electronics Visual Mixtape*. 2019. Uploaded to *Vimeo* May 26, 2020.

———. "Southern Electronics and Grassroots Technologies." *Are.na*, December 22, 2020.

———. "Techno as a Pedagogy of Suggestion." *A Black History of Electronic Dance Music: The Lecture Series*, Season One, Harvard University, Cambridge, Massachusetts, November 2, 2023. *YouTube* video, 1 hr., 28 min.

———. "Where's the Drop?: Notes on Dance Music Ecologies." *Soap Ear*, no. 10 (n.d.).

Clover, Joshua. *The Totality for Kids*. University of California Press, 2006.

———. *Red Epic*. Commune Editions, 2015.

———. *Riot. Strike. Riot.: The New Era of Uprisings*. Verso, 2016.

Coulthard, Glen. *Red Skin, White Masks: Rejecting the Colonial Politics of Reconciliation*. University of Minnesota Press, 2014.

Couvillion, Brady R., Holly Beck, Donald Schoolmaster, and Michelle Fischer, "Land Area Change in Coastal Louisiana (1932 to 2016)," *US Geological Survey Scientific Investigations Map 3381*, 16 p. pamphlet, 2017.

Daigle, Michelle. "The Spectacle of Reconciliation: On (the) Unsettling Responsibilities to Indigenous Peoples in the Academy," *Society and Space* 37, no. 4 (2019): 703–721.

Davey, Moyra. *Index Cards*. New Directions, 2020.

Davies, Kevin. *Comp*. Edge Books, 2000.

———. *FPO*. Edge Books, 2020.

———. *The Golden Age of Paraphernalia*. Edge Books, 2008.

———. *Pause Button*. Tsunami Editions, 1992.

Davies, Kevin, and Diane Ward. "Episode Fifteen: Kevin Davies and Diane Ward." PhillyTalks, January 18, 2000. *PennSound*. MP3, 96 minutes.

Davis, Heather, and Zoe Todd. "On the Importance of a Date, or, Decolonizing the Anthropocene." *ACME: An International Journal for Critical Geographies* 16, no. 4 (2017): 761–780.

De Landa, Manuel. "An Interview with Manuel De Landa." By Konrad Becker and Miss M. at Virtual Futures, *Future Non Stop*, 1996.

Derksen, Jeff. *After Euphoria*. JRP|Ringier and Les Presses Du Reel, 2013.

———. *Annihilated Time: Poetry and Other Politics*. Talonbooks, 2009.

Douglas, Stan, ed. *Vancouver Anthology*. 2nd ed. Talonbooks, 2009.

Giroux, Dalie. *L'oeil du maître: Figures de l'imaginaire colonial québécois*. Mémoire d'encrier: 2020.

Glück, Robert. *Communal Nude: Collected Essays*. Semiotext(e), 2016.

Greenaway, Peter, dir. *Four American Composers*. Channel 4, UK, 1983. 220 min.

Han, Byung-Chul. *Shanzhai: Deconstruction in Chinese*. Translated by Philippa Hurd. The MIT Press, 2017.

Hejinian, Lyn. *The Language of Inquiry*. University of California Press, 2000.

Huidobro, Vicente. *Altazor*. Translated by Eliot Weinberger. Graywolf Press, 1988.

Homer. *The Odyssey*. Translated by Emily Wilson. W.W. Norton, 2017.

Hupfield, Maria, editor. *Breaking Protocol*. Inventory Press / Vera List Center for Art and Politics at The New School, 2023.

Illich, Ivan. *Tools for Convitiality*. Harper and Row, 1973.

Jacobs, Claude F. "Benevolent Societies of New Orleans Blacks during the Late Nineteenth and Early Twentieth Centuries." *Louisiana History: The Journal of the Louisiana Historical Association* 29, no. 1 (1988): 21–33.

Kawagley, Angayuqaq Oscar. *A Yupiaq Worldview: A Pathway to Ecology and Spirit*, 2nd ed. Waveland Press, 2006.

King, Tiffany Lethabo. *The Black Shoals: Offshore Formations of Black and Native Studies*. Duke University Press, 2019.

Kulchyski, Peter. *Like the Sound of a Drum: Aboriginal Cultural Politics in Denendeh and Nunavut*. University of Manitoba Press, 2005.

Lewis, George. "A Small Act of Curation." *On Curating* 44, 2020.

———. "Lifting the Cone of Silence from Black Composers." *The New York Times*, July 3, 2020.

Long Soldier, Layli. *WHEREAS*. Graywolf Press, 2017.

Lukin Linklater, Tanya. *My mind is with the weather*. Contemporary Art Gallery, 2023.

———. *Slow Scrape*. 2nd ed. Talonbooks, 2022.

Mitsch, William J. et al., "Reducing Nitrogen Loading to the Gulf of Mexico from the Mississippi River Basin: Strategies to Counter a Persistent Ecological Problem," *BioScience* 51, no. 5 (May 2001): 373–388.

Moten, Fred. *Stolen Life*. Duke University Press, 2018.

Nardone, Michael, ed. "Aural Poetics." *OEI* 98–99 (February 2023).

———. "Sonic Materialities." *textsound* 21 (2016).

Nicholson, Cecily. *From the Poplars*. Talonbooks, 2014.

———. *HARROWINGS*. Talonbooks, 2022.

———. *Triage*. Talonbooks, 2011.

———. *Wayside Sang*. Talonbooks, 2017.

Nienhuis, J.H., et al., "Global-Scale Human Impact on Delta Morphology Has Led to Net Land Area Gain," *Nature* 577 (January 2020): 514–518.

Nowak, Mark. *Coal Mountain Elementary*. Coffee House Press, 2009.

Pesutic, Sergio. *La Hinteligencia Militar*. Tercera Prensa, 1992.

Pope, S.W. "Decentering 'Race' and (Re)presenting 'Black' Performance in Sport History: Basketball and Jazz in American Culture, 1920–1950." In *Deconstructing Sport History: A Postmodern Analysis*, edited by Murray G. Phillips. SUNY Press, 2006.

Qikiqtani Inuit Association. *Qikiqtani Truth Commission: Thematic Reports and Special Studies, 1950–1975*. Inhabit Media, 2013.

Regis, Helen A. "Blackness and the Politics of Memory in the New Orleans Second Line." *American Ethnologist* 28 (2001): 752–777.

Reznikoff, Charles. *Holocaust*. Black Sparrow Press, 1975.

Risam, Roopika. *New Digital Worlds: Postcolonial Digital Humanities in Theory, Praxis, and Pedagogy.* Northwestern University Press, 2018.

Robertson, Lisa. *The Baudelaire Fractal.* Coach House, 2020.

———. *Occasional Work and Seven Walks from the Office for Soft Architecture.* Coach House, 2010.

Robinson, Dylan. *Hungry Listening: Resonant Theory for Indigenous Sound Studies.* University of Minnesota Press, 2020.

Rosenthal, Sarah, ed. *A Community Writing Itself: Conversations with Vanguard Writers of the Bay Area.* Dalkey Archive, 2010.

Scott, Gail. *Heroine.* Coach House, 2019.

———. *Main Brides.* Talonbooks, 1993.

———. *The Obituary.* Coach House, 2010.

———. *Permanent Revolution: Essays.* Book*hug, 2021.

———. *Spaces Like Stairs: Essays.* Women's Press, 1989.

———. *Spare Parts Plus Two.* Coach House, 2002.

Scott, Gail, Robert Glück, and Camille Roy, eds. *Biting the Error: Writers Explore Narrative,* Coach House, 2004.

Silva, Max. "Heard Utopia vs. Utopian Hearing: Haas's *in vain* and Political Ambivalence in New Music," *Twentieth-Century Music* 15, no. 1 (February 2018): 75–102.

Shklovsky, Viktor. "Art as Technique." In *Russian Formalist Criticism: Four Essays,* edited by Lee T. Lemon and Marion J. Reis. University of Nebraska Press, 1965 [1917].

Simpson, Leanne Betasamosake. "Being with the Land, Protects the Land." *Abolition Journal,* February 21, 2020.

———. "Dancing the World into Being: A Conversation with Idle No More's Leanne Simpson." Interview by Naomi Klein. *Yes!,* March 6, 2013.

Soto Román, Carlos. *11.* Ugly Duckling Presse, 2023.

———. *Bluff.* Commune Editions, 2018.

———. *Chile Project: [Re-Classified].* Gauss PDF, 2013.

———. *Common Sense.* Make Now, 2019.

———. *Haiku Minero.* Pez Espiral, [2007] 2021.

Spicer, Jack. *The Collected Books of Jack Spicer.* Black Sparrow Press, 1975.

Susskind, Rob. "Faith, Certainty and the Presidency of George W. Bush." *The New York Times Magazine,* October 17, 2004.

Ultra-red. *Ten Preliminary Theses on Militant Sound Investigation.* Printed Matter, 2008.

Victor, Divya. *Curb.* Nightboat Books, 2021.

———. *Kith.* Fence Books / Book*hug, 2017.

———. *Natural Subjects.* Trembling Pillow Press, 2014.

———. *Partial Directory of the Unnameable*. Troll Thread, 2011.

———. "Strangers in Our Own Homes: The Pandemic's Xenophobic Discourse." *The Yale Review*, September 20, 2021.

———. *Things to Do with Your Mouth*. Les Figues, 2014.

Weintraub, Scott. "Narrating (The Other 9/)*11*: The Poetics of Carlos Soto Román," *Asymptote* (website), January 3, 2019.

Wilson, Jordan. *qeqen: House Posts: A walking tour of Musqueam House Posts at UBC*. Belkin Art Gallery, 2018.

Wolfe, Patrick. *Settler Colonialism and the Transformation of Anthropology*. Bloomsbury Press, 1999.

Wu, Fan. "Shanzhai Lyric: LOOSELY ASSEMBLED CYCLE 3: J'ai besoin d'a Of North 1986." *C Magazine* 144 (2019).

Xiang, Zairong. "Inbuilt Errans: What Is and Is Not 'Radical Indifference.'" In *Errans: Going Astray, Being Adrift, Coming to Nothing*, edited by Chrisoph F.E. Holzhey and Arndt Wedememeyer. ICI Press, 2022.

"Yellow Towel." *Neon Lobster* (website). nd.

Contributor Copyright

"Convivialities" © 2025 Michael Nardone
"No Fixed Positions: A Dialogue with Dana Michel" © 2025 Michael Nardone and Dana Michel, live artist
"Can Struggle Be Shared? A Dialogue with Joshua Clover and Jasper Bernes" © 2025 Michael Nardone, Joshua Clover, and Jasper Bernes
"A Collectively Authored, Ever-Unfinished Landscape: A Dialogue with Shanzhai Lyric" © 2025 Michael Nardone and Shanzhai Lyric
"We Need to Ground It in the Real: A Dialogue with Cecily Nicholson" © 2025 Michael Nardone and Cecily Nicholson
"Contrary Motions: A Dialogue with Raven Chacon" © 2025 Michael Nardone and Raven Chacon
"Tracking the Traffic of Glyphs Across Oceans: A Dialogue with Divya Victor" © 2025 Michael Nardone and Divya Victor
"An Alternative Set of Procedures: A Dialogue with Carlos Soto Román" © 2025 Michael Nardone and Carlos Soto Román
"Documenting Physical Investigations with Language: A Dialogue with Tanya Lukin Linklater" © 2025 Michael Nardone and Tanya Lukin Linklater
"Permanent [Upside Down] Revolution: A Dialogue with Gail Scott" © 2025 Michael Nardone and Gail Scott
"The Mystery of Indexicals: A Dialogue with Kevin Davies" © 2025 Michael Nardone and Kevin Davies
"Sensate Sovereignty: A Dialogue with the Culture and Technology Discussion and Working Group" © 2025 Michael Nardone, Sadie Couture, Randolph Jordan, Andy Kelleher Stuhl, Burç Köstem, Landon Morrison, Shirley Roburn, Allyson Rogers, Mehak Sawhney, Jonathan Sterne, and Hannah Tollefson
"A Sediment Diversion for the Audible World: A Dialogue with Ryan C. Clarke" © 2025 Michael Nardone and Ryan C. Clarke

MICHAEL NARDONE is a poet and editor based in Montréal. His recent and forthcoming works include: *Aural Poetics* (an edition on listening practices across the arts), *Yellow Towel: A Score* (a collaboration with Dana Michel), *Border Tuner | Sintonizador Fronterizo* (a monograph on Rafael Lozano-Hemmer, co-edited with Edgar Picazo Merino), the Documents on Expanded Poetics book series (co-edited with Nathan Brown), *The Transatlantic Conversation* (a translation of Abigail Lang's monograph on contemporary French and US poetry), and *The Ritualites* (a book of poems). Beginning in 2024, he is a writer-in-residence at the SETI Institute.